Fiction of the Home Place

Fiction of the Home Place

Jewett, Cather, Glasgow, Porter, Welty, and Naylor

Helen Fiddyment Levy

University Press of Mississippi
Jackson

Copyright © 1992 by the University Press of Mississippi
All rights reserved
Manufactured in the United States of America

96 95 94 93   4 3 2 1

The paper in this book meets the guidelines for permanence and durability of
the Committee on Production Guidelines for Book Longevity of the Council
on Library Resources.

Library of Congress Cataloging-in-Publication Data

Levy, Helen Fiddyment.
    Fiction of the home place: Jewett, Cather, Glasgow, Porter, Welty, and
Naylor / Helen Fiddyment Levy.
        p.   cm.
    Includes bibliographical references and index.
    ISBN 0-87805-663-7 (pbk.),—ISBN 0-87805-554-1 (cloth)
    1. Domestic fiction, American—History and criticism. 2. American
fiction—Women authors—History and criticism. 3. Women and
literature—United States. 4. Social problems in literature.
5. Sex role in literature. 6. Family in literature. 7. Home in
literature. I. Title.
PS374.D57L48 1993
813.009'355—dc20
                                                              93-7679
                                                              CIP
British Library Cataloging-in-Publication data available

To those who have sewn in my family,
but especially
Joanie.

Remember this—
A wave over a patch of zinnias and the scarlet petals
take flight.
And this—
Winged marigolds follow them into the air.
Listen—
A thump of the stick: morning glories start to sing.
The other place. Butterflies and hummingbirds. And the
wisdom to draw them.
Ancient eyes, sad and tired: it's time you knew. An old
house with a big garden. And it's seen its share of pain.

—Gloria Naylor
Mama Day (1988).

Success breeds. There are few overriding community interests
to check the leader's impetus. The greater his influence, the
more support he attracts. . . . He has made [his followers']
lineages and ancestral shrines less meaningful for them than
his own favour. . . . Recruited and harnessed to a competition
which seems to hold glittering rewards for all, they find themselves trying to work a complex system of rules. In the name
of the rules the Big Men justify their demands. Whether it be
rules of monetary exchange, debt and credit, or rules of eti-
quette and hospitality, the system constitutes an oppressive
grid. Londoners too know what this can mean. As a system of
control industrial society is impersonal. Some more than others feel their lives controlled, not by persons, but by things.
They wander through a forest of regulations, imponderable
forces are represented by forms to complete in triplicate,
parking meters, inexorable laws. Their cosmos is dominated
by objects of which they and fellow humans are victims. The
essential difference between a cosmos dominated by persons
and one dominated by objects is the impossibility of bringing moral pressures to bear upon the controllers: there is no
person-to-person communication with them.

—Mary Douglas
*Natural Symbols: Explorations
in Cosmology.*

Contents

Acknowledgments

The occupation of independent scholar makes for short acknowledgments. But I have been blessed with the help of those who believed in the community of scholars and who acted on their beliefs. First, thanks are due to those colleagues and friends who read sections of the manuscript and the whole in various stages of readiness: Connie Johnson, Bud Hamilton, Lisa MacFarlane, Bob and Gene Berkhofer. Especially gracious and industrious were my dear friends and colleagues, Mary Corbin Sies, Gary Magruder, and Rosemary Kowalski. Susan Rosowski showed great generosity in reading and giving thoughtful commentary on the introductory chapter and the Cather criticism of a writer whom she met at a conference and who then presumed on that acquaintance. My dissertation director, Lyall Powers, has offered me valuable criticism and much good conversation on matters literary and cultural throughout my career. The engaged scholarship and teaching of John O. King during my graduate career and beyond, along with his inestimable direct help with methodology and style, set a high standard for my work and for that of all his students. The combined contributions of these dedicated colleagues saved me from many errors both of commission and omission. Even more, they saved me from the self-pity that overtakes those who work alone and receive little bureaucratic compensation or validation.

The staff of the University Press of Mississippi deserves particular mention as well. My editor, Seetha A-Srinivasan, believed in the project from the beginning and offered insightful and tactful guidance throughout the revision and production process. Her understanding and tough gentleness got me over the inevitable rough spots on the way to publication. My copy editor, Ann Finlayson, displayed a wide range of knowledge and great good sense as well as a fair amount of patience. The librarians of the Library of Congress must be mentioned, especially Victoria Hill, head of the Main Reading Room, and Bruce Martin, the research facilities officer, who shortened research time immeasurably by their professionalism and courtesy. Any errors that remain after all of this help must of course be laid at my doorstep.

My daughters, Liz and Elena, inspired this writing through their love, their achievements, and their respective intelligences, so different one from the other but both crucial to my work. Elena, who completes her doctoral degree in English this year, has been a beloved intellectual companion who heartened and inspired me, and Liz, from various airports, has unstintingly given me both sympathy and encouragement despite an incredibly busy schedule. Both have read the manuscript and contributed valuable insights throughout the writing. Finally, of course, my husband, Bernardo Levy-Navarro, never allowed us to doubt that we could achieve anything we set ourselves to do. Bernardo supported me in many ways, caring for Liz and Elena in the early years when I returned to college, cooking superbly while I prepared the manuscript, and saving me repeatedly from abysmal computer illiteracy. A strong man of grace and decision, he gave his daughters and his wife an enduring example of masculine kindness and purpose.

Fiction of the Home Place

Introduction

THE OTHER PLACE

IN *Herland*, Charlotte Perkins Gilman surveys the perimeters of the home place, an ideal pastoral domestic setting. The home place as it appears in the fiction of many American women writers is presided over by an elder wise woman who embodies the care and wisdom associated with maternity:

> They had no enemies; they themselves were all sisters and friends. The land was fair before them, and a great future began to form itself in their minds.
>
> The religion they had to begin with was much like that of old Greece— a number of gods and goddesses; but they lost all interest in deities of war and plunder, and gradually centered on their Mother Goddess altogether. Then, as they grew more intelligent, this turned into a sort of Maternal Pantheism.
>
> Here was Mother Earth, bearing fruit. All that they ate was the fruit of motherhood, from seed to egg or their product. By motherhood they were born and by motherhood they lived—life was to them, just the long cycle of motherhood. (59)

The feminist utopian novel progresses from the discovery of Herland by three American men to the salvation of two of them by acceptance of the maternal example and the cooperative, egalitarian morality of the female community. The children of Herland are conceived without male fertilization. Gilman explicitly presents her egalitarian female community as an alternative to the cultural ideal of competitive individualism which she perceived at the base of the modern American society.

The outlines of her utopian homeland suggest similar imaginary female communities in the writing of a group of American women writers of the twentieth century: Willa Cather, Sarah Orne Jewett, Ellen Glasgow, Katherine Anne Porter, Eudora Welty, and Gloria Naylor. Although other American women writers could have been treated, I do not claim universality for this imaginative paradigm among American women writers. Nonetheless, by its persistence and prevalence in this important group of women, the home place deserves attention. Some of its outlines were established in the plots and characterization of the nineteenth-century domestic novel, and the latest author, Gloria Naylor, evokes the seer's homeland in *Mama Day* published in 1988. Throughout this period the home place has challenged both the forest and the marketplace, arenas of male competition.

Several features of the above condensed description appear repeatedly in the portrait of the home place by the twentieth-century women literary artists discussed here. First, the author summons a semidivine wise woman, most often a grandmother, whose own experience of birth and care has informed her relationship to the American natural world. The seer addresses the natural world as a beloved, living partner in her labors of creativity, thereby refuting the concept of a objectified, supine nature common in works by American men. (Kolodny, *Lay of the Land*, 134–37). Along with the other authors in this study, Gilman sees the home place as existing seamlessly within the natural environment, women's domestic craft and nature's abundance enriching each other constantly. The American home place is established in a setting in which care of garden or field is viewed as growing out of labor in kitchen or nursery. As Alice Walker writes of the dooryard of the home place in "Everyday Use," "A yard like this is more comfortable than most people know. It is not a yard. It is like an extended living room"

(2004). Gilman's neat "Dutch kitchen"—an ideal setting, shedding warmth on the whole of the neighborhood, garden, and fields—welcomes all women, honors their range of choices. It also includes men who eschew the morality and rewards of the social competition for individual dominance. Maternity in *Herland* offers a pattern for cooperative womanly creativity, not a biological demand; therefore here, as in Ellen Glasgow's *Beyond Defeat*, Sarah Orne Jewett's *The Country of the Pointed Firs*, or Gloria Naylor's *Mama Day*, the female leader of the community need not experience childbirth herself—the seers in those books are all middle-aged and unmarried or widowed—but she must practice the wisdom and acceptance associated with a long life of care of the natural world and of the human beings around her. Notably, the ideal mothers of Herland do not claim their daughters as belonging to a single mother. They refuse to mark their children with name and possessions as an extension and expression of their own respective personalities, but rather their daughters remain the responsibility and pride of all the women in the community of Herland. Moreover, neither the claims of "romance" nor the promise of material gifts tempt them. As Frances Bartkowski points out in *Feminist Utopias*, the visitors' ideas about marriage, formed in their contemporary America, center on words with no meaning in the female pastoral, "privacy," "possession," "wife," and "home"—the "home" Gilman rejects in her early work such as *The Home and Its Work and Influence* (1903).

Maternal abundance and creativity does not burden the daughter with guilt in these authors but rather inspires her intellectual and artistic labors. The matrix replaces the phallus as the source of art, as the female body itself creates and nurtures the community through both body and spirit. In *The Madwoman in the Attic*, Sandra Gilbert and Susan Gubar pose a question that the woman writer in England and America confronts in the face of a traditionally male lineage and language: "[W]hat if the male generative power is not just the only legitimate power but the only power there is?" (7). The elder wise woman offers the younger woman an alternate explanatory story for the emergence of female art, one that replaces the "anxiety of [patriarchal] influence" with a direct, irrefutable pattern for a lineage of female creativity.

Throughout this discussion, I will use the word "lineage" to indicate the descent of the daughter, and her art, from the wise woman's creativity. As Gilman depicts through the explicit parthenogenesis in *Her-land*, the line of descent from an ancestor (as dictionaries define "lineage") is not purely an intellectual or spiritual one but one that involves the younger woman's discovery of her connection to those women who have gone before in body, mind, and spirit. The authors in this study refuse to allow female creativity to reside purely in the reason or in the imagination, thereby rejecting a split between body and mind. The writers often designate the female seer as sole creator of her world and her children, both physically and morally through the office of maternity; as Porter's Granny Weatherall says of her children, "There they were, made out of her, and they couldn't get away from that" (83).

By reaching as mature artists toward a female-created pastoral setting, these writing women find an end to the crucial search for female creative models for authorship. The elder wise woman—in Gilman, the Mother Goddess—becomes the sole or equal creator of a woman's homeland with power often stolen from a lord and master, either male deity or earthly authority. The home place affirmatively, joyously, transcends the fears and hesitations generated by acceptance of male theories of authorship and a male creator of the cosmos.

The wise woman serves as the model of female creativity, the repository of woman's history, and the provider of the mother's enduring care. The seer's creative labors anticipate those of the female writer. In the cooperative, egalitarian setting, the daughter gains greater freedom to follow her own path without maternal, or paternal, defensiveness; the friction between the all-powerful parent and the helpless girl child is removed. Moreover, by removing this ideal one generation in the case of the grandmother or through the chosen mother, the authors further avoid the dangers of psychic absorption of the daughter's personality by the mother (Chodorow, *Reproduction of Mothering*, 108–10). Instead of the adversarial relationship fostered in the culture of competitive individualism, the relationship between female biological body and woman's artistic, intellectual creativity is healed; the body is reclaimed and celebrated by its labors of creativity, which constantly inspires the daughter's own task. As Gloria Feman Orenstein writes in *The Reflowering of the Goddess*, "The symbol of a woman Creator bringing forth both life and art, nature and culture, seems to represent in the most poignant way possible, the point at which many of the themes espoused by contemporary feminists converge" (6).

The convergence between physical labor and artistic creativity is most dramatically suggested by the connection of the house with the natural world and by the twin creativities of garden and sewing room. The female ideal creates a floral display of both plenitude and beauty, joining together the personalities of her family as she stitches a quilt out of scraps, gathering together the stories of her family history. The figures of garden and quilt become the inspiration for the daughter's book, music, painting, or intellectual labors. Domestic crafts inspire literary arts, a heritage of female creativity passing from mother to daughter. The home place rejects the polar thinking, the body-mind division and the winner-loser model, prevalent within the social competition the writer and her creations leave behind.

The home place offers a metaphorical explanation for individual female authorship as well, depicting a powerful example of ongoing womanly creativity and strength, which extends to all women. Nina Auerbach's *Communities of Women* identifies a literary trope in writing by women, which culminates in the creation of a woman's community whose central goal is "rootedness" in a particular place such as a city or school where the women gain "self-possession" (8). In the United States, however, the tendencies Auerbach cites are reshaped by many women authors into the very specific outlines of the home place with the inclusion of a harmonious nature joined with a creative, independent domesticity and a chosen circle of relationships.

In its particular emphasis on the reclaiming of male legend and religion to empower female creativity, the passage from *Herland* anticipates similar fictional strategies in the most fully realized works of a significant group: Jewett, Cather, Glasgow, Porter, Welty, and Naylor. Gilman also addresses patterns established by the earlier literary craftswomen of the domestic novel, although her novel and those by the six self-conscious authors refuse the nod toward paternalistic control. Moreover, these authors intend the home place to serve as a metaphoric representative of democratic egalitarianism and community action to the American reader. The authors often explicitly retell the legend of the founding of the particular American neighborhood to include women's contribution, whether the setting be the island home of Naylor's Willow Springs, the prairie *patria* of Cather's Nebraska, the fishing village of Jewett's New England, the farm of Porter's Texas, the mountain home of Welty's West Virginia, or the valley settlement of Glasgow's *Virginia*. By evoking a nurturing American homeland set within a vital, domesticated nature, the women writers create an alternate female vision, which directly challenges a social competition that they perceive as devoted to an unrelentingly pragmatic morality. Because the paradigm of the home place addresses and challenges a central cultural myth in heroic individualism, the writers take two paths to reach it. The high road, or positive narrative, treats the continuity of the woman's community and the creativity of the wise woman's female wisdom and language, whereas the low road, or negative narrative, criticizes through precautionary tales the venality and dehumanization of women under competitive individualism.

This group of modern women artists write within a social order of expanding rationalized bureaucratic organizations. This social order valorizes the individual, encouraging the self-aggrandizement of a small group of white male winners in the social competition for dominance and wealth. A very few women—often the female kin of the male leadership—and a smattering of minorities are included near, but seldom at, the top of the pyramid. The supporting social structures that enact the directives of the dominant individuals govern their followers by an ever-elaborating maze of impersonal laws, spawned by the bureaucracy, but among themselves the Big Men operate through a web of personal contacts and individual influence. Such a social order offers few religious legends or other cultural examples of female creativity, whether manifested through domestic craft, reformed social circles, or self-conscious art. Instead, it privileges the unique male individual in positive, even heroic, presentation, through such cultural messages as self-conscious fiction, popular culture, advertising, and political pronouncements. In addressing the competitive individualism that underlies the American social structure, the psychological and social stakes of the writing game are especially high for the woman author who has experience as a daughter of a communal female history. She must repudiate both her female physical and her female cultural communal experience. Therefore, in their earlier writings these women writers attempt to adapt the plot of the socially unconnected heroic male individual to their narratives of female protagonists, unable as yet to overcome either the patriarchal model of authorship or the cultural ideal of the dominant individual. This pattern appears in women authors such as Cather in *O Pioneers!*, Jewett in *A Country Doctor*, Glasgow in *Barren Ground*, and Wharton in *The Fruit of the Tree.* They adapt the individualistic fictional strategies generated by the dominant discourse of the large-scale, male-controlled social structures.[1]

In summoning nothing less than a new homeland, the authors change the definition and uses of the American natural world. The often semidivine protagonist encounters the land as a midwife or as the mother who guards life and death. The elder wise woman finds a special kinship with the American earth as she partakes of the same creative rhythms of seedtime and harvest and rest. As in Walker and Gilman, nature may be portrayed as a "living room," an extension of the home place. The wise woman brings her separate homeland to life in its natural, domestic, and artistic manifestations through her sympathetic identification with the physical environment, a sympathy that arises directly from her own abundant womanliness.

Language too is reshaped in the seer's personal, private world. In this female pastoral setting, communication between the members comes almost telepathically, arising out of daily, loving encounters. The interaction between female characters occurs in spare, colloquial language, often with excision of logical connectives, augmented expressions of emotional connection, reference to shared places, acquaintance, and memories. As noted above, myth and legend abound, redolent with the bonding emotions of woman's communal ritual. All these women hear the tales of a patriarchal communal history, which they rewrite as challenging female narrative to counter the cultural emphasis on the individual. Woven out of memories, the narrative is brought out to the public world by the imagination and the sophistication of the daughter as in Porter's *The Old Order*, Welty's *The Optimist's Daughter*, or Jewett's *The Country of the Pointed Firs*; or by female authorial voice itself as in Glasgow's *Beyond Defeat* and *Vein of Iron* or Cather's *My Ántonia*; or by the voice of the female community as in Naylor's *Mama Day*. The writer-daughter, a type of Persephone, visits the sterile impersonal public world in her exile. As the stories are passed directly from the older woman to the younger woman, so too is the knowledge of the essential crafts which she learns at the seer's side—a clear contrast to the dominant culture's education in the official history of the Big Men, offered by the hired experts of the impersonal educational bureaucracies, reminiscent of Toennies' concept of gemeinschaft.

The women's writing under discussion has at its base a didactic, quasi-religious intent accompanying the artistic vision, an intent that arises out of the bonding achieved by the local language. Art here has a serious intent far beyond serving the readership with a competing form of leisure entertainment. The spiritual emphasis of these women's writing also asserts the morality of the home place by offering a vision of a purer American democracy, one which admits cooperative communal relationships and undertakings as an alternative both to the competitive individualism of their contemporary dominant discourse and the repressive hierarchy of the earlier paternalistic family. The home place throughout serves the ideal of moderation. Whether placed in a traditional pastoral rural setting, the most usual case, or in the village, the home place holds neither the smoke and dust of the modern city nor the terror and brutality of untouched nature. Emotionally, it stands between the acquisitive egotism of the heroic individual and the reactionary oppression of the patriarch. In Jewett, Cather, Glasgow, Porter, Gilman, Naylor, and Welty, we can perceive a conscious, explicit attempt to re-view history by adding the female contribution. The movement in most of these writers is from individual to female comradeship to home place; the movement in all is from the competitive individual to the loving community. It cannot be said too often that these writers counter the dominant individuals and their supporting impersonal bureaucracies with a persistent focus on the local neighborhood as the authentic American homeland, a concept Cather makes explicit in *My Ántonia* through her extended reference to Virgil's concept of the *patria*. The home place fulfills more completely the original American "errand into the wilderness," bringing art and knowledge to all the community's members, offering care to those who need it in their turn, for the authors fully realize that the old, the sick, the young, the discouraged have their claims and that all members of the social order must in their turn depend on others.

Although the narrative addresses the transmission of woman's lore and memories, the authors insist that men are equally welcome, always provided that they eschew the competitive, pragmatic values of the Big Man culture and accept the morality of the home place. (Gilman, for one, is skeptical that this is possible, given the rewards accruing to males from both the paternalistic and marketplace arrangements that have constituted American public life.) In contrast to the dim or missing social background behind the heroic individual, who occupies so much of the horizon of American male literature, these women bring the egalitarian community to the fore, implying that their visions have the power if heeded to inspire both social policy and individual creativity.[2]

Through the outlines of the imaginative portrayal, the women writers depict the isolation from the present American cultural center of any female roles of crucial importance, even as they insist on woman's contribution to the building of the American homeland. The unconscious result of the American competitive emphasis is to proclaim a successful individual as "self-made," meaning that he has gained success by his own efforts. But the crucial adjective "self" as applied to the male winner of the material competition, suggests the cultural worship of rugged individualism; if one is "self-made," then social context, especially family history, falls away. In her introduction to *Of Woman Born*, Adrienne Rich remarks that in other times and places motherhood has endowed "all women with respect, even with awe," but in the United States, Rich continues, this has not been so (xv). Writers of such diverse sensibilities as Porter and Cather confirm Rich's observation as they contrast woman's situation in modern America with that of women in idealized foreign communities, Indian Mexico in Porter or early Quebec in Cather, because in their opinion America offers little acknowledgment beyond lip service to women's contribution as creator of its civilization. By summoning the wise woman, these women counter the dramas of the American cultural mainstream, placing the home place within a larger European or African mythological and historical framework.

With the exception of Gloria Naylor, whose African-American parents, in her characterization, *"aspired* to be working class," these women writers all come from the white middle or upper classes (*American Audio Prose Library*, emphasis Naylor's). Although Glasgow and Jewett had the means to devote their lives to writing, Naylor first studied and worked to support her writing, and Porter, Welty (for a short while), and Cather were journalists. With the exception of Gilman, all of these women remained unmarried for much or all of their lives, although Cather and Jewett had long-lasting committed relationships with women. Only Gilman had a child. Their biographies reinforce Tillie Olsen's insights in *Silences* on the difficulties of combining female authorship with maternity.

Except for Gilman's *Herland*, which serves as the template for the imaginative constructions that follow, these authors will be treated developmentally because discussion of major works over time reveals the full complexity and consistency of this fictional strategy. To pluck a metaphor here and a quote there out of the context of the work and the oeuvre is to risk misrepresentation both of the intent of the work itself and its place within the woman's career. Those works will be discussed that have as their central impelling circumstance the moment at which the female protagonist achieves insight into her connection with her own female identity within the American social context. This may be the realization of the dangers of immoderate romantic passion, or it may involve the individual woman's discovery of her membership in the female community as the source of her own creativity; both involve renunciation of competitive individualism. The positive portrayals of the home place, which show woman's understanding of her relationship to the maternal home, include Cather's *My Ántonia* and *The Song of the Lark*, Glasgow's *They Stooped to Folly, Beyond Defeat*, and especially *Vein of Iron*, Jewett's *The Country of the Pointed Firs* and "The Foreigner," Porter's *The Old Order*, Welty's *The Optimist's Daughter* and *The Golden Apples*, and Naylor's *Mama Day*. Several works will be included that show the woman writer trying to adapt the plot of heroic individualism to women of achievement: Cather's *O Pioneers!*, Jewett's *A Woman Doctor*, and Glasgow's *Barren Ground*.

Cautionary tales such as Naylor's *The Women of Brewster Place* and especially *Linden Hills*, Glasgow's *The Sheltered Life*, Welty's *The Golden Apples*, Cather's "The Bohemian Girl" and *My Mortal Enemy*, Jewett's story of Joanna Todd in *The Country of the Pointed Firs*, Porter's "Old Mortality," and Gilman's "The Yellow Wallpaper" all tell of woman's susceptibility to immersion in the life and interests of the male in the Big Man social order.[3] In these authors' careers, the female protagonist suffers because of alienation from her own self-identity and from the community of women, as she is subsumed into a man's life and interests, most often through an immoderate immersion in romance.[4] If the home place is an imaginative vision, this is the social reality that they fear: a loss of identity, which brings women in these works to madness, death, disgrace, or nonlife—all manifestations of fragmentation of the female identity—as they transform into mannequins for display of the Big Man's wealth. Such works prepare the way for the home place, illustrating the costs and the traps for women in the male-controlled social competition.

The discussion of the home place and the elder wise woman proceeds from my understanding of several sources in sociology and anthropology. First, these authors respond most forcibly to several aspects of Max Weber's model of the process of rationalization: the erasure of received traditional identities arising out of long-established, stable family, neighborhood, and other local relationships; the replacement of the master-apprentice method of passing on knowledge with specialized educational bureaucracies; the organization of the social structure to maximize economic productivity and to reward individual success; and the objectification of nature into malleable material for individual and corporate exploitation. Moreover, the drive for more efficient outer control of the worker-citizen leads to a cultural devaluation and even denial of the aspects of the female body involved in the female biological processes designated by Sara Ruddick as "birthing labor." The process of rationalization moves steadily toward increased predictability of performance; therefore any aspect of humanity that produces a (possibly) less efficient worker such as youth or age, strong emotion—whether in the religious or personal realm—or female biology, marks the individual as less predictable, less identified with the bureaucratic structures at the social center. The movement is toward making the human being as uniform as the machine; a standard of absolute predictability in the rules that govern daily life is also desirable. This process affects the web of human relationships as well, facilitating the movement toward the large-scale, specialized, role-differentiated bureaucratic structures described by British anthropologist Mary Douglas as supportive of the Big Man competition.

Ideally, consideration of the difficult personal case is eliminated, as are other judgments or definitions of meaning on the part of the lower bureaucratic functionaries who actually deal with the public at large. The individual faced with proliferating impersonal laws is often caught between the contradictory demands of conflicting social structures with no chance of mediation or appeal without great expenditure of effort. The cultural insistence on the ultimately responsible individual ironically leads to increased control as each person finds himself or herself subject to control of rationalized bureaucracies in ever-increasing areas of their daily life, areas previously considered as his or her own personal, intimate concern. At the same time, the legacy of individualism places more burdens for the care of those unable to participate fully in the social competition on the reduced and weakened personal networks; there is no model under rationalized individualism for communal solutions to "private" matters although there is increased bureaucratic oversight and punitive action in those same areas (the "war" on drugs, for example, with its emphasis on technology and penalties rather than on treatment and social rehabilitation, or legal penalties for "child neglect" without corresponding communal "child care"). Previous collective American efforts in areas such as public education, public health programs, and public transportation have been given over to massive national bureaucracies at the expense of local communal action.

As the authors of *Habits of the Heart* examine the rhetoric of what they deem Neocapitalism through the speeches of its primary spokesperson, Ronald Reagan, they find that it evokes private, rather than civic, virtues. The president's inaugural address, as they read it, considers the American nation to be an economy not a polity. The authors' extrapolate from this rhetoric that this vision considers government's primary duty to preserve the security "necessary to allow self-reliant individuals to pursue their largely economic aims in freedom" (262). The evolving American vision of the human as a self-created, autonomous actor in a central economic competition opposes that of the home place.

The pressures generated on the individual creator of literary work by the social order are illustrated in this discussion through use of a community-social structure model, terms having roughly the same general outlines of Toennies's concepts of gemeinschaft and gesellschaft. I will, however, center more extensively on modes of communication, ritual, and language, using the model developed by British anthropologist Mary Douglas in *Natural Symbols* and *Purity and Danger*. It should be noted that these categories are suggestive, explanatory models, as they are in Weber's social schema; therefore they are almost never exclusive one from the other, all people in the modern media-saturated society having at least some access to both of the language codes. The models are utilized to explain the shared approach to language and metaphor evidenced in these women authors.

Coming from a symbolic anthropological approach, Mary Douglas describes the expansion of the modern bureaucratic system within the large-scale industrial society. She concentrates on language as the guardian of the categories of social reference. Stating that different sorts of social matrices generate particular patterns of language, Douglas builds on the work of linguist Basil Bernstein. The discussion focuses on two of those language and social interactions, the codes, elaborated and restricted, and the social matrices from which both arise and with which they interact. The elaborated code, which I call the associational language, arises from the large-scale, role-differentiated rationalized social order, whereas the restricted code, which I call the local language, emerges from and reinforces the small, face-to-face, ritualistic community. The individual who grows to maturity primarily under sway of local language will have a different sense of self from that of the person who is educated in childhood primarily through the associational language. The human being shaped by the local language, which continually reinforces the stable community, assumes the continuance of his or her relationships throughout a lifetime; in contrast, the individual molded by the categories of the associational language will experience life as a free agent, unconstrained by the duties, traditions, and history of the group, in an ever more specialized vocational identity.

Douglas describes the dynamic by which industrial society generates the associational language. This always innovating language centers on the individual, allowing him or her to "make his [or her] own intentions explicit, to elucidate general principles" (44). Language thus fosters the separation of the individual from his or her fellows, reflecting the competitive nature of the culture. This separation can lead either to social dominance (in the case of the dominant individual) or to social control (in the case of the subjects of its directives).

In the competitive cosmology, represented in fiction by the urban setting or the impersonal bureaucracy, individual actors seek to impose their own personalities on and dictate their own interests to the rest of the population. The Big Man at the top of the social pyramid survives there only as long as he wields power, only while his strength lasts. The arrangement gives its strongest approval to the individual who gains enough social influence to shape the lives of his or her fellows. There is no stable morality; a succession of dominant individuals repeatedly redefine the meaning of such terms as "worth," "obligation," and "bravery" as they gain or lose power (*Natural Symbols*, 44). As a result of the emphasis on public and occupational life, traditional female discourse, which is founded on communal roles, suffers devaluation, becoming irrelevant, a distracting drain on the progress of the male material achiever; at best it serves as a respite from social competition. Private life finds itself more and more at the service of the expanding public sector as Nancy Cott posits in *The Bonds of Womanhood*. Evidence of the female biological role, with its cycles of menstruation, pregnancy, and menopause, becomes a sign of unfitness for competition in the arena of occupational identity, which demands that emotion and evidences of the primacy of the vulnerable human body be suppressed in the interest of predictability and thus complete control of the worker. Therefore the woman who would succeed in public roles must repudiate manifestations of her gender and devalue the private domestic role. As Elizabeth Fox-Genovese writes, "Shorn of its conviction of salvation and transcendence, the vision of androgyny collapses into the gray interchangeability of cogs in some machine" (*Feminism Without Illusions*, 228). Alienated from their own history, encouraged to shape their bodies for subsidiary roles in either nationalized "business" or sexual "romance," their mothers' lives and examples cast off and left behind, women risk transformation into commodities—"female eunuchs" in Germaine Greer's perceptive phrase. The fictional "town girls" of Cather, Glasgow, Welty, and Porter and the "third sex" of Gilman appear as genderless, emotionless "consumers"—beautiful, lifeless mannequins, markers for the display of the Big Man's success in the social competition. In the later novels as well as Gilman's later nonfiction, they serve the dominant male individuals as acquiescent, available sexual partners, unencumbered by the competing demands of child rearing and female kin and friendship. Although such women are often sexually active, they are seldom sensuous. Sex becomes for them a commodity to ensure female advancement within the social competition.

In contrast to the social arrangements and language of the competitive cosmology, Douglas, building on Bernstein's theories of language and social context, posits a second relevant language arising from another set of social arrangements, a small-scale community based on oral transmission of cultural socialization. It is, as I understand it, prevalent in the family itself and the neighborhood in traditional communities at some distance from the governing bureaucratic center.

In the shift from community to social structure, communication changes not only in degree but in kind. A face-to-face community of stable social hierarchy and custom produces artistic communications—"literature" as we understand it is too specialized a term—that are meant to address and unite the whole social order through elements of religious ritual. In contrast, the large-scale social order gives birth to purchased, individualistic written literary productions, marketed and sold by specialized publishers to a particular audience as a leisure entertainment. The smaller social organization tends to have very clear and stringently enforced boundaries between the community and the outside world. Because this small community operates within an interlocking network of interdependent human beings, crucial roles for women exist, despite the often tyrannical control of the patriarchal head. Custom and skills are transmitted directly along with responsibilities of the social role accompanying them, and art, as we understand it, is inextricably entwined with religion, economics, politics, and, above all, personal relationships, especially family.

As might be expected, in the patriarchal community, "literature" is seldom an essentially private, even leisure activity. The conditions of artistic creation change in the shift from small-scale community to national state. In the community, emotion is integrated into the prescribed formulas of ritual priestly communication. Whatever his or her own circumstance, abilities, or interests, any participant in the group celebration can receive, feel, and understand the meaning of the ritual message. Despite the individual's social situation and despite questions of justice, no member misunderstands or has a feeling of incomplete participation. These rituals orchestrate human emotions—awe, joy, fear, and love are engendered by the familiar act that celebrates and reinforces the boundaries of the interconnected community.

Artistic communication retains much of this religious identity and didactic intent. The artistic communications of the community are generally experienced as a group in a central meeting place and feature actors who represent whole categories of people. The women in this discussion attempt to capture both the bonding power of ritual and the didactic intent of earlier literature for their own art, to restore the emotional force of the integrated community within an egalitarian harmonious community under the leadership of the accepting wise woman, not the controlling patriarch. The local language strengthens the bonding of the social group and partakes of some of the immediacy and inclusiveness of ritual. The utterances of the local language within the community have, as Douglas explains, "a double purpose: they convey information, yes, but they also reinforce it. The second function is the dominant one" (*Natural Symbols* 44). The bonding, and bounding, local language exists at the edges of dominant discourse of the social center. This is where the authors place the home place under the care of the wise woman, and this is the language they seek to evoke.

Placing these models in the American context will suggest how these two languages and their social matrices generated the concept of the home place as a counter to the "self-made" man. Although the ritualistic community never existed in the fullest degree in the New World—for example, the complex argumentation of the male leadership, intellectual and religious, moved far away from the immediate communication of ritual—the small-scale Puritan community nevertheless retains significant relationships and communications: its authoritarian nature and its lack of role specialization, its emphasis on shared lands and facilities, its moralistic cosmos, and its pervasive religious life.[5] The early communities of the South evolved a particular aberrant pattern of the patriarchal community. As commentators on the American South have noted, from the redoubtable W. J. Cash onward, this communal arrangement explicitly subordinates black men and black and white women to the rule of the white patriarch.

In both New England and Southern models, however, the potentially disruptive individual was isolated from the exercise of conscience by an interlocking network of roles and institutions to which all members of the community belonged. Politics, religion, and history mixed with artistic aims in this order, just as one human encompassed several overlapping, crucial identities that reinforced each other. In such a tightly woven cloth of relationships and duties, the strands of written and spoken communication clearly served more general functions than does the single thread of the specialized literary activity of today. Retaining much of the didactic and communal components of ritual, the written word served directly to carry the messages of the political and religious leaders to the rest of the community. Early American literature consists of journals, sermons, orations, instructional books, and didactic poetry. The didactic, often religious, communal aim outweighed the artistic. In its undifferentiated functions, the literary activity thus both reflected the system and guarded its narrow boundaries.

As the American social order expands in the eighteenth and especially the nineteenth century, with the process of industrial takeoff, the development of interlocking, rationalized structures parallels the expansion of population and territory, reaching out to undergo both horizontal and vertical organization. The identity of the human being is increasingly defined as separate from collective traditional social structures such as family, church, and neighborhood. Although this shift is characteristic of large-scale bureaucratic social orders, the move toward material competition between freestanding individuals encounters few obstacles in the New World within a "virgin" landscape holding no equally powerful competing societies. In the United States, as cultural commentators such as Myra Jehlen and T. J. Jackson Lears have noted, support for liberal individualism is more pronounced than it is in the Europe that produced the first wave of immigrants. In *No Place of Grace*, Lears suggests that the absence of competing communal authorities such as church and nobility offers one central explanation for this cultural phenomenon—without them the process of rationalization proceeded unfettered (4). As Lears concludes, American "individualism was less openly challenged, its optimism more brazen and banal" (6).

The competitive, rational, expansionist social structure and universe replace the cooperative, moralistic, tightly interrelated community. As the process of rationalization continues, the natural environment becomes for the dominant male leaders an available resource to be utilized, rather than a savage wilderness boundary to be avoided. These leaders play out their individualistic competition in the arena of the marketplace, the successful entrepreneur becoming almost a law unto himself, the followers subject to a growing body of impersonal law devised and administered by unknown persons far beyond their influence. This process parallels Douglas's strong grid cosmology of the Big Man and his followers (88–92). Those who support the leaders make up the staffs of the burgeoning bureaucracies, whose impersonal rules now reach not only into vocational settings but increasingly into the remnants of traditionally private and informal communal relationships.[6] The complex, large-scale society encourages and values individual initiative and assigns personal responsibility and control to events and outcomes. The losers in the social competition at the center cannot console themselves with extrapersonal explanations; as Douglas observes, the only sin is stupidity. Failure is a personal, not a social, condition.

At the time that women began to write prose fiction, the leadership of politics, religion, trade, and science were separating into distinct disciplines, each with its own specialized language. Literature was more and more the province of the socially devalued emotion and imagination as religion itself became ever more rationalized. The secular order captures the symbolism that now centers on the dominant material achiever, "the self-made man," as its representative figure. Women writers quite naturally attempted to capture the attention of the American audience by recasting this pattern into female terms, by changing the gender of the protagonist but not the essential outlines of the characterization. Although Cather, Porter, and Jewett initially present the autonomous female individual, who enters spheres of achievement deemed male, they later move toward portrayals of the female seer within a nurturing egalitarian homeland.

Mary P. Ryan details how the cultural valorization of individualism has worked to create an adversarial relationship between woman and the family, creating a progressive historical paradigm, in which increased movement away from communal family relationships is portrayed as liberation. Ryan asserts that the assumption that women enter history as fully developed individuals pursuing autonomous goals is erroneous, a paradigm influenced by the cultural model. She states that woman's history often presumes an individualized female subject and, further, that it overemphasizes the lives of women who have the time and inclination to write diaries and letters; this could also be noted about the writing women here treated. Such women also have been educated in the associational language and the educational bureaucracies at the cultural center, thus diminishing the influence of domesticity and local language. Ryan makes a further observation: many of these women are young and single, suspended between parental and conjugal home, therefore "likely to deposit disproportionate evidence of female individuality and subjectivity into the historical record" (*Mother* 7). As these writers grow older, they often move from an individualistic viewpoint, whether of triumph or despair, to a communal female context.

Intellectuals of several disciplinary stripes have long described the paradigmatic male figure influenced by the outlines of the successful Big Man of industrial society: an autonomous individual, who seeks to move out of time and space, defeating the constraints of history and social custom, even denying the limits of death as he has already shed birth and the woman in his self-creation. Psychologist Erik Erikson, for example, sees a historical basis for this figure in John Henry, who represents the "*child who abandoned the mother*" (296, emphasis Erikson's). Erikson considers this folk hero to represent the "motherless" man who "faced new geographic and technological worlds as men and without a past" (296).

Another example comes from Ruth Benedict's classic *Patterns of Culture*, whose profligate, cannibalistic Kwakiutls represented the traits the author saw in her contemporary America: "All these prerogatives (titles, material goods, names) though they remained in a blood lineage, were nevertheless not held in common, but were owned for the time being by an individual who singly and exclusively exercised the rights which they conveyed" (183). In the male-dominated individualistic society, women's primary occupation was the production of goods for the potlatches, which determined the men's status, rather than "household routine." Ultimately, even the children themselves become commodities for destruction in the competition between dominant males. In contrast, Benedict idealized the civilization of the pueblo peoples of New Mexico, whose matrilineal, peaceful, ritual-reverent society she contrasts sharply with the equally altered (by Benedict) acquisitive, wasteful Kwakiutls—as the material competition at the American center differs from the fictional home place. Benedict notes that among the pueblos there is "no delight in any situation in which the individual stands alone" (122) and, moreover, in this egalitarian community life is lived according to the order of nature as the "seasons unroll themselves before us, and man's life also" and they pray that they "shall be one person" (128). As John O. King observes in conversation and lectures, these ideal constructions respond to the

American process of rationalization, but they also represent, more particularly, a type of the female home place and reflect Benedict's portrayal of the costs of the individualistic competition.

In literary criticism this tendency has been especially marked. In *The American Adam*, R. W. B. Lewis offers the most concise and cogent description of this representative male personality who "is an individual emancipated from history, happily bereft of ancestry, untouched and undefiled by the usual inheritances of family and race; an individual standing alone, self-reliant and self-propelling, ready to confront whatever awaited him with the aid of his own unique and inherent resources" (5). Free from competing human definition, he creates a simpler, happier retreat in a natural setting amenable to his imaginative world-building. In Quentin Anderson's perceptive phrase, this literary individual becomes an "imperial self," blotting out competing social authority. Moreover, Richard Slotkin notes that whereas Jefferson praised the farmer, a figure which implied a settled home and family, as the model citizen, the American introspective and popular literature, in reality, celebrated the frontiersman of "adventure and exploit," a characterization "more prophetic of future developments than are the agrarian panegyrics of Jefferson and his intellectual heirs" ("Myth and the Production of History," 84). The appeal of this figure in the nineteenth century, as Slotkin notes, comes from his identity as a double for the self-styled self-made man of the emerging industrial social order who leaves group constraints behind.

Fictional circumstance replicates metaphorically the ideal experience of the individual in the competitive nation, as the single human being faces an elaborating social structure with fewer markers of stable identity. The plot and characterization of individual world-building reflect a corresponding impulse in the underlying industrial and post-industrial American culture, one in which, as Douglas writes in *Natural Symbols*, "[T]here are few overriding community interests to check the leader's impetus. . . . He has made their lineages and ancestral shrines less meaningful for them than his own favour" (89–90). Day in, day out, the assumptions of the dominant discourse through manifestations of public institutions and law underline the cultural insistence on the dominant individual.

The plot of heroic individualism allows the artist and the reader to experience imaginatively the personal expansiveness promised to the

winner of the social competition. All members of the literary community are influenced by this model and must address it if only to reject
it. Repeatedly women authors discuss the influence of the "mainstream" tradition or, alternately, they borrow and adapt its characterization and plots to their uses. Here is the very moment where the
problem of conflicting identities becomes especially problematic for
the woman author, the more if she is a woman of color or a lesbian.
Many central works of American mainstream canon valorize the morality of the competitive cosmology, especially the subjugation of the
natural and social environments to the will and vision of the heroic
individual. There is little space for the woman, except for victimized
women such as Hester Prynne, Lady Brett, Lena Grove, Eula Varner,
Zenobia, or Isabel Archer, women undone by their self-assertion, their
naivety, or their passions. The woman writer finds no models of female
creativity; most often fictional characters with natures like her own are
shaped to the needs of the male protagonist.

The women's fictional homes attempt to manipulate the symbolism
of the male myth; as Rachel Blau DuPlessis observes of such twentieth-
century American poets as H. D. and Adrienne Rich, these authors
also attempt a re-vision of male myths familiar to their readers. In
DuPlessis's formulation, women poets reshape ritualistic, religious,
and legendary materials, as the voice of women's communities overcomes the individualistic language of the father. The reformulation of
myth is especially apparent in poetry, which retains its public, ritualistic function, but it appears in prose as well. Douglas observes that
those who are ignored by the bureaucratic social structures as they
wander among a maze of impersonal rules "should act strongly against
non-differentiation and seek to establish clear categories and distinc-
tions which the oppressors would be forced to recognize" ("Control of
Symbols," *Natural Symbols*, 183).

By conflating elements of the Jeffersonian vision with the biblical
idea of the New Jerusalem—as writers such as Cather and Glasgow
explicitly do—or by manipulating the pastoral ideal around a Demeter
figure within a local American context—as Porter and Welty do—or
by placing the seer's home far away from the public competition—as
Gilman, Naylor, and Jewett do—these women illustrate metaphorically the isolation of the woman's contribution from the dominant cultural discourse.[7] (When these writers leave the landscape for the

American city or town, they portray artistic and biological sterility.) By capturing these references, the writers create a suggestive model of democratic collective action as an alternative to a morality of calculation and competition, which they consider antithetical to a civilized human life. Through the creation of the home place and the evocation of a semidivine wise woman, they hope to offer an alternate imaginative narrative of American beginnings, one which challenges the legends of the womanless woodsman moving ever farther away from woman and home.

At the same time that the writers deplore the impersonality and regimentation of the social order, they have no yearning for a past, which they consider repressive and paternalistic. More than simple antimodernist pleading underlies this repeated narrative. Even though Porter and Welty, the most problematic in this regard, ultimately rewrite the past as matriarchal, they nonetheless make clear the visionary nature of the home place. Instead of simply representing nostalgia, the setting, which joins the natural and domestic worlds, forms a clearly imaginary exemplar for a human existence, which acknowledges the claims of community. In its shared productive labors and its immediate emotional communication, the home place rejects the usual detached contemplative yearning associated with the traditional pastoral, the detachment which Raymond Williams describes as "that of the scientist or the tourist, rather than of the working countryman" (*The Country and the City*, 20). The "other place" seeks to bring the reader into the full, feeling membership of ritual communication, to destroy distances between genders, generations, and classes. To do this, the authors have frequent recourse to myths and oral tradition.

The women's literature, early and late, intends to address the woman's community, present and future, to insist upon the neglected female power as its creators take their place within the lineage. In Jane Tompkins's witty turn of phrase, they have "designs" on the American audience (*Sensational Designs*). As they mature in their art, these writers imply that the woman's body itself serves as the transcendent model of creativity. The wise women they depict perform prodigies of creativity: human, through their power of procreation and nurture—the demigoddesses have attended childbirth as midwife or have given birth themselves; natural, through the gardens they plant and tend—not only the essential vegetable patch but wonders of floral display; domestic, through sewing and knitting—especially the creation of quilts, each scrap of which comes from a remembered piece of clothing with its own story—and finally, literary and historical, through their remembered stories of their respective families or their sponsorship of art.

In many of the works, the central female character does nothing less than rewrite the history of her American homeland, her neighborhood—it cannot be emphasized too strongly—not the nation. For example, Grandmother Fincastle retells the story of the coming of Glasgow's own Scotch-Irish ancestors to Virginia, adding the costs to the women pioneers and depicting the violence toward the native people; Porter's Miss Sophia Jane and Nanny of *The Old Order* as well as Granny Weatherall detail their labors in creating the Texas neighborhood despite the fecklessness and failures of the male family; Miss Katie Rainey of *The Golden Apples*, Ellen Fairchild of *Delta Wedding*, and Becky McKelva of *The Optimist's Daughter* narrate a history of Welty's own small corner of Mississippi, and Naylor's Miranda recounts the founding of Willow Springs by the determination and courage of the female slave Sapphira Wade, who wrested the land from a white slaveholder. In all, women by wit, endurance, and strength overcome both male domination and natural wilderness to create a just homeland.

And for each introspective woman writer, the discovery of her own place as autonomous woman artist within her own female history emerges as a central developmental task. The resolution of the conflict between the wise woman's communal memory and the daughter's individual aspirations forms the dramatic center of Jewett's *Country of the Pointed Firs*, Cather's *The Song of the Lark*, Glasgow's *Vein of Iron* and *Beyond Defeat*, Porter's *The Old Order*, Welty's *The Golden Apples*, Naylor's *Mama Day* as well as Louise Erdrich's *Tracks* and Joan Didion's *A Book of Common Prayer*. This resolution occurs through the evocation of demigoddess, whose womanly identity, memory, emotions, and body itself generate and bless all forms of creativity, male and female. In strikingly similar scenes from Wharton's *The Gods Arrive*, Cather's *My Ántonia*, and Glasgow's *Vein of Iron*, the female authors show the silencing of male art and language before the ultimate creative source. In all, the authors insist that male creativity issues from the "eternal feminine," thus creativity is more easily available to the woman artist through the model of her own body. Moreover, by their own female authorship of the scene, they claim their own places as daughters of the matrix of creativity.

In rebellion from the father's language, from narratives of patriarchal creativity, and from male social dominance, these women writers summon the female seer and thus reclaim authority for their own artistic tasks. Maternal wise women such as Jewett's Mrs. Blackett, Cather's Ántonia Shimerda, Glasgow's Grandmother Fincastle, Porter's Granny Weatherall, Nannie, and Miss Sophia Jane, Welty's Ellen Fairchild, Miss Katie Rainey, Granny Vaughn, and Becky McKelva, and Naylor's Sapphira Jane, Abigail, and Miranda embody the woman's history, which is exiled from the dominant discourse and often first rejected by the author.

Language is crucial in the development of the protagonist, for she must struggle to hear the female demigoddess, who cannot be summoned through the associational language—she must reclaim lost childhood memories and hear the mother's language. The massive social order accepts the individual as its base unit and suspects traditional communal language and relationships. The male family and lovers often use, however unwillingly, the women around them as instruments of their own self-aggrandizement. Jason Greylock, for example, exploits both Dorinda Oakley and Geneva Ellgood in Glasgow's *Barren Ground*, as Oswald Henshawe marries Myra Driscoll in Cather's *My Mortal Enemy*, as Battle Fairchild submerges Ellen in Welty's *Delta Wedding*. Through the powerful, resonant female imagery, the authors summon the elemental creative power they see embodied in the wise woman; at the same time they insist on the limits of the associational language. In their latter-day emphasis on memory and their suspicion of the expanding social structures, the woman writer mirrors her writing brothers, but always within a context and toward a meaning specifically female. Gilman, Jewett, Glasgow, Cather, Porter, Welty, and Naylor, as well as the earlier domestic novelists witness to the isolation of female influence from the American centers of power. Caught in bureaucratic structures by a tight net of an abstract language and addressing a tradition which privileges the autonomous male individual, the woman writer finds few references to connect with the memories of the women's history. Restrained by the patriarchal past and its male-centered myths, she must rework those materials into her own narratives of creativity. These writers attempt to reconstruct a context for a female communal vision, interweaving vivid emblematic scenes using recaptured biblical or classical myth within the linear narrative, reusing cast-off materials into new women's stories—like the beloved scraps that make up the mother's quilt. They attempt to stop the narrative's forward motion in order to engage in emotional visual language and to defeat for a moment the innovating language, which denies the past and the mother. Their language paradoxically tries to *become* ritual, although of course it will always express a tension between its aim and its success because it must begin and end in the associational language of the dominant discourse.

The female protagonist of both the domestic and the self-conscious fiction steps into a dangerous competitive social order; to save her humanity, the isolated heroine must find the home place to recover her own woman's language, discover her own woman's history. To complete her developmental task successfully, she must connect with the female seer and the home place. When she succeeds in this journey back, she finds her "voice," a process most marked and literal in Cather's *The Song of the Lark* and Jewett's *The Country of the Pointed Firs*. The use of the alternate myth portrays a psychic woman's journey, which parallels the American version of the male quest but ends in the return to a social order and to the generations.

The home place grants the revolutionary discovery to the writing woman that, whereas her own literary works are a product of her individual genius, their beginnings are communal, arising out of a shared history and ongoing connections. The authors bring this knowledge to other cultural activities as well. The central figure for female literary creativity is the quilt, which represents the rejoining of diverse female experience into literature and reflects the less linear nature of this narrative by women. In the writings of these women, the text resembles the quilt. Thus work, memory, art, and language are reunited in the present, in the past, and in the future. Not only as "memory," but in a real physical artifact, thus the implication that human relationships have actual, lasting effects on the material world. By consonance, the demigoddess wise women created by these writers need not envision a spiritual heaven; their immortality arises from their bodies and their creative natures, both spiritual and physical manifestations of creativity. This plot heals the split between mind and body, human artifact and natural creativity, individual and group.

Accordingly, the language assumes an almost physical presence, resonant with ritual inclusiveness. When her "child" Cocoa prepares to marry, for example, Mama Day makes her a honeymoon quilt, an emblem of the position in the family's history that the young woman is preparing to assume:

> Down and up, a stitch at a time. She's almost knee deep in bags of colored rags, sorted together by shades. The rings lay on a solid backing of cotton flannel; from a distance it looks like she's bending over a patch of sand at the bottom of the bluff when it's caught the first rays of a spring moon—an evening cream. . . . A bit of her daddy's Sunday shirt is matched with Abigail's lace slip, the collar from Hope's graduation dress, the palm of Grace's baptismal gloves. . . . The front of Mother's gingham shirtwaist. . . . I'll just use a sliver, no longer than the joint of my thumb. Put a little bit of her in here somewhere. . . . When it's done right you can't tell where one ring ends and the other begins. It's like they ain't been sewn at all, they grew up out of nowhere. (137–38)

The quilt expresses perfectly how the female narrative grows out of female memory, as Naylor evokes the living experience of the home place. In the refashioning of old, emotion-imbued materials—the quilts are often stitched together of scraps of cloth from central events of beloved lives—into new forms of art, the author-daughters discover the link between their self-conscious art and their grandmothers' lives. The use of quilting and sewing is exceedingly persistent in the writing of American women; they are a central metaphor in other works such as Jewett's "The Foreigner," Cather's *O Pioneers!*, "The Joy of Nelly Deane," and *Shadows on the Rock*, Welty's *The Golden Apples* and *The Optimist's Daughter*, Porter's *The Old Order*, and Glasgow's *Virginia* and *Vein of Iron*. In all the image of women sewing inspires the daughter's artistic method.[8]

In Alice Walker's "Everyday Use," the quilt, representing the female history and narrative, is withheld by the mother from the urban, professionalized daughter in favor of the homebound daughter. The narrative issues from the local context, just as the stories held in the quilt are woven of the local language of oral narrative. Most often, as the quilt is made, the stories are recited and the memories of family members, living and dead, are reunited. As Walker's title illustrates, this quilt of artistically arranged scraps of beloved memory is for "everyday use"; the woman's art thus belongs to a living context, healing the split between the place of work and the place of residence, between art and daily existence, between past and future. Together, the repeated metaphors of the garden and the quilt show female care as a unifying creative social force. Through the garden, the wise woman works with nature and produces harmony, just as she labors with female body and creates civilization—she is not defined purely by biological procreation but more fully by her power to join individuals in community. Through the quilt, she starts with discarded materials and creates a work of beauty as these women writers start with lost female narratives and shape them into an artistic whole.

With their evocation of reworked myth and ritual, their recourse to a communal language, their valorization of the domestic arts, and their re-creation of a pastoral female home, the authors move from the hesitations and doubts of their first writings, when they employ the male model of competitive individualism, to their later work, when they understand their own artistic endeavors and their experience as part of a vital lineage with a communal history, arts, and language.

The women writers in this discussion come together in an imaginative social world that operates on much the same dynamic as those social feminists who used the powerful symbolism of the family against that of the self-made man. The shared plot of the home place borrows from both the individual as defined in the early republic and from the crucial roles of the small-scale community. The emphasis on individual achievement may be seen in the acceptance of the daughter's art and in the wise women's leadership of the community. They bring together the figure of the individual woman of achievement and display the displaced human connections and suppressed emotional ties they perceive in their contemporary social order. They achieve this by bringing the independent daughter back into the home place for replenishment for the competition "outside." The legacy of the small-scale traditional community appears in the emphasis on the female family and friendship, in the retention of didactic purpose, in its recreation of stock communal characters, and in its abiding suspicion of the exclusive male-female bond with its dependence on the competitive, individualistic public world. These women, however, imagine something in the domestic homeland far different from the satellite of consumerism, which supports and participates in exchange morality. Instead, they create an exemplary egalitarian neighborhood gathered around the wise woman, which shows forth as a creative center for

both nature, through her garden, and for art, through her quilt of stories sewed for the community's individualistic artist daughter.

Like their male literary counterparts, the women authors also play
out the drama of the movement away from the commercial center, but
with different metaphor and plot. Although influenced by the plot of
American heroic individualism, most of the women realize that the
plot necessarily excludes cooperative emotion, the female family, and
woman's creativity, symbolized in these women by the wise woman.
Repeatedly the authors in this study mourn the lack of any central social institution that offers acknowledgment of their identity as women,
and they protest the devaluation of the female community. They suggest that the separation of women from the social center traps all individuals, both men and women, in the time and experiences of the
one single lifetime. As writers such as Willa Cather, Ellen Glasgow,
Gloria Naylor, Eudora Welty, Katherine Anne Porter, and Sarah Orne
Jewett progress through their careers, they reject the flight of individual aspiration as a childish fancy. These American women artists
will not have to paint over a canvas to create their narratives on blankness; the social order itself supplies it.

They themselves were a unit, a conscious group;
they thought in terms of community. As such,
their time-sense was not limited to the hopes
and ambitions of an individual life. Therefore,
they habitually considered and carried out
plans for improvement which might cover
centuries.

> —Charlotte Perkins Gilman
> *Herland*

2.

Home-Made

SARAH ORNE JEWETT

IN THE GROWING social organization of the later nineteenth-century
America, impersonal rules enforced by faceless, distant administrators
increasingly controlled the individual; Sarah Orne Jewett detailed the
effects of these changes on small New England towns during the final
twenty years of the nineteenth century:

> [C]rowded towns and the open country were to be brought together in
> new association and dependence on each other. It appeared as if a sec-
> ond Harvey had discovered a new and national circulation of vitality
> along the fast-multiplying railroads that spun their webs to bind together
> men who had once lived far apart. (*Deephaven*, 31)

As Jewett understood, the ideas and mores of the city had changed
small-town "rustic" New England irrevocably. The single human being now associated with strangers, as customers or competitors in the
same occupation, instead of daily encountering a wide range of familiar members of a tightly bounded social order. The process of bureau-

cratization accelerated, producing the results on association and language that Mary Douglas details as characteristic of the modern social order. More and more, received identities and connections were separated out from public activity and isolated in the move toward bureaucratization, causing the changes for women of which Nancy Cott writes so eloquently. Glenna Matthews describes the effect of the process of rationalization on the home with its demand for further predictability and standardization and its scorn for the craft tradition of women's domestic arts. Matthews demonstrates how this personally transmitted and modified body of knowledge is rejected by the corporate and intellectual leadership as wasteful, unreliable, and even unhealthy. Even such feminist reformers and visionaries as Gilman herself in *Women and Economics* (1900) and *The Home: Its Work and Influence* (1903) and Edward Bellamy in *Looking Backward* (1888) deemed the domestic tradition outmoded and worthless. In *"Just a Housewife,"* Matthews assesses the effect of those reformists' attitudes—their insistence that the bureaucratically organized public life was the important sphere—on the devaluation of most women's daily work. The reformists gave scant interest to the home as virtuous human setting and crucial component of society, a problem which had engaged earlier thinkers. As Matthews concludes, "Ironically, the long-term consequence was not to liberate women, who were still ascribed to the home, but to trivialize the home, thereby rendering it a much less satisfactory work environment" (114). As Matthews realizes, the domestic arrangements promoted in the nineteenth century, often by male clerics, were strongly paternalistic; nonetheless, like other socially subordinate groups, women created arts and skills of great sophistication, developed local language, and accumulated knowledge, which the women writers early and late celebrate.

In addition, as Dolores Hayden contends in *The Grand Domestic Revolution*, two developments had hastened the repudiation of domestic traditions that encouraged multigenerational families. By the late nineteenth century, such home economics specialists as Ellen Swallow Richards and Mary Hinman Abel had begun to urge that the home be "rationalized"; the public kitchen, for example, associated with the settlement house which served the working poor, had taken "the form of a scientific laboratory" (Hayden, 157). These specialists put aside the personal relationships and the domestic craft tradition of "home" cooking as old-fashioned, inefficient, and perhaps unsanitary. More-over domestic tasks such as clothing manufacture and food prepara-tion had become part of the public market economy, controlled by dis-tant bureaucracies. Having rejected the female craft tradition under local female leadership in favor of efficiency and control by experts, these reformers found their own female-headed communal solutions rejected. Ultimately, the national leadership replaced the communal aspect of these plans for domestic rationalization with an ideal of the one-generational home, headed by a man, thus supporting the male's public roles and duties, and thus returning to the cultural valorization of the dominant male individual. Hayden details several developments signifying the shift to "one man's family." In 1931, for example, Presi-dent Hoover called a national conference on home building and home ownership, which proposed the nuclear family home as an antidote to the depressed economy and to labor unrest (275). The male leadership denounced the communal nature of the reformists' domestic arrange-ments, implying that nonnuclear-family living was foreign and un-natural to the American social environment. Hayden relates that the Red Scare of the 1920s attacked the socialists in the material feminist movement and ultimately the "collective home" as under the sway of Soviet models.

Once both the corporate leadership and the material feminists had appropriated and standardized the domestic tasks, it only remained, as happened in the 1920s, for the mass woman's magazines, under pres-sure from changing fashions, to promote the isolated house—a house needing to be "managed" like a small business. The ideal home now sheltered the nuclear family, headed by a male—rather than several generations that often included members of the wife's family—the husband's children demanding socialization, and a "tasteful" display of goods purchased by a passive female under the direction of a horde of "experts." In a segment on a popular woman's magazine, *The Wom-an's Home Companion,* Hayden describes how the periodical turned from its 1923 support of women's cooperatives to its 1927 promotion of the nuclear family home, stocked with a full array of purchased goods and services. (275). The individual woman—her traditional crafts and domestic labor devalued, herself isolated from the competi-tive public world except in her functions as consumer and operative, her domestic tasks diminished—experienced the conflicting impersonal roles of followers of the Big Man culture. As Hayden concludes, the earlier material feminists recruited women whose basic activity was domestic labor, even as they rejected the craft tradition, but "contemporary feminists who have attacked the family home have had little to offer housewives as an alternate ideal of home life" (303).

Many women authors, however, have refused even to the present day to cede this central homemaking activity to either the governmental and commercial bureaucracies; still less do they hark back to the male-controlled, socially isolated nuclear-family home that some reactionary groups demand under the rubric of "tradition." A significant group of women writers (including Matthews) center on the woman's area of traditional craft knowledge, created despite the paternalistic social framework, and they focus (as does Hayden) on women's potential to unite despite class, ethnic, and vocational divisions; this knowledge and this strength, the critics and the women authors agree, have the potential to enrich the lives of both women and men, presenting the woman's home place as a model to the society of more equitable human relationships and more vigorous cooperative social action. Barbara Ehrenreich and Deirdre English neatly summarize the losses and gains of the domestic sphere under the process of rationalization: "Industrial capitalism freed women from the endless round of household productive labor, and in one and the same gesture tore away the skills which had been the source of women's unique dignity. It loosed the bonds of patriarchy, and at once imposed the chains of wage labor" (*For Her Own Good*, 14).

The "other place" existed in the novels of American women from their beginnings, as they tried to imagine models of strength arising from women's daily activities and associations. Written under lingering paternalistic influence, the domestic novels clearly differ from the later self-consciously artistic novels. Creating a pattern, these craftswomen and artists evolved a plot whose elements were drawn from women's daily activities and women's relationships with female family and friends. Its outlines change and evolve from the midnineteenth century to the present, but its criticism of the social emphasis on exchange, competition, and individual dominance remains. And, of course, in the work of these women, we as readers see the communal, didactic intent most clearly.

Nina Baym in *Woman's Fiction* identifies one basic plot in the domestic novel that remained significant for later generations of female authors, "In essence, it is the story of a young girl who is deprived of the supports she had rightly or wrongly depended on to sustain her through-out life and is faced with the necessity of winning her own way in the world" (11). Domestic fiction most often depicts a socially isolated heroine who establishes a family and redeems a network of supportive friends and family from a barren and often mercenary social order, thus reversing the repeated male plot of the individual moving away toward a promising frontier and leaving a corrupt social order behind. Despite its lip service to previous paternalistic social arrangements— the ending, as Baym notes, most often ends with the marriage of the heroine—the plot subverted patterns of male dominance as the heroine undertakes the creation of the home. She, for the most part, chooses her own husband and creates a circle of family and friends from the fragmented society around her. The search often takes place in the face of the absence or the opposition of those materially ambitious protectors—fathers and brothers—who might have guided or sup-ported the girl's choice in the paternalistic community. The absence of an effective, caring mother or female family is central to this narrative, suggesting the depreciation of female roles and history in the imper-sonal social order. Placing the American woman at the center of a redeemed familial, cooperative context, the narrative criticizes the separation of woman's influence from the national social order.

As Baym writes, this domestic plot assumes that men and women reach their greatest humanity through the home, which is defined not simply as the nuclear family but a range of human relationships "based on love, support, and mutual responsibility" (27). Despite the fulsome panegyrics granted maternity in their contemporary litera-ture, the domestics know better. They seek to imagine a woman-centered social alternative, one in which, as Baym notes, the domestic setting is posited as "a value scheme for ordering all of life, in compe-tition with the ethos of money and exploitation that is perceived to prevail in American society" (27). The woman's domestic world was to be the home for all, not simply an adjunct to the public competition. The fictional patterns of later self-conscious women writers indicate that much of this American vision remains, albeit with variations, until the late twentieth century.

In many domestic novels, the ties of womanhood defeat spatial and temporal ties through the letters of a distant sister or death through the remembered counsel of a beloved dead mother. Thus they suggest the isolation of female networks through the disappearance of the physical presence. At the same time, they insist on the moral presence of female family, which defeats pure materiality. By contrasting the cooperation of the woman's community with the competition of the male-controlled social structures, the authors betray their opinion of their contemporary American society.

For many middle-class women readers, the themes and character-ization of the domestic novel offered an alternative both to the advice of popular writers and the directives of the impersonal marketplace. By their portrayals of such vigorous female figures, often mothers in training, as Isabel of Maria McIntosh's *Two Lives* (1846), domestic novelists implicitly refuted the attitudes found in such best-selling ad-vice books as John Abbott's *The Mother at Home; or, The Principles of Maternal Duty* (1834). As Abbott presents it, maternity is an intellec-tually and spiritually passive occupation, which has as its central charge the duty to relay to sons the directives of the male deity as interpreted by male clergy. Mothers, in short, were a sort of spiritual switchboard operator. Woman had little authority but great responsibility for the spiritual and ethical welfare of the American nation: "When our land is filled with virtuous and patriotic mothers, then it will be filled with virtuous and patriotic men. She who was first in the transgression, must be yet the principal earthly instrument in the restoration" (166). Jane Tompkins convincingly outlines the "cultural work" of the do-mestic novel's spiritual component as it challenges the dominant dis-course of competitive materialism. The morality of the home place Isabel founds at the end of *Two Lives* contrasts starkly with the ethics and practice of the New York social and financial spheres depicted in the novel's early pages. In a work that stands midway between domestic novel and introspective fiction, *Pink and White Tyranny* (1871), Harriet Beecher Stowe contrasts the women's American homes and gardens of small-town Springdale with the French-influenced mansions and landscaping of New York as the author juxtaposes the paternalistic business practices of John Seymour with the individualis-tic, pragmatic calculation of Dick Follingsbee. Both authors insist that the American home and its female founder directly determine the character of the nation itself. Whereas the advice books counseled obedience to both male deity and paternalistic earthly authority, the domestic novels shifted the emphasis to a creative, dynamic maternity within a vital, ongoing, and socially significant woman's community. Remaining evidence of the communal, didactic intent in later woman's introspective novels, however, has not been so clearly delineated. Through the ideal female home place, self-consciously artistic writers such as Cather, Jewett, Welty, Naylor, Porter, and Glasgow address the woman reader, presenting their alternative to the plot of the triumphant male individual.

From the beginning, defenders of early paternalistic domesticity and those of the later competitive society have criticized the domestic novels in intemperate terms. Dee Garrison details the adverse reactions to woman's fiction by identifying the qualities that caused many of their books to be withdrawn from libraries in 1881. Those banned bestsellers, Garrison writes, all reject traditional male authority particularly in regard to social hierarchy, religious faith, and domestic life (74). In sum, the challenge to the male control of domestic life was rebuffed. Modern critical practice seeks the unique language of the singular individual; it therefore mistakenly cites didactic content as a failure of imagination. Henry Nash Smith, for example, appears to criticize the domestics for their cultivation of a communal sensibility, as opposed to the individualistic practice of the contemporary social order. He damns *The Wide, Wide World* for its spiritual emphasis, its chipping away at the borders between natural and supernatural spheres. Smith presents the works of Hawthorne and Melville as exemplars of the excellent novels inundated by the tidal wave of domestic writing, an argument Tompkins persuasively refutes. Above all, he objects to the "Rise of . . . the Common Woman." The critic senses the opposition between the communal assumptions of the domestics and the individualistic practices of the heroic male individual.

In the present discussion, McIntosh's *Two Lives* serves as the exemplary text for the mother's home as it appears in the domestic novel. This novel, which went through seven editions in four years, evidences fictional strategies found in the novels that follow, both domestic and self-conscious. *Two Lives* opens at the grave of the two protagonists' male protector, Mr. Elliott, who was the father of Grace Elliott and the uncle of the orphaned Isabel Duncan. Both motherless girls have been supported by Mr. Elliott and cared for by his unmarried sister Aunt

Nancy. From the beginning McIntosh makes the clear distinction between Grace—small, blond, emotionally dependent, physically weak, and charming—and Isabel—vigorous, dark, handsome, erect, and plainspoken, who represents the independent woman who by her physical nature differs from other women.

Carroll Smith-Rosenberg addresses both the androgynous nature of the New Woman and her ties to the woman's community, connecting the androgynous figure with the familiar problem of language for feminists, who must seek to bring their female experience to the dominant discourse through its own language. Smith-Rosenberg notes that by adopting a male symbolic system, women lose the power to create language; basing her work in part on Mary Douglas's work, Smith-Rosenberg understands the difficulty of overcoming cultural categories. She asks two important questions: If marginal groups have lost the power to create language, how can they survive? How can they frame alternate communal, ritual modes of experience in associational language? ("Androgynes," 266). These questions, of course, touch on the questions of patriarchal literary influence. Stating the problem differently, the woman writer must undertake to promote female symbolism and histories within a culture that privileges male symbolism and histories. The texts suggest that this problem has plagued women writers as well, causing them to begin a writing career by creating the somewhat androgynous woman who challenges the assigned social roles.

Isabel's description anticipates such protagonists of women's introspective narratives as Cather's Ántonia Shimerda of *My Ántonia*, Kate Chopin's Edna Pontellier of *The Awakening*, Glasgow's Susan Treadwell of *Virginia*, Dorinda Oakley of *Barren Ground*, Ada Fincastle of *Vein of Iron*, and Roy Timberlake of *In This Our Life* and *Beyond Defeat*, Edith Wharton's Justine Brent of *The Fruit of the Tree*, Ellen Olenska of *The Age of Innocence*, and Laura Testvalley of *The Buccaneers*, Porter's Miranda of *The Old Order*, "Pale Horse, Pale Rider," and "Old Mortality," and Welty's Miss Julia Mortimer of *Losing Battles*. Isabel is "handsome . . . though not so beautiful as Grace, or so engaging in her manners" (32). These outlines appear within the domestic novel as well in Gertrude of Maria Cummins's *The Lamplighter*, Gabriella Lynn of Caroline Lee Hentz's *Ernest Linwood*, and Ellen Montgomery of Susan Warner's *The Wide, Wide World*, among others. The characterization allows the author to address female achievement obliquely, thus not threatening the tasks and aspirations of women completely engaged in domesticity. The androgynous protagonist serves a function as well in the self-conscious woman writers who follow, as the authors struggle with the fact of female biological identity. The writers understand that the female body with its biological cycles—which refute the rule of the rationalized alarm, the classroom bell, the closing whistle, the tyranny of artificial time—conflicts with the modern demand for the rationalized worker under bureaucratic control. Moreover, these physiological markers belie the ideal of the autonomous individual in control of his or her world; the body too clearly has a claim on the intellect and the imagination. Only by shedding the female body, these writers' plots imply, can the woman undertake achievement in the male realm.

Grace's appearance also introduces a stock figure, the blond male-dependent woman who contrasts with the independent woman. Through this figure, the writer obliquely criticizes the cultural ideal of feminity as a diminution of female creativity and power. At the graveside, the childlike Grace manifests the extreme emotion that anticipates her later career as romantic victim: "Let me alone, Isabel! . . . Let me die here, for there are none left to love me now!" (20). In her incessant demand for "love," her whole career is forecast as a cautionary tale on the dangers of female romantic dependence. McIntosh contrasts Grace's hysterical dependency with Isabel's mature generosity and appropriate emotion. The male-identified woman, sometimes hysterical, will often be blond like Grace, Chopin's Madame Ratignolle of *The Awakening*, Stowe's Lillie Seymour, Wharton's Bessy Westmore of *The Fruit of the Tree*, Glasgow's Geneva Ellgood of *Barren Ground* and Stanley Timberlake of *In This Our Life*, and Cather's Lena Lingard of *My Ántonia* and Lily Fisher of *The Song of the Lark*. This precautionary figure depicts the authors' rejection of dependence on male support, showing it as leading to either the life-in-death of the mannequin or the reduction to childishness.

Sent north from their warm Southern home and loving Aunt Nancy to be educated by their uncle and aunt, the fashionable New York Elliotts, the girls experience this change of residence in radically different ways. Their new "parents" represent the morality of the emerging industrial social order. Mr. Elliott spends all of his time at his place of business; his wife spends most of her time and their money on fashionable display. Grace falls easily under the tutelage of frivolous Mrs. Elliott. Grace is described as "a plant that has no roots" (anticipating the central description of Wharton's Lily Bart of *The House of Mirth*)— that is, she has no inner beliefs, no abiding mother's home, to counter her romantic dreams. Therefore, Grace sees no need for membership in the private woman's community, accepting in its stead the homage of the commercial center and acquiescing in her own life in death as an emotional infant. For example, when the family's washwoman is burned out of her home, Grace keeps her contribution to spend on her own clothes in contrast to Isabel's generosity. And like Lily Bart, she considers those women less brilliant or less well-placed as being almost of another species. McIntosh characterizes Grace's reaction to her social successes: "While all smiled on her and caressed her, her heaven was attained" (43). Like protagonists in the introspective novels, courtship display and romantic illusion rapidly turn sour for the woman as the underlying power relationship between the sexes surfaces after marriage. Here Grace falls under the sway of a dissolute French marquis. Like other writers such as Cather, Wharton, and Glasgow, McIntosh contrasts the injustice of the paternalistic Old World with the display of the competitive New World center; the true American homeland will be found in neither extreme but in the woman-centered family. In an extended passage, McIntosh uses dance—in these authors, the metaphor for romance—to contrast Isabel's gentle devotion with the marquis's sophisticated sexuality. The contrast of the unselfish affection between women with the possessive love of the male romance adds another strand to the fabric of American female authorship. In the whirl of male romance, the woman necessarily loses control of her own life as she separates from other women. As Baym summarizes, "Merely to feel strongly is to be at the mercy of oneself and others. . . ." (*Woman's Fiction*, 25).

When their guardian loses his money, Isabel supports the family through her music lessons, thereby showing that the strong womanly protagonist can function in the public world. In *Two Lives*, the encroachment of vocational and economic demands on the family appears through Mr. Elliott's career. When first we see him, Mr. Elliott is harassed by business demands and by the requirements of maintaining his social positions through his fashionable wife's expenditures—

here the competitive marketplace subsumes the private sphere, putting it at the service of social competition. After his exile from the public sphere by bankruptcy, defeat in economic competition, Mr. Elliott discovers the value of Isabel's woman-centered home. He never returns to business, choosing instead to spend his life with Isabel's family. Mr. Elliott's career calls attention both to the possibility of male redemption and the voraciousness of the public sphere. In his renunciation of the public sphere in favor of the female-centered home, we see the "sensational [cultural] designs" the domestic writer has on her American readership (Tompkins).

Having reflected a social order they perceive as impersonal and scattered, the authors depict the female heroines, like their sophisticated successors, as reforming the family and the community. Isabel, for example, is an orphan, who at the beginning of the book once again loses her second "parents," her uncle and aunt, the Southern Elliotts. Sent to yet another family in New York, she nonetheless comes into womanhood by creating an emotional home in the midst of the commercial capital. Through no action of her own, and thus no personal responsibility, the heroine finds herself isolated, forced to reconstruct the roles of mother and wife within the impersonal, competitive social environment, often more than once. After removing the received network of social support and control, the domestic novelists show the woman alone in a hostile and faithless world, re-creating a community based on love and domesticity—often only through letters, contemplation, and memory; here, for example, Isabel writes to Aunt Nancy and Grace during their separation. Whereas the typical male heroic individual finds opportunity in a society that increasingly devalues personal identities, the women find barrenness.

Domestic fiction flourished until after the Civil War. As the movement toward rationalization of the woman's sphere matured, the developments detailed by Matthews and Hayden, the domestic novel atrophied. At the time, as Baym observes, the main movements of woman's popular fiction were to the Gothic romance or the children's book.[1] Novels featuring adult heroines took place in distant exotic settings, an escape fiction similar in effect to nostalgic local-color pieces, especially those of the "moonlight on the magnolias" of male Southern writers like Thomas Nelson Page, who clearly had a reactionary social agenda.

At this time, Josephine Donovan sees the emerging group of female New England local-colorists, Jewett chief among them, as the creators of a woman's world counter to the elaborating social structures.[2] Donovan identifies such writers as Mary Wilkins Freeman and Elizabeth Stuart Phelps as envisioning a woman-identified literary realism, and roughly at this time Ellen Glasgow began to write her woman-centered "social history of Virginia" (*New England Local Color*, 3). The early writers in this discussion, Gilman, Jewett, Cather, and Glasgow, borrowed the fragmented families, the female-centered home—albeit without the paternalistic emphasis—and the didactic spiritual content from the domestic novelists, the female writers that Nina Baym notes first turned American women into readers and writers (*Woman's Fiction*, 11). This flight from literal realism surfaces not only in the reclaiming of male myth but also in the numerous ghost stories written by Edith Wharton, Glasgow, and Jewett. In all these writers, the added dimension, whether moral or supranatural, appears. Repeatedly, these women undercut the authority of the scientifically delineated environment even as they insist on the power of extrarational human experience.

Moreover, the woman writer must address organizational changes in the business of publishing, which affect both men and women literary workers.[3] Portrayals of the "here and now" and excision of the spiritual from public communications serve to isolate and specialize the activity we now deem as literature. At the century's end, only leisure time, time spent escaping from the "real" world of economic and professional competition, remains to the writer for the fictional experience of connection and depiction of the maternal home. The shrunken parameters of imagination enclose the fictional landscape into which Jewett steps and whose narrow limits she seeks to expand. In the late nineteenth century, through the growth of female higher education and the limited acceptance of women in careers such as social work and education, middle-class women gained limited recognition in a wider range of public roles. And women had also become writers through the domestic fiction.

This constellation of literary and social forces coalesced at the end of the nineteenth century as an unprecedented number of women turned from the craft of writing to the art of literature. In *Private Woman, Public Stage*, Mary Kelley details the attitude held by such domestic writers as E. D. E. N. Southworth, Susan Warner, and Augusta Evans Wilson toward their participation in an occupation that put them in public view. The ambivalence that haunts many American women writers to the present first appears then. On the one hand, the woman writer responds to the value the social order places on individual distinction, desiring the increased economic and social status awarded a professional career; on the other, she desires to present her communal experience and history to American society. The minds and hearts of women writers try to resolve at least two contrasting cultural visions, the dominant male literary lineage, both popular and introspective, which elevates the heroic male individual, and their own female history and literary practice, which immersed them and their readership in personal networks and within a tradition of domestic arts. Mary Wilkins Freeman, Kate Chopin, Gilman, Jewett, and Glasgow were among the women authors who participated in the movement toward self-conscious authorship. Jewett's *A Country Doctor* (1884) and her later *The Country of the Pointed Firs* (1896) serve to introduce the themes of the later women writers.

An impersonal, mercenary social structure allows no place for the female generations, a circumstance shown by the breaking of the mother-daughter bond and the intrusion of the male public sphere and the dominant discourse on private life. The self-conscious women authors, like their domestic predecessors, try to counter the growing public sphere both by creating an alternate communal homeland and by rejecting the romantic male-female relationship as reflective of male drives toward material possession and personal dominance. Now women aspire to self-conscious authorship as they attempt to join the competitive public world of individual influence. Nonetheless, certain key elements of the domestic novels remain, even though the fictional techniques and authorial viewpoint are increasingly innovative and introspective. For example, the emphasis of the narrative still centers on the woman, and the social background into which she steps is still impoverished, holding few positive family or other personal relationships. The protagonist must strive to create the vital, continuing community. In such a barren social context, emotionalism and sexual promiscuity still expose the woman to loss of life or sanity. Personal relationships, especially romantic affairs and marriage, more and more serve the male's competitive interests in the woman's narrative, as, for example, in "The Awakening" Leonce Pontellier evaluates his wife and home as a business asset, or in *The House of Mirth* Rosedale insists on Lily Bart's retaining her social value for marriage. The failure to integrate women's contributions into the center of American society impoverishes male characters as well, the novelists say, weakening their ability to be dependable romantic partners and husbands and understanding fathers. Given the American emphasis on individual dominance, the strength of the economic structures' pragmatic morality, and the solidly white male leadership of the social order, these women writers continually question the honesty and vitality of the exclusive male-female bond. The language of romance and the institution of marriage now most often appear as instruments of female subordination to a male dream of individual expansiveness. Female romantic dreams lead inevitably to abandonment or exploitation by men. As Nina Auerbach cogently suggests, the community of women challenges the ideal of a woman devoting her energies to a man's interest, "attaining citizenship in the community of adulthood through masculine approval alone" (*Communities of Women*, 8).

A literature celebrating mother-to-daughter transmission of skills, local language, and received relationships, as Jewett implies, finds it increasingly difficult to reach an audience in a social order centered on impersonal rules and individual responsibility. Looking back at her youthful self, before she summoned the home place and the maternal ideal, Jewett judges *Deephaven* to be an attempt to *explain* the city and the country to each other; therefore the earlier work is much more "realistic," that is, tied to the social status quo, than the later *The Country of the Pointed Firs* (1896) and "The Foreigner" (1900). In *Deephaven* the protagonists are two female friends from Boston who discover and report back to the city about the characters and events of a rustic village with almost an anthropological exactness in the recreation of speech and custom.

A particular and consistent constellation of personal relationships appears in many of these works by American women. Indeed, the constellation is remarkable for its consistency and its persistence. Repeatedly, the authors draw shattered families within the American social environment; they portray missing, mad, sick, or ineffectual mothers, missing, impoverished, or unsympathetic fathers, and unreliable, insensitive lovers and husbands. The young protagonist finds herself without maternal support or example in a society that sees evidence of her female body or of "other-regarding" emotions, in Wharton's phrase, as invitations to personal and social disaster. She finds herself at the same time without the emotional and economic support of the paternalistic family.

Due to the recent efforts of feminist critics such as Donovan and Sarah Sherman, the work of Sarah Orne Jewett is being reread, reclaimed from the misreadings that relegated it to the "nostalgic" local-color backwater along with the work of other talented women writers. But before she could summon the home place, Jewett addressed the plot of the heroic individual in *A Country Doctor* (1884). As will Glasgow in *Barren Ground* and Cather in *O Pioneers!*, and like Edith Wharton in *The Fruit of the Tree*, early in her career Jewett creates the woman who succeeds in self-assertion in roles defined as belonging to the male and in repudiation of customary female communal and domestic roles. The imposition of the individual personality upon the lives of her neighbors, however, requires the sacrifice of sexual expression. The protagonists impose their will and vision on the male profession, the stubborn soil, or an uncaring social order, against the opposition, or absence, of family and neighbors. The adaptation of the cultural plot of heroic individualism by the substitution of a female heroine occurs relatively early in writers' careers when the maturing author is most under the sway of the existing models of male authorship, when she is trying to gain access to the male literary establishment. Moreover, the women writer flees from the cultural tendency to identify the female with the second-rate. The woman's domestic realm, at least initially, seems at best confined, a reminder of childish helplessness and female boundaries.

A Country Doctor introduces Nan Prince, who, the author insists, is different from other women—a constant in all such early identifications of the protagonist. Nan has no drive toward romance or maternity, undertakings that subordinate her to a man's interests and needs. Nan instead becomes a doctor, justifying it to herself and her readers as a sort of parallel maternity in her care of the community's children. Sherman has skillfully traced the genesis of the plot in Jewett's own life and her relationship with her beloved physician father. As with Alexandra Bergson in Cather's *O Pioneers!* and Dorinda Oakley in Glasgow's *Barren Ground*, Nan Prince takes over the "father's" task, entering a competitive public sphere customarily reserved for men. Like the other heroic individualistic female protagonists, the women's networks surrounding Nan have no lessons for the young girl in her individualistic quest at the cultural center; Nan must be rescued from an ignorant, harsh woman's world at the social margins by the "father," Dr. Leslie. Along with Cather's *O Pioneers!* and Glasgow's *Barren Ground, A Country Doctor* represents the attempt of the woman author to grasp male creativity through a protagonist who embodies "male" characteristics. Therefore, the quest parallels the male success story of the dominant discourse. Nan journeys out, away from her female family, to take her place in the professional competition; she repudiates learning passed from mother to daughter in favor of the education of the bureaucratic institution. For survival in the public sphere, Nan must learn the language of Dr. Leslie's library, not Grandmother Thacher's kitchen. To succeed, she must learn the associational language, and she must eschew romance.

Nan's father is dead, as is her alcoholic mother, who lived only long enough to bring the child back to a rough rural setting in the house of the ignorant and coarse Grandmother Thacher. Her mother had submerged herself in a passionate romantic relationship, which ended with the death of both of Nan's parents. Even though Nan's father dies, he retains his family's allegiance, but his wife and his daughter have no claim on their regard. The message is clear: in a male-controlled social order, the woman, even one of undoubted spirit and gifts, cannot act on her own or her daughter's behalf. She becomes the victim, while her daughter is attaining independence through her pursuit of male profession and her refusal of romantic involvement.

Throughout the story, Nan sees the workings of the Heavenly Father in her life choices—Jewett, as Sherman points out, doubles the meaning of the narrative. Her ending evokes the possibility of a female pastoral home place and rejoins the daughter with her long-dead mother, "Perhaps, made pure and strong in a better world . . . [her mother] had helped to make sure of the blessing her own life had lost . . . bringing her child in her arms toward the great shelter and home" (259). Through her subtle undercutting of the male-identified deity, Jewett suggests, despite the weakness of the mother, the female pastoral centered on the wise woman. Despite the obeisance given to the father God, the woman's touch and female nature itself reach to the daughter. At the end we cannot be sure that the God she addresses directly is not embodied in maternity. Moreover, like Cather's Alexandra Bergson, Wharton's Justine Brent, and Glasgow's Dorinda Oakley, among so many other female protagonists, Nan Prince receives replenishment of spirit and energy from contact with the American earth.

As Jewett insists, Nan has no models for independent female achievement as she undertakes a parallel quest to that of the young boy. The solution found in *A Country Doctor* is one that answers the need for the woman writer to reconcile professional commitment with traditional female roles. Its costs are high to the protagonist. It demands the shedding of her female past, here portrayed as parochial and ineffectual. In addition, the woman must reject a personal and sexual life beyond the professional comradeship Nan shares with her male guardian and mentor.

Acceptance of the individual quest of sovereignty over nature and society gives way, in this group of women authors, to an urgent need for the female generations to rejoin under one powerful ideal female figure for a more just and loving social order. For a social order that seems to define human beings as individual competitors, they seek to substitute a model that promotes an ideal of civic virtue. Jewett moves from the ideal of individual achievement embodied by Nan Prince to the imaginative home place represented by the female acolyte of Mrs. Todd in *The Country of the Pointed Firs.* Her movement anticipates other such shifts in plot and characterization found in this group of American writers. Cather, for example, moves from the individualistic stance of *O Pioneers!* to the communal themes of *My Ántonia;* Glasgow from *Barren Ground* to *Vein of Iron* and *Beyond Defeat*, and Porter from "Old Mortality" to *The Old Order.* Ultimately, Jewett and later writers declare the dream of individual dominance to be an immature fantasy. They then replace it with the home place at the center of a reconstituted community arising out of the emotions, memory, and body of one woman.

Jewett's acknowledged masterwork, *The Country of Pointed Firs,* depicts the wise woman in her full strength and mature wisdom, enshrined in the isolated home place, like Ántonia Shimerda's farm in Cather, Mama Day's island in Naylor, the Mother's Herland in Gilman, Kate Oliver's Hunter's Fare in Glasgow, Miss Sophia Jane's Texas farm in Porter, and Miss Katie Rainey's home in Morgana in

Welty. Jewett carefully avoids placing Dunnet Landing on a map of New England, thereby indicating the imaginative nature of the female pastoral. True enough, we know it is located "somewhere 'along shore' between the region of Tenants Harbor and Boothbay," but Jewett forthrightly states that Dunnet Landing is not a "real 'landing' or real harbor." Jewett as omniscient author tells us "the mixture of remoteness, and childish certainty of being the centre of civilization of which her affectionate dreams had told" draws the woman writer back to the mother's landscape (*Pointed Firs*, 12). From the first words of the novel, Dunnet Landing is portrayed as "more attractive than the other maritime villages of eastern Maine," thus the reader is alerted that Dunnet Landing is indeed *not* the nostalgic re-creation of an actual past way of life or cherished place, but indeed an ideal female community (11). Only after these perimeters are established is the visiting writing daughter allowed to claim the narrative from the author, for now she, and we as readers, are ready to begin our shared education at the knee of the female seer. Through her first-person narrative, she will pass to her readers, directly with her own voice, the lessons she received orally from Almira Todd; the novel itself brings us into the narrative by shifting from a detached third-person narrator to the account of the city visitor. Significantly, the woman author arrives as a "single passenger." She will leave with Mrs. Todd's coral pin as a symbol of her glowing, constant love and a herbal bouquet of southernwood and bay, a gift which Gwen L. Nagel identifies as an acknowledgment of her literary talents ("Jewett's New England Gardens," 43). These symbolic tokens signal the city woman's successful mastery of the female lore and traditions. Dunnet Landing and the even more remote Green Island—"a sudden revelation of the world beyond this which some believe to be so near" (44)—depict the female seer in her full glory, enshrined in the isolated home place. As Elizabeth Ammons observes, the narrative operates in a series of circles as the narrator moves ever closer to the Celestial City of the Bowden reunion at which Mrs. Blackett will be crowned "queen." The Bowden family home and its reunion stand as the matrix, the creative source, of the American nation, from which all the male adventurers journey forth and to which they will return in life or in death. Like Porter's *The Old Order*, Welty's *The Golden Apples*, Naylor's *The Women of Brewster Place*, and Cather's *O Pioneers!* and *My Ántonia*, Jewett takes seemingly unrelated women's narratives and stitches together a coherent work of art. *The Country of the Pointed Firs* has been criticized for its lack of a linear, progressive plot line, but, feminist critics such as Donovan prefer to describe its innovative structure as more "unified than a collection of sketches, yet looser than the traditional novel" (*Sarah Orne Jewett*, 99). Here the text is pieced together like the quilt, each individual memory or voice united by the female artist into a distinctive work, which expresses both the creator and her community. Jewett's fictional structure in *The Country of the Pointed Firs*, a webbed shape, contrasts with standard dramatic structure. The work consists of single strands that always return to the central relationship of the seer and the daughter (Ammons, "Going in Circles," 85). Further, Donovan writes that Jewett particularly disliked the intrusion of the typical male author's personality into his work; instead, she aims for an effect of a work of art produced by the narrator and her community. Here, the novel seems not so much produced as it appears to arise organically, almost magically, from the female realm to which the narrator learns to listen as she journeys ever closer to the female center.

Both community and island are ruled by the two demigoddesses, Mrs. Blackett and her daughter, Almira Todd. From our first glimpse of Mrs. Todd, her wisdom, her size, and even divinity, as numerous commentators have noted, indicate that she, like her homeland, is above and beyond the simply human: "Her height and massiveness in the low room gave her the look of a huge sibyl, while the strange fragrance of the mysterious herb blew in from the little garden" (18). Jewett insists that the "mateless," childless wise woman participates in maternity as fully as does the biological mother. The creation of unmarried or widowed teachers and artists—Cather's Thea Kronborg and Evangeline Knightly of "The Best Years," Jewett's Mrs. Todd, Glasgow's Louisa Goddard, Porter's Aunt Eliza, Cousin Eva Parrington, and Miranda, and Welty's Miss Eckhart, Miss Julia Mortimer, Adele Courtland, and Naylor's Miranda—indicates the writer's move toward resolution of the conflict between her female heritage and those of her profession. All women who understand their connection to the female history work in their parallel ways to carry the generations forward. The individual woman's talent is brought into cooperative harmony with the female community.

These individual protagonists may initially desire to fit into the competitive model, but they must learn through the course of their work to embrace their female tradition. All of these wise women, mother or artist-teacher, undertake the intellectual training of the daughter, educating her in the ways of nature and initiating her in the mysteries of the wise woman's own chosen life's work. The split so often portrayed between the unmarried woman and her married sister is healed ultimately through the writing of the narrative, which gives both female priestess and maternal ideal their full due in the creation of the daughter. The mother in her garden, the grandmother stitching her quilt, the musician in her rehearsal hall, and the teacher in her schoolroom, all must retain their connections with their female histories, memories, and bodies represented by the home place to achieve their full potential.

Along with the knitting, which is so integral a part of the female stories of Joanna Todd and Mrs. Captain Tolland of "The Foreigner," the metaphor of the garden assumes central importance, as indeed it will in the authors who follow. The garden, as Alice Walker has written, proclaims the mother's creativity, both natural and aesthetic (*In Search of Our Mothers' Gardens*). It offers an example of the female Eden, the woman-shaped natural world joined seamlessly with the female-created domestic home. Its diversity, its harmonious blending of different colors and species, suggests the acceptance of a range of women's choices and their own forms of creativity. The idea of the many different blooms brought into harmony by the woman's creative gifts and physical labor indicates the writers' vision of the democratic community, a balance between individual talent and civic responsibility. Transformed into the farm, the garden is redeemed from male failure by woman's care in Cather's *O Pioneers!* and *My Ántonia,* Porter's *The Old Order,* and Glasgow's *Barren Ground, In This Our Life,* and *Beyond Defeat.* As Gwen Nagel points out, Mrs. Todd's garden is a proper New England garden, in contrast to the great Western Garden of the World; Jewett portrays gardens that are "small, tidy plots, confined by fences, associated with the past and not the future, and lovingly cultivated by women" ("New England Gardens," 43). Although I would insist that the garden is an emblem of the woman's living present and a promise of the future (as every garden is), Nagel's point is well-taken. These women's gardens, "lovingly cultivated," through generations, represent American nature at its best, brought to fruition by woman's cooperative labor in cooperation with the native earth. Further, the herbs symbolize the local language, the silent communication, which foils the patriarchal language of the mainland.

The relation of the female body to the woman's identity has excited many an inharmonious feminist discussion. The most forthright approach is found in Sara Ruddick's *Maternal Thinking*. Ruddick draws a firm distinction between the emotional and physical tasks of maternity, which any member of the social order who renounces individual dominance can undertake, and "birthing labor," which pertains to the biological tasks of maternity: gestation, birth, and breastfeeding. The writers in this discussion share Ruddick's suspicion of the devaluation of woman's biological identity. As she notes, both men and women in the large-scale social order minimize the procreative aspects of the female body—men because they claim a higher creativity for themselves, women because they fear to classify themselves purely by these aspects (192–98). Like them, the critic fears that the ungendering of birth leads to the growth of a "technocratic and legal apparatus," the absolute perfection of Weberian rationalization and Douglasian impersonal rules, which will exploit the female body for profit, reducing the woman to a commodity in ways only now being understood. As Ruddick remarks, "To deny the different relations of women and men to human birth founds the entire egalitarian project on an illusion" (49). Ruddick points out that birth is "indelibly a social relationship" acting against the individuation of bodies, their rationalization into inhuman machine (191). Minimizing the importance of the female body allows men to envision themselves as "self-made," claiming privilege of mind over body. Ruddick concludes that as "long as we fear and deny the distinctly female character of birth, we risk losing the symbolic, emotional, and ultimately political significance of birth itself" (49). As anthropologist Sherry Ortner contends and literary critic Margaret Homans demonstrates, male intellectuals have defined cultural categories in exactly this mode by insisting on contrasting and competing dichotomies that place the woman as "simpler" because of the powerful and obviously creative matrix. These authors insist that female art, in the last account, comes through not only acceptance of the body but celebration of its potential. After attempting to appropriate male cultural models of creativity, they come to the home place, understanding that any alternate social order must repudiate insofar as possible the categories of the male-defined rationalized society. Their body forms an important part of their journey to creativity. Although they find that they themselves need not become mothers in order to reach creativity, that shared woman's body offers a forceful example of integral female creativity, which challenges the pen/phallus male model.

In Jewett's *The Country of the Pointed Firs* the unnamed woman narrator at first finds herself impatient with Mrs. Todd's demand that she immerse herself in the old female arts and in the women's networks of care and joys. Newly arrived, seeking inspiration from a change to a more picturesque setting—a little like the sentimental "local colorist," which Jewett may have feared in herself, the writer-narrator is deep into her own professional task. She considers her art as an individualistic, commercial obligation separate from and competing with the women's lives and stories around her. She is not yet ready to hear the mother's voice, to journey to the still center of Green Island; therefore, Jewett reduces the young woman to childlike status, emphasizing her need to be reeducated in female knowledge. The comings and goings of Mrs. Todd's herbal customers distract her, as does the gentle, maternal world of civilized nature; her pen remains "idle" in her hand. To escape the mother's world, to reassert her individual profession, the narrator hires the schoolhouse in which to write—by this neat stroke Jewett criticizes the removal of the educational function from the rest of woman's daily life as dangerous to female literary art. And as Paul Voelker observes, Jewett points up the guest's reduced status with such remarks as "the small scholar hung her hat," which indicate her status as a "child." The narrator herself begins to feel uneasy about her patterns of thought borrowed from the now-distant mainland. She begins the rationale for her retreat with the words, "Selfish as it may appear . . ." (20).

Remembering "a long piece of writing, sadly belated now, which I was bound to do," she says "unkind words of withdrawal" to Mrs. Todd, who only becomes more affectionate, implying that she will be her young guest's friend and teacher, passing on her woman's lore, preparing her to reach a greater depth of personal expression in her chosen life's work. The older woman sees the depth of insight in the writing daughter, who will carry her knowledge back to other women because Almira Todd "never had nobody I could so trust. All you lack is a few qualities, but with time you'd gain judgment an' experience, an' be very able in the business" (17). The seer implies that the daughter's art will reach its potential after she becomes proficient in the old arts and religion, possibly those of the witch of the full moon, as Ammons outlines it in "Jewett's Witches."

With the funeral of the venerable old wise woman, Mrs. Begg, the narrator begins to sense her isolation. As she sits alone in her schoolroom, she glimpses the funeral procession, which "looked futile and helpless on the edge of the rocky shore"; the lonely writer feels strongly her own mortality. Even though she returns to her work, the "anxious scribe," shaped by her urban experience, still accepting the model of rationalized professionalism, and still held by the paternal language, fails "to catch these lovely summer cadences" (24). She wonders if she should not have joined the procession of mourners and immersed herself in life and death, realizing that she "had now made myself and my friends remember that I did not really belong to Dunnet Landing" (25). She must pass through the borrowed male language and its literary tradition before she, like later women protagonists, can find her way home to the inner circle of experience of Green Island and the creative maternal ideal.

Given the daughter's struggle to reclaim her female artistic heritage, the visit of Captain Littlepage becomes of crucial importance to understanding the narrative. As she is writing in her lonely hideaway, the old captain comes to give her an unexpected lesson in the American individualistic cultural myth and in the hazards of too-easy acceptance of male literary models. His first words are a quote from Milton, threatening the narrator with the "anxiety of influence." As Jean Rohoff concludes, Captain "Little-page" remains captive to an "intertextual nightmare. The layers of narrative—those of Milton, Shakespeare, Gaffett, and Littlepage himself—have rendered the old sea captain a prisoner of discourse" ("A Quicker Signal," 41). The captain always removes himself from the experience of the community; as Mrs. Todd remarks, he had "overset his mind with too much reading" (27). This remark comes as the writer struggles to reconcile her membership in the community of the passing female generations with her individualistic profession of authorship, Jewett encourages us as readers to focus on the problem of woman's artistic creativity. Further, the demented old man's narrative, like many another mainstream lit-

erary work, takes him away from the women and home he finds so
confining into an uncharted natural wilderness. In contrast to the
comments of Mrs. Todd and the narrator, which insist that the community is representative of human types all over the world, the captain sees each port as different, detached, fragmented, an exotic piece
of human experience, and he views the landscape as objectified, in-
hospitable nature to be explored and overcome. This journey into
nature is undertaken in a ship named the *Minerva*—a symbol of
female-free intellectual procreation—which soon founders, suggesting the revenge of nature on the cold, intellectual alienation that the
captain represents. This leaves the wanderer isolated in an icy country
far up north, away from Dunnet Landing, the "next world . . . where
there was neither living or dead" (37–38). Captain Littlepage's, a
fantastic narrative captive to male literary models and abstracted
from ongoing human relationships and local landscape, threatens
the young woman author's art by negating her experience. She must
instead accompany Mrs. Todd to the mother's island "where pennyroyal grew," the magic woman's herb, which brings to the writer the
emotionally freighted memories that summon real, living female art.
Clearly the icy shades of the captain's narrative prepare the woman
writer and the reader in her turn to enter the vibrant life of Jewett's
warm maternal Green Island and to learn the local language, which
unites the women of Dunnet Landing, Green Island, and the road to
the Bowden reunion.

To highlight the significance of the captain's tale, Jewett introduces
the repeated metaphor of the bird and flight as representative of the
female artistic quest; a frightened swallow comes into the schoolroom
as if pursued by a "kingbird." Flying wildly against the schoolhouse
walls, it escapes back to nature. Immersed as he is in his fantastic,
borrowed tales, the captain sees none of this natural, deadly drama,
which replays in the small the woman's own quest. The schoolhouse
will imprison the woman's art through its male perimeters and models;
the woman must step out. As the fantastic tale unfolds, she hears the
sound of the sea, "a strange warning wave that gives notice of the turn
of the tide" (33). She is warned by these two natural portents that she
needs to turn from the male language and the American narrative of
individual adventuring represented by the trapped bird and enter the
home place. Just then, "A late golden robin, with the most joyful and

eager of voices" sings, announcing the narrator's readiness to accept the wise woman's guidance into the mysteries of her mother's island.

After she parts from the old seafarer, the narrator sees Green Island illuminated with warm sunlight in a "compelling way," another contrast with the icy, dim "literary" world. Later the priestess-seer offers the visitor some of her beer, a brew she gives only to those who enter her inner circle, in a sort of communion. Still under the influence of the old man's tales, the younger woman experiences it as part of a "spell and incantation," expecting that her "enchantress" will assume the cobweb shapes of the mad story. Instead, she discovers that Mrs. Todd offers, in Chopin's words, "no extraordinary flights," but rather the real comforts of home and the abiding promise of "clear sunshine and the blue sky of another day" (46); in sum, she brings the miracle of the continuity of the home place.

By coming to the island, the narrator has entered the creative center of the community, the mother's home place. She realizes the source of Mrs. Todd's elemental force. Almira Todd, Jewett suggests, gained her wisdom and generosity and female creativity from her mother's training and love. As Elijah Tilley observes, correctly, of Mrs. Todd, "No, there ain't a better-hearted woman in the State of Maine. . . . She's had the best of mothers" (162). In the mother's island, the magic pennyroyal brings the widowed Mrs. Todd to talk of her brief marriage. In the second of Mrs. Todd's discussions of her romantic past, the demigoddess underscores the common belief in this group of authors: relationships with men pass—"It was but a dream with us"—but relationships with women continue (68). There in the old house overlooking the sea, filled with the needlework, and surrounded by the lovingly tended gardens, the visitor at last finds a home. Here too she discovers the "language of the heart," the immediate connection that foils the impersonal language of the mainland's dominant discourse.

At the matrix of creativity, as such commentators as Marcia McClintock Folsom, Francis Fike, and Rohoff have noted, the mother's language of genuine love banishes the intellectual constructions of Captain Littlepage and the chilly "theoretical love," as Fike characterizes it, of the ministers. The male language recedes as the woman narrator comes home to the local language. Folsom and Rohoff outline the immediate mind reading between the women of the home place. United by the traditional domestic rituals, which Ann Romines details, the women connect their homes and their lives by a sort of task-based telepathic communication of the heart, which arises from the wholeness of that female domestic world (Folsom 80).

After repeated visits, the narrator is at last ready to receive the language, although as yet only within the sacred sheltered center itself. Through individual creation placed within the woman's community, the author hopes to reassert those discarded visionary elements and instinctual emotions of ritual in a social order that seems, as recent metaphoric patterns suggest, to allow less and less regard for enduring personal relationships and more and more control of public life by abstract rules promulgated by distant experts. As I say, the woman writer must seek to join her national culture through use of the associational language, but at the same time she must try to evoke the communal language. Like Jewett and other introspective women writers, the narrator partakes of a double cultural experience. In anticipation of Jewett's own discovery, the protagonist breaks through this double vision by the discovery of the home place and by the subversion of the associational language.

As the public language of cultural differentiation and specialization makes woman's communal experience of relationships, transmitted knowledge, and communal roles harder to portray, Jewett, Cather, Glasgow, Porter, Welty, and Naylor place highly visual, emblematic scenes and references appealing to classic or biblical references—moving their writing as close as possible to the communal ritual, rich with the incense of emotion and memory—words that seek to wield the emotional impact of T. S. Eliot's "objective correlative," the integrated feeling and intellect at the center of the restricted language of the community. In Porter's "The Grave," for example, the adult Miranda understands how far she has come from her childhood innocence but also how much her grandmother's home, which she has left, has shaped her as she remembers in living immediacy her brother smiling at the silver dove. Incantatory phrases, conventional metaphor, earlier literary elements—orally transmitted legends, folk stories, songs—indicate the didactic, communal intent implicit in these writings, an attempt to replace the emotions of the communal ritual experience. Dreams, visions, and memories of rejoined family and community occur in works by all the writers as they witness to their isolation. They mourn the restorative, emotional language that reinforces the arts and connections of female family and community. The tendency to reassert communal relationships, to assert alternate artistic lineages, and to restore ritualistic modes of expression parallel those of such modern male artists as T. S. Eliot and Ezra Pound, but with specifically female content toward an American woman's tradition.

Moreover, women characters communicate without language through dance and music, the authors reaching for an immediate heartfelt communication, paralleling ritual in its physical as well as emotional component. Some notable examples central to the meaning of the respective works include the whirling dance between Porter's female narrator and the shattered, inarticulate Ottilie at the end of her short story "Holiday," the furious playing of Miss Eckhart before her uncomprehending girl students in Welty's "June Recital," the dance of courtship in Glasgow's *Virginia*, Porter's "Old Mortality," and Welty's *Delta Wedding*, and Thea Kronborg's discovery of her "voice" in Cather's *The Song of the Lark*. In dance people are joined, experiencing the breathing, moving partner, and in music the protagonists overcome the deficiencies of language, achieving the serenity of a continuing separate woman's community. Here the connection is achieved through the voices of the "old singers," William and "Mother" Blackett and also through the music and dance of Mrs. Tolland, who sings so much better than the women under sway of the male ministers. Moreover, with song, the woman undertakes an artistic creativity that mirrors that of the female body, the throat, as Cather's central metaphor in *The Song of the Lark* illustrates, resembling in shape and function the matrix. Paula Gunn Allen writes of the strength of the Native-American Singing Woman, who sings the world into being, "That power is not so much the power to give birth, as we have noted, but the power to make, to create, to transform" (*Sacred Hoop*, 29). With music, many of the women writers indicate, the power of the father's language is defeated and the woman's creativity is come to life.

When Almira Todd takes the narrator to "where pennyroyal grew," a sacred place thus far known only to herself and her mother, she is ready to penetrate the woman's mysteries and understand the woman's language. The pilgrim realizes that she has journeyed to the presence of a great female spirit unlike any other human being she has encountered in her regimented urban environment; she is at last "not incompetent at herb-gathering":

There was something lonely and solitary about her great determined shape. She might have been Antigone alone on the Theban plain. . . . She seemed like a renewal of some historic soul, with her sorrows and the remoteness of a daily life busied with rustic simplicities and the scent of primeval herbs. (68)

The female lineage is extended in Green Island as the guest comes into her full artistry. She claims her place in the chain of life, carrying on the woman's tradition and community through her art. She has passed from the outer circle, the City of Destruction, journeyed through the captain's Slough of Despond, to the gates of the female mysteries. Surrounded by the woman's herb, the guest learns that deep love between a man and a woman is deeply satisfying, an instinctive need, yet leading to grief and ultimate isolation. The bonds of love between the rejoined generations of women, in contrast, abide.

Amplifying this theme of the eternal bonds between the mother and her children is Jewett's late story, "The Foreigner," only recovered by Richard Cary in the recent *The Uncollected Short Stories of Sarah Orne Jewett* (1971). Once again the metaphor of the woven text is the center as Mrs. Todd relates her tale to the daughter narrator; the sibyl knits as she "spins" out the story of Mrs. Captain Tolland and transcendent mother love, the two women safe together against the storm and thinking of Mrs. Blackett on her island. It is the end of summer, the turn of the seasons that will, as Sherman notes, return Persephone back to the outer circle of the city. The tale therefore has a consolatory meaning, which extends, as DuPlessis suggests "beyond the ending," through its embedded message of the restored, ongoing female generations.

Left alone, widowed and childless, Mrs. Captain Tolland, for that is how she is known, is brought from Jamaica by her sea captain husband to Dunnet Landing. In a strange land, she has no access to her maternal traditions; even song and dance, the usual metaphor for the language of the heart, alienates her from the women who are under the sway of a paternalistic religion. When she attempts to dance in the vestry at a meeting of the women, to communicate her own feelings and defeat the limitation of language, she is rejected. Thereafter she lives a lonely life, until Mrs. Blackett, with her sure maternal understanding, tells her daughter to visit the stranger and that is the beginning of their friendship. Mrs. Tolland is wondrously learned in the domestic arts of sewing, gardening, and cooking; she even manages to teach Almira Todd "a sight of things about herbs" because she too is attuned to life beyond the purely human. When the captain dies at sea, as so many male wanderers die away from Dunnet Landing, she is devastated. Dependent as she is on her relationship to the captain, the foreigner sickens and comes to her deathbed—in contrast to Almira Todd's reaction to her loss. After Mrs. Blackett gives her comfort by summoning a priest to administer Extreme Unction, she is ready to die. As Mrs. Todd comes to the climax of her tale, she reaches the feelings of great art, becoming the very spirit of the female Muse, "an old prophetess" "posed for some great painter," as "unconscious and mysterious as any sibyl of the Sistine chapel" (321). The watcher suddenly sees "a woman's dark face lookin' right at us" with a "kind of expectin' look" (322–23), and Mrs. Todd assures her that she "ain't never goin' to feel strange and lonesome no more" (323). Mrs. Captain Tolland now regains her name, her history, and her language through her return to the mother, caretaker of the gates of life and death. The semidivine mother's home, Jewett suggests throughout the Dunnet Landing story cycle, resembles the dying vision Glasgow grants to John Fincastle of *Vein of Iron* and to Victoria Littlepage* in *They Stooped to Folly*, the "beatific rapture" Porter allows Miranda in "Pale Horse, Pale Rider," and the home to which Naylor returns Abigail in *Mama Day*; all portray a final reality presided over by a powerful maternal figure. These visions challenge the male myth of creation directly with the mother portrayed as the source from which life comes and to which it returns. In all, there is no sense of punishment, of the wrath of the male lawgiver, but rather the dying child is comforted by an accepting mother, who represents the generosity of creation, the joyful plenitude of the natural world itself. In Jewett, as in the other women writers represented here, existence is seamless—there is no abrupt break between states of being, between the human, the animals, and the whole creation of rich green and riotous flowers.

The "lesson" the female narrator learns here is explicitly stated by Mrs. Todd: "There's somethin' of us that must still live on; we've got to join both worlds together an' live in one but for the other" (323). In contrast to the proper balancing of life and eternity as evidenced

---

*Both Jewett and Glasgow use the name "Littlepage" to refer to paternalistic, foolish old men. In Glasgow's novel, Virginius Littlepage is Victoria's husband.

by Mrs. Todd, the story of Joanna Todd stands as a precautionary tale. As numerous commentators have noted, Joanna Todd's Shell-Heap Island offers a contrast to the mother's home. Jewett, as do all of the artists in the present discussion, warns against the too-passionate romantic involvement. Almira and Joanna have both been involved in romances that came to unsuccessful conclusions; the crucial difference, Jewett suggests, is their experience of mothering. Joanna's mother "had the grim streak, and never knew what 't was to be happy" (98), thus the girl came to womanhood vulnerable to the myth of romance, with no countering positive association to cushion her against disillusionment. Almira recounts that Joanna had "given him her whole heart. . . . All her hopes were built on marryin', an' havin' a real home and somebody to look to; she acted just like a bird when its nest is spoilt" (88). Unlike Almira who grows more monumental when her romances are past, Joanna shrinks to a small island, to her father's "dreadful small" bachelor house; she even undergoes a physical diminution, like Cather's Myra Driscoll. She shrinks into her own sour mother. Mrs. Todd believes that "the love in mother's heart would warm her," and offers Mrs. Blackett as a visitor and companion, but Joanna refuses. Unlike the narrator, she refuses the gift of love offered by Mrs. Todd, the coral pin.

Perhaps fearing a like fate, the narrator is driven to see the island where Joanna lived and died twenty-two years before; Shell-Heap Island shows the barren nature of the mother's missing hand, a "few wind-bent trees" which are mostly "dead and gray" and the "fresh green of June" changed to a "sunburnt brown that made them look like stone" (107). Unlike the abiding homes of Mrs. Blackett and Mrs. Todd, "Poor Joanna's house was gone except the stones of its foundation, and there was little trace of her lower garden" (109). Like Cather's Clara Vavrika of "The Bohemian Girl," Marie Tovesky of O Pioneers!, Myra Driscoll of My Mortal Enemy, and Lucy Gayheart, like Glasgow's Eva Birdsong of The Sheltered Life, like Porter's Aunt Amy Rhea, like Welty's Rachel Sojourner and Virgie Rainey, and like Ruby of Naylor's Mama Day, Joanna builds no lasting house, sews no quilt, plants no garden, and vanishes into the man's romantic drama.

That Jewett intends Mrs. Blackett as the spiritual and bodily source of Dunnet Landing, and by extension, America, appears in the climax of the narrative, the Bowden reunion. Although numerous commentators have noted this incident as the culminating episode, no one has yet observed how Jewett magnifies the local experience into a national context. As the assembled family members and guests prepare for their procession, the narrator-writer perceives the importance of the home place, of which Mrs. Blackett is "queen," as source and center of the American nation: "We could see now that there were different footpaths from along shore and across country. In all these there were straggling processions walking in single file, like old illustrations of the Pilgrim's Progress" (130). Jewett explicitly crowns her American mother goddess and her ancestral home as the source of male activity; unlike Captain Littlepage's yearning for the distant, shadow land "away," the aim of the earthly Pilgrim's Progress is the maternal source and her home place. Here Jewett announces the maternal ideal's divinity and simultaneously her refutation of the American heroic individual. Those male wanderers have died, far away, with no decorum, no mourning at the moment to mark their passing. As Sherman observes, both Mrs. Blackett and Mrs. Todd partake of the death-dealing impulse of the Great Mother as well as the positive aspects of the birth impulse. Further, Jewett unites the American earth, the American mother's home, and the American community with the eternal, claiming it as a model of the mother's heaven, observing that they had passed from being simply one New England family and had moved into representing all families through time possessing "the instincts of a far forgotten childhood" (132). By this leap into timelessness, Jewett defeats the dominant discourse of competitive individualism, and by the narrator-pilgrim's progress from city to Dunnet Landing to Green Island to the Bowden home place, the meaning of the sibyl and the mother become clear. Here is the center. At the end of the passage, the writer-daughter has found her place in the maternal lineage as she comes "near to feeling like a true Bowden" (144). Now she, unlike Glasgow's philosopher John Fincastle and Cather's estranged lawyer Jim Burden, finds her mother tongue, can depart and return, but never separate. What she could not find in the schoolhouse or learn from the captain's voyages and secondhand Milton, the narrator finds in the Bowden homestead.

As the narrator returns to the city, we as reader know that she will endlessly return through the book, which has brought her readers back with her. By learning the natural and domestic arts, by immersing herself in the daily lives of the women of Dunnet Landing, the narrator has found her woman's voice. In *The Country of the Pointed Firs*, we see the earliest example of the author-daughter's journey back to her own tradition. The certitude that supports this book suggests a coming together of a constellation of women's history, female myth, personal identity, and artistic skill. Jewett's resolution anticipates other such books as *The Optimist's Daughter, Song of the Lark, Vein of Iron, The Old Order,* and *Mama Day.* In all, the home place offers a vision of order, plenitude, and acceptance unavailable in the social center where calculation and competition reign.

Fictional circumstance replicates metaphorically the experience of the isolated individual in the emerging competitive, differentiated nation. The quintessence of this literary plot appears in these women's writing from their early careers, here illustrated by Jewett: the author depicts her protagonist's entry into and triumph within the male public sphere, taking her away from her female family. Nan's quest illustrates the isolation, and the moral distinction, of the individual protagonist, and the subsequent creation of a purer alternate retreat or relationship expressive of the hero's self-definition. Along with the rest of these literary women, Jewett questions the emphasis on competition and individualism, the American dream of imposition of the self on the social or natural landscape. Because of the centrality of this individualistic cultural drama, the overarching society has a definite interest in ignoring or misreading these women by insisting that their social criticisms are limited to "woman's" experience and do not address the categories of the dominant discourse or that they represent simply a sentimental harking back to a "golden age."

From the end of the nineteenth century to the present, however, a significant group of American women authors has, in the last account, noted and questioned the strong cultural emphasis on the accidents and achievements of the individual life. In their opinion, the heroic individual's desire to step out of history, here illustrated by Captain Littlepage's mad dreams, is a foolish one, deadly both to the person himself and to all around him. The pragmatic morality of the self-made individual directly opposes those of the female pastoral. Finally, these writers insist that roles of strength for women have not existed in the past, and they will not be found in the future, as long as women adapt male definitions of womanliness. Writers such as Jewett suggest the barrenness of unredeemed paternalistic myth and female roles. Excision of gender, in contrast, as demanded by the large-scale bureaucratic social structures, is equally futile. It proves to be ill-logic indeed, as visionary as the farthest reaches of the home place. Another place and another way must be found.

She had only to stand in the orchard, to put her hand on a little crab tree and look up at the apples, to make you feel the goodness of planting and tending and harvesting at last. All the strong things of her heart came out in her body. . . . She was a rich mine of life, like the founders of early races.

—Willa Cather
My Ántonia

3.

Damming the Stream

WILLA CATHER

LIKE SARAH ORNE JEWETT, her friend and mentor, Willa Cather first creates the heroic celibate female individual and later celebrates the female maternal source of the home place as the matrix of civilization.[1] From her lost "beautiful past," Cather early draws statuesque immigrant heroines, who replicate in many respects the heroic male individuals of the "male mainstream" plot. (Lest her readers miss her intention to rewrite American literary history by the addition of woman's contribution, Cather titles the first of her "prairie" novels *O Pioneers!* after Whitman's poem of the same name). To issue a challenge to the tough Nebraska soil, to enter the kingdom of art, and to create the lasting community, the author first felt she needed to bring to life female figures of such emotional and physical size as to appear demigoddesses. In her three "prairie" novels, *O Pioneers!*, *The Song of the Lark*, and *My Ántonia*, these figures serve as the creative matrix for an ideal neighborhood away from the city, the factory, and the railroad of modern America.

Born in Virginia in 1873, Cather migrated with her family at the age of nine to the Nebraska plains that serve as the setting for the prairie novels and stories.[2] In her childhood rambles, she heard and remembered the women's tales that would become the basis for her early Nebraska stories. In an early interview, she tells of her "unreasonable" excitement visiting old immigrant women, some of whom spoke very little English, at their morning baking or butter making; she "always felt as if they told me so much more than they said—as if I had actually got inside another person's skin."[3]

Along with that emotional communication, which bridged the chasm of language between girl child and immigrant women, Cather internalized the landscape, recognizing its outlines and seasons emotionally as well as intellectually and filling it with the previously unconnected stories of the peoples of other countries and times. Her childhood experiences combined with the historical moment and her own artistic sensitivity to bring a new story of the creation of the American homeland. In the unformed pioneer country of her youth, Cather began her lifelong search for a language arising from that shared past that would redeem the history of the American earth—always her Middle West neighborhoods—from its modern insistence on profit and change. As her childhood had shown, the women had a central, if subordinate, place in Old World civilizations.[4] By purging that European past of its paternalistic bias, a revolutionary, more truly democratic American order would come into being. Cather's belief in her New Jerusalem is indicated by a persistent plot circumstance in which the European father, through death or incompetence, cedes the responsibility for the renewal of the family to his American-born daughter. The passing of the European "father" is central to all of the prairie novels, the New World *Shadows on the Rock, My Mortal Enemy,* and *Lucy Gayheart.* In addition, the failure of the American "father" is seen in *A Lost Lady,* "Old Mrs. Harris," "The Joy of Nelly Deane," and *Sapphira and the Slave Girl,* to name a representative group. To achieve America's full potential as a civilization, woman's physical and cultural contribution must be acknowledged.

Like Jewett, Porter, Welty, Naylor, and Glasgow, Cather creates the Earth-Goddess, who represents the elemental creative force of female biological creativity—the heroine of *The Song of the Lark* bears the name "Thea" lest the reader miss the author's intent! Cather first consciously delineated an American homeland that centered on woman's social contribution in *O Pioneers!* (1913), most fully evoked it through classical and biblical allusion in *My Ántonia* (1918), and finally resigned it as a vision for America in the later work *My Mortal Enemy* (1926). These three novels, along with "The Joy of Nelly Deane," "The Bohemian Girl," *The Song of the Lark* (1915), *Shadows on the Rock* (1931), and "Old Mrs. Harris" (1932), indicate Cather's growing discovery of her own connection as a female artist to the home place and, more specifically, acceptance of her place within an ongoing American literary tradition of writing women. Moreover, the plots and characterization of the strongly autobiographical "prairie" novels suggest a resolution of her attitudes toward her gender.

"The Joy of Nelly Deane" (1911) and "The Bohemian Girl" (1912) introduce Cather's major themes. As "The Joy of Nelly Deane" opens, the protagonist is the queen of her social setting, surrounded by her three older women attendants, Mrs. Spinny, Mrs. Dow, and Mrs. Freeze, and viewed by the narrator, her adoring friend "Peggy."[5] Like Edith Wharton's protagonist Lily Bart in the tableau vivant of *The House of Mirth*, Nelly stands above the other women in a theatrical production, which in effect places her as object of an auction. She sings the title role in a cantata based on the Old Testament story of Queen Esther, suggesting her "royalty" and the dominance of the patriarchal past.

Nelly Deane shows the gaiety of the Cather quicksilver heroine, who lives through emotional and personal magnetism like such later Cather protagonists as Clara Vavrika of "The Bohemian Girl," Marie Tovesky of *O Pioneers!*, Marian Forrester of *A Lost Lady*, Myra Driscoll of *My Mortal Enemy*, and Lucy Gayheart. She shows little of the inner drive of Cather's independent, consecrated heroines. For example, when Nelly talks of Chicago, she emphasizes its spectacle and amusements. (Thea Kronborg, in contrast, looks forward to the fulfillment of a life's work.)

Cather draws a central scene between Nelly and Peggy in Nelly's bedroom. As they share confidences, Nelly drifts off to sleep, but Margaret lies awake. "In that snug, warm little bed I had a sense of imminent change and danger. I was somehow afraid for Nelly . . . and I put my arm about her protectingly as we drifted toward sleep" (61). The similarities to the setting and emotional impact of this scene

with that between Wharton's Lily and Gerty Farish after the protagonist's discovery of how crudely she has been "sold" at her auction are
striking; again the author depicts the lovely woman taking sympathy
from her drabber female companion as they lie together, comforting
each other before they prepare to enter the uncaring public world. As
in the Wharton novel, the author contrasts the public exposure of the
crowded stage presentation and its male onlookers who judge and ad-
mire, who seek to possess but do not love, with the private shelter of
the friend's bed and the companion who both loves and admires, who
seeks to comfort. The public stage, sanctified by the presence of the
male leaders of religion, business, and farming in the town, contrasts
with the narrow women's space.

The assertion by Sharon O'Brien that this scene, so like the scene between Lily and Gerty, depicts covert homosexuality is problematic.
Writing that nineteenth-century women often kissed, called each other
pet names, slept together, and wrote to each other in terms now considered at least romantic, if not overtly sexual, Carroll Smith-
Rosenberg contends that those friendships are often misunderstood,
because they are wrenched out of their place in a whole network of
women's relations by a presentist emphasis on individual psycho-
sexual development rather than the communal historical and social
context. Moreover, as Eve Kosofsky Sedgwick notes, paralleling Smith-
Rosenberg, one of the new developments at the turn of the century was
the "world-mapping" by which every one, along with their gender
identity, was also designated as either homosexual or heterosexual (2).
Within the social context, it is uncertain just what emotions are intended to be portrayed in the scene between the two female friends;
Cather may not have seen it as a matter for definition.

As the story progresses, the impoverished social background of the
male-dominated public order emerges in its starkest outlines. Nelly
finds herself left without the social network of support upon which her
royalty rested: her female friend gone to college, her mother dead,
and her father tied by financial obligation to Spinny, she is forced to
make a financially expedient marriage to a "hard man" with a face like
the "castings he sold" because of a failure of expected parental support. Nelly's singing falls still as she sets out with few resources to
regain her happiness. Her death comes directly from her "sale" to the
troll-like merchant Scott Spinny with the "strong, cold hands." Unlike

the larger-than-life Cather heroine, she is defeated by forces larger than she.

Ten years later, Peggy, now a writer, yearns for her friend, who symbolized her own childhood place and time. Mrs. Dow, one of the Fates who weave together the lives and stories of the women, writes that Nelly has recently died giving birth to her son. Later in the small town of Riverbend, as Mrs. Dow sits with her sewing, she offers Peggy the consolation that Nelly has found not only happiness, but a joy in her life, which came not from the romance about which Nelly dreamed but from the rejoining of the generations through the affection of her mother-in-law: "But we must remember that Nelly always had Mrs. Spinny. I never saw anything like the love there was between those two. . . . And then Nelly took great comfort of her little girl" (66). The generations of grandmother, daughter, and granddaughter are reknit into an ongoing woman's lineage.

When Peggy meets Margaret, Nelly's little girl, she sees her friend reborn. To emphasize Cather's theme, the last scene takes place in a darkened church, where once again the three women attend Nelly's son, who appears as the Christ Child, the central figure in another church pageant. The season is Christmas, a favorite one in Cather's fiction, symbolizing rebirth within the dying season and the passing years. As Marilyn Arnold and Sharon O'Brien observe, the scene suggests the Nativity. As it will in *Shadows on the Rock*, it suggests the birth of a new community under the protection of the three old women, the Three Magi, who honor Nelly's child; the holy natural cycle of life begins again. Hidden away from the outside society, the neglected circle of womanly concern nevertheless suggests renewal for the neighborhood, even as the Old Testament patriarchal law is replaced by New Testament redemption. The author implies as well that Nelly's maternity presents Peggy with a model for her own literary creativity and a sense of proportion that extends her life beyond its individual limits.

As in the plot of Jewett's *The Country of the Pointed Firs*, the single-woman writer in "The Joy of Nelly Deane" finds herself inspired by the model of maternity. With the outside writing daughter's return to the female homeland and its older generation of wise women and its generous shelter, Cather forecasts the bridging of the chasm between individual, self-conscious female artistry and traditional female domestic craft and tasks, which she achieves in her later novels. In a parallel to Jewett's early *Deephaven*, the educated urban dweller will carry away the experience of the woman's community to the city; like those other visiting but resolutely urban dwellers, Peggy also displays the mingled wonder and bemusement before the joy and peace of the rejoined female circle.

In "The Joy of Nelly Deane," Cather has already established the centrality of women's relationships to the formation of the neighborhood and the power of female biological creativity to lift the individual artist out of the purely personal and transitory. She presents Peggy, the woman writer, as homeless language weaver who journeys back to discover the social and artistic patterns generated by the woman's community. Finally, Cather contrasts the pragmatism of the public sphere with the generosity of the woman's private space.

In its pictorial nature, the final tableau of "The Joy of Nelly Deane" suggests Cather's search for a language that will both address her modern readership and reproduce the communal feelings of the woman's homeland. As the public language of cultural differentiation and specialization makes woman's communal experience harder to portray, Cather, along with Jewett, Glasgow, Porter, Welty, and Naylor place highly visual, emblematic scenes and references appealing to classic or biblical scenes. Literature thus returns as closely as possible under associational language to the communal ritual, rich with the incense of emotion and memory. All seek to restore the echoes of experience and memory integral to ritual communication. By understanding the sacramental element to Cather's work, as well as that of the other writers here treated, we as readers can trace their extrarational, didactic intent. The pictographic language reinforces the meaning of the numerous goddess figures as Jewett understood in *The Country of the Pointed Firs*, giving the woman's literature a depth beyond the individual experience, a path out of modern literary solipsism. As ritual evolves to woman's local language to memory, it falls in danger of shrinking to the personal, private vision, to being captured in the net of individualism. Thus the recourse to mythic and religious symbolism, which elevates even the most private of moments into an ongoing community of female experience. Incantatory phrases, conventional metaphor, earlier literary elements—orally transmitted legends, folk stories, songs—indicate the didactic, communal intent implicit in these writings. Dreams, visions, and memories of rejoined family and community occur in works by all the writers as they witness to their isolation from female homeland. They seek the restorative, emotional language that reinforces the human connections, the biological roles, and the social traditions of the female family and community. Through individual creation placed within the woman's community, Cather hopes to reassert those discarded visionary elements and instinctual emotions of ritual in a social order that seems, as recent metaphoric patterns suggest, to allow less and less regard for enduring personal relationships and more and more control of public life by abstract rules promulgated by distant experts. Thus Cather, like the others in this discussion, must seek to address her national culture through use of the associational language, but at the same time she must try to evoke the communal language, its emotions and relationships.

Several commentators have discussed aspects of Cather's pictorial language. Bernice Slote describes her attempt to transcend the associational language and linear rationality, noting that the author eschewed realism. Imaginative artistry, Cather felt, existed by "its own vivid life," "one not subject to the laws of everyday life"; as Slote points out, "it is not a lesson in sociology" (64). Cather felt that capturing the highest ideal of the artist's quest in "more exact words" was an impossibility. "It had to be said by indirection and in ritualistic invocation" (*Kingdom*, 65). A later commentator, Robert Nelson, focuses on Cather's use of the pictographic—the evocative, visual language, which in its pictorial intent comes close to ritual itself, considering it an attempt to rediscover the "lost language" of immediate emotional communication. Nelson astutely connects language and ritual; because of Cather's interest in the religious and spiritual elements of art, the successful pictographic passage promotes the language and culture as "sacramental signifiers" (16). Judith Fryer sees Cather's narrative in *My Ántonia* as exemplary of the oral community's art, whose formulaic nature retains the bonding elements of ritual (279). In her references to the unspoken connection between women, Cather reaches to the immediate communication of ritual. The local language is explicitly tied to shared domestic arts in her interviews and fiction; the very pots of the woman's kitchen become the vessels of transformation of nature into culture, the creative matrix.

The local language, as I say, passes from elder to younger directly, through touch and intonation. Its rhythms and its meaning rest on the confidence of a continuing relationship. The daughter, therefore, has great freedom to bring to the tradition her own particular vision, a characteristic of the stories of the oral community. Cather repeatedly seeks to reproduce the effect of local language through visually based scenes, which evoke the emotions of universal myth; in *My Ántonia*, for example, even the unreliable narrator Jim Burden realizes, "Ántonia had always been one to leave images in the mind that did not fade—that grew stronger with time" (352). The listing of those images, Ántonia at the entrance of the fruit cave, Ántonia with her work team against the sky, Ántonia at her father's grave in winter, brings forth the pictorial images, which glow with the reflected memories and emotions of biblical and classical sources, enlarging the individual's emotional parameters and escaping the associational language that she as a modern author must use. Through these fictional patterns, Cather suggests that the woman's community and its language, despite addressing a readership composed of citizens of the rationalized society, is not simply a matter of sentimental, passive nostalgia. Instead, it is an exemplary, vital community transcending material competition and physical life. It exists, however, in emotional reality; like Herland, it is created from a desire for the female home so strong that it possesses a spiritual reality.

With the writing of the lengthy short story, "The Bohemian Girl" (1912), Cather introduces the characterization of her mature work, presenting two women, Clara Vavrika and her mother-in-law, Grandmother Ericson, who stand in symbolic opposition. At first thought, it appears an unbalanced presentation, with Mrs. Ericson hardly a factor at all. The nominal heroine, Clara Vavrika, the Bohemian girl of the title, displays the fiery temperament of the romantic heroine, whereas Mrs. Ericson possesses none of the flash of attractiveness or little of the gentleness of the conventionally feminine. Moreover, Mrs. Ericson seldom actually appears in the action, but she dominates much of the other characters' thoughts, offering by her person and her creative labors commentary on the choices of Nils and Clara.

Cather creates Clara body and spirit in the outlines of the female rebel; she is said to have a "strain of Tartar or Gypsy blood" and an often sullen expression. When Nils observes that Clara is losing her joy in life among his dour family, he uses the imagery of the bird, "you've caught a wild bird in your hand, haven't you. . . . Well, you used to be just like that, a slender eager thing with a wild delight inside you" (37). In this group of women writers, the authorial attitude toward the possibilities for women in traditionally male public roles most often appears through a repeated metaphor: that of the bird in flight or caged. The theme of the caged and soaring bird is remarkable for its consistency and durability as a representation of woman's relation to her social roles and individual aspiration.

An ambiguous symbol, flight comes to take on a particular meaning in the literature that arises from the American context, standing for the casting off from the female body and its social connections through the practice of art or, more negatively, through flight from the woman's community. The ambivalence behind the presentation of flight indicates the authors' anxiety over the perceived conflict between the female biological identity and the human imagination culturally identified with the male; flight represents the imagination unrestrained by the demands and connections of the body. The figure represents the especially acute conflict for the American woman author between the transcendent aspirations of heroic individualism and the emotional sustenance of the woman's community. The repeated symbolism of the bird and flight not only appears but claims its place as a central metaphor in Glasgow's *Virginia* and *The Sheltered Life*, Cather's *The Song of the Lark*, Porter's "The Grave" and "The Fig Tree," Jewett's *The Country of the Pointed Firs*, and Welty's *The Golden Apples* and *The Optimist's Daughter*; it appears as an important figure in other works by self-conscious women writers and domestic novelists as well. In *A Country Doctor*, the eagle circling above the grave of Nan Prince's dead mother forecasts Nan's own triumph over female body and feminine role. Ellen Moers in *Literary Women* sees a divergence of associations clustered around the imagery over a range of time and location; in the American group, however, the imagery displays more consistency.

Unlike most of the women in the community, Clara cares very little for the household arts. She leaves the running of her house to her doting unmarried aunt, Johanna Vavrika, and takes a perverse enjoyment from her defiance of local custom and rules, especially those of her stolid, unimaginative husband, Olaf Ericson, and his traditional, unimaginative mother. Motherless throughout the story, the spoiled and sensuous Clara prefers to spend her time instead with her wid-

owed father and the men in his tavern. Finally, she leaves her marriage
to elope with her own brother-in-law. Like the other impulsive Cather
women, Clara chooses romance over any larger consideration. The female character who chooses personal emotion over cultural commitment, whether it be to the woman's community, the earth, or art itself,
suffers destruction. She vanishes from the life of her people into Nils's
romantic "legend."

To commentators who concentrate only on the compelling figure of
Clara, the concluding section poses the same sort of critical problem
as "The White Mulberry Tree" in the next narrative, *O Pioneers!*. Once
Mrs. Ericson, the maternal representative of the immigrant women's
community, receives her full due in the narrative, these difficulties disappear. The mother of three of the male characters in the book, Mrs.
Ericson has the strength and dedication of Cather's later pioneer heroines. In her seventies, with thirty-one grandchildren, Mrs. Ericson
does her own work, drives and repairs her own automobile, and serves
as the leader of the family. None of Clara's outward energy enlivens
Mrs. Ericson, whose placid personality and massive body resemble the
great figures of the epic.

Clara Vavrika and Mrs. Ericson contend for the love of Nils and the
younger brother Eric and for the moral authority of the narrative.
Cather herself is drawn in this early narrative to Clara's rebellion even
as she acknowledges the older generation's labors. Cather makes the
contrast between the two women explicit in a long set piece at a barn
raising at Olaf Ericson's farm. Nils finds himself admiring a group of
old immigrant women watching the dance; his musing leads inevitably
to a comparison of Clara with these mother-women. He marvels at the
"Herculean" labor the fifteen women have completed—cows milked,
butter churned, gardens planted, children and grandchildren tended,
floors swept, "mountains of food" prepared. He is forced to conclude
that the woman walking alone—the woman Clara whom he loves—is
not like those women, that she is a heroine for his romance, incapable
within "a hundred years" of accomplishing the labors undertaken by
his own mother (29).

The final section takes place a year later. Again a train brings one of
Mrs. Ericson's sons back to home and mother. Her youngest son Eric
has abandoned his plan to join Clara and Nils, after the Ericson family
suspected him of complicity in the pair's escape. Like other unmarried

male wanderers in Cather's later work, Carl Linstrum, Anton Rosicky, and Anton Cuzak, Eric is drawn back to the maternal source. When the young man comes into the house, fearing his mother's rejection, she instead grants him her blessing in an emblematic scene in which she rests her hand on his head, fingers twining within his hair, and, Cather tells us, "happiness filled his heart" (41). Instead of being an unsatisfactory ending, the reunion of the maternally founded family contrasts with the relationship of the lovers, which threatens to tear apart family and destroy the homeland. David Stouck concludes, "We cannot help feeling that [Eric's] choice involves the author's deepest sympathies and emotional preferences" (*Cather's Imagination*, 22).

Although Mrs. Ericson holds less appeal than Clara, just as Alexandra Bergson possesses fewer charms than Marie Tovesky, she nonetheless accepts the duties of the creative individual in Cather's work. Stouck writes that Cather creates such characters as Mrs. Ericson and Alexandra in the mold of the heroine of the primary epic, who appears as a one-dimensional representative of her people against the forces that threaten the community's survival (*Imagination*, 23). But the silence behind the epic figure also fits in with Cather's idea of the ineffable nature of the female experience, its inability to be confined by the abstract linearity of the associational language. Cather's emblematic scenes, the bathing of Mrs. Harris's feet, Thea's artistic epiphany, and the apotheosis of Ántonia as mother of the homeland—all express the individual's entrance into the human community. Mrs. Ericson and Alexandra have great womanly creativity precisely because they do not spend their time in amusement or romance. They do not beguile; they create.

In its themes and characterization, "The Bohemian Girl" suggests that Cather has not yet found the rationale for her own leave-taking. The massive figure of Mrs. Ericson, however, prepares us for the great figures of female creativity in Cather's prairie novels, especially Alexandra Bergson of *O Pioneers!* (1913). James Woodress notes the parallels between "The Bohemian Girl" and *O Pioneers!*: the Nils–Clara and the Emil–Marie relationships, the time of both works, and the portrayals of the two pairs of plodding brothers (*Life and Art*, 148). The first of the prairie novels shares additional elements with the preceding story: the Bohemian and Scandinavian immigrants, the two central female figures, and the homeland's creation. Cather presents contrasting stories of women's choices, Alexandra's creation of a country, and Marie Tovesky's romance and death.

Of *O Pioneers!*, Willa Cather wrote, "In this one I hit the home pasture."[6] Alexandra Bergson is chosen by her dying father to succeed in taming the wild Nebraska earth and to lead the family he has brought to the New World. Cather indicates that the stubborn Nebraska earth will yield to female nurture what it refuses to male conquest. Unable to accept life in America, the European father, whose vigorous daughter assumes leadership of the family, appears in Cather's work from *O Pioneers!* to *Shadows on the Rock* as the author suggests that the patriarchal Old World order must yield to the woman's nurturing, egalitarian community to achieve the promise of a new order in the New World. Even though she is not yet a woman, Alexandra's strength and identification with the soil far surpass that of her conventional brothers. Not only does her dying father violate the expected gender order, but also Alexandra's immigrant mother cannot offer her daughter a pattern for homemaking on the prairies, which bear no mark of cultural tradition and few marks of human continuity. In fact, Alexandra serves as parent to her own mother, a shadowy background figure who seeks to re-create her European domestic life in America.

When she comes of age in body and wisdom, Alexandra puts her physical and emotional energy into the creation of a separate agrarian community, Cather illustrating the nature of Alexandra's commitment to the land by the erotic, poetic manifestation of the Divide—the visitations of a Corn God. Annis Pratt identifies the figure as Alexandra's complementary figure of Death, Cather thus removing the destructive aspect of the maternal archetype. Alexandra considers the men she sees around her as comrades, "work fellows." In Cather, the soil itself offers a genius for the immigrant woman who, by the combination of her female nature and her European tradition, is instinctively and physically attuned to the earth's rhythms, "There were certain days . . . when she was close to the flat, fallow world about her, and felt, as it were, in her own body the joyous germination in the soil" (*O Pioneers!* 203–204). Alexandra evidences the identification with the American earth that informs so much of the national literature. Unlike the westering frontiersman and the expansive entrepreneur, Cather's woman pioneer meets the land as a mother-sister-lover.

The heroine Alexandra differs from other women in physical size

and in prophetic vision as well as in role and background. Like Chopin's Edna Pontellier of "The Awakening," Wharton's Justine Brent of
The Fruit of the Tree, Glasgow's Dorinda Oakley of *Barren Ground,*
and Cather's Clara Vavrika of "The Bohemian Girl," Alexandra has
androgynous outlines, which suggest her essential difference from the
rest of her sex—her size, her interests, and her appearance. Fryer
notes her primary connection with the fields and the pastures, continuing that, unlike the more domestic women, she cannot be expressed by
her house (256). In this early novel, as with "The Bohemian Girl,"
Cather indicates that domesticity and creativity do not exist in the
same female personality, but now the protagonist appreciates the
women who make the home, the domestic traditions, and the shared
history through their homely arts; Cather thereby implies that their
domestic work supports and inspires autonomous individual female
creators such as Alexandra, Kronborg, or Vickie Templeton.

That Cather intended for her novel to reverberate with the references and language of the classic pastoral has been amply demonstrated. Tracing the parallels between *O Pioneers!* and Virgil's *Ec-
loques,* Susan Rosowski cites such characteristics as the linking of
unrelated subjects, the discarding of the linear narrative, and Alexandra's place as "privileged noble peasant-shepherd" given her by her
father (*Voyage Perilous,* 50). Evelyn Helmick's essay further identifies
the composition of *O Pioneers!* as an attempt to bring classical and
contemporary myths to her work, especially that of the maternal archetype Demeter. Cather, however, through the integration of wom-
en's metaphors such as sewing, suggests the renovation of the patriarchal dramas.

The use of such heroic figures as discussed by C. G. Jung and his
interpreter Erich Neumann evokes a pattern of transcultural symbolism, which particularly valorizes the feminine. In *The Great Mother,*
Neumann writes that the Great Mother Goddess is the goddess of
grain and agriculture, hence all growth, an observation which illumi-
nates Alexandra's portrayal. Kathryn Rabuzzi reminds us that the
Jungian maternal archetype also connects to death, which leads to rebirth in the cyclical natural cycle; therefore, the dead who return to
"the maternal womb of earth" will be revived (23). Those beloved mor-
tals around Alexandra die, but Cather emphasizes that death is neither
the threshold to a religious heaven nor the final step to the abyss. Al-

exandra dies into the life cycle of the land, only living as individual self in the memories of the women in the homesteads, fed and nurtured by her land. Her promise of immortality appears in the novel's last lines: "Fortunate country, that is one day to receive hearts like Alexandra's into its bosom, to give them out again in the yellow wheat, in the rustling corn, in the shining eyes of youth!" (309). Through the use of such emblematic figures and their epic creation of the American homeland, the author hopes to reshape male myths into female narratives of heroism. Unlike the male quest, and the American pioneer legend, Alexandra receives her strength from connection with the earth and with other women and their domestic arts.

Alexandra's career shows the extreme constraints Cather puts on the woman who would take on the role of heroic individual. The needs of American literary individualism and classic quest myth dovetail neatly in Alexandra's career. She cannot, for example, express her sexuality with a human lover while she is young and able to bear children. She consecrates all of her sexual energy, female fertility, and maternal care to the creation of the new country. Cather emphasizes the platonic nature of her protagonist's relationship with her childhood friend Carl; she can only be with Carl as long as he accepts the land and honors her—in sum, only as long as he refuses to make her his own. Alexandra marries after the homeland is established, and she herself has passed childbearing age. Woodress notes the shrinking of Alexandra into a mere mortal after her labors are complete (*A Literary Life*, 246). After her fertility has created the homeland, the personal, diminished Alexandra is left, much like the shell that is Kronborg after her performance; in both, the womanly vitality is transferred into the communal task.

Not only does Alexandra lack parents and husband as support in her difficult task, but her unimaginative brothers continually misunderstand the proper use of the land and the correctness of Alexandra's "unwomanly" and lonely life. She has no supportive community except for old and young women powerless to aid her physically in her task but who offer emotional backing. Fryer identifies the quilting undertaken by Alexandra, Marie, and old Mrs. Lee as a symbol of the stitching together of the stories of the book (257). As these women weave past and present in their stories with Alexandra's vision of the future, they themselves join their affections and experiences. The independent woman finds no hostility in her friends who have made different choices. As the earth outside rests, so does Alexandra, renewed by her friends and their "winter memories" of the Old World domestic arts and customs. The woman's community creates a homeland from memories and matrix—as *The Song of the Lark* shows clearly, the American neighborhood arises from Alexandra's physical fruitfulness fully as much as it emerges from her generous emotions and far-sighted imagination.

Cather commented, "Restlessness such as ours, success such as ours, striving such as ours, do not make for beauty. Other things must come first: good cookery; cottages that are homes, not playthings; gardens; repose." Cather continues that she rejects the "Americanizing" of the immigrant culture, the demand for rationalization represented by "[s]peed, uniformity, dispatch."[7] Alexandra's creativity connects with and arises from the kitchens and gardens of the other immigrant women. In Alexandra, the strength of the pioneer is joined with a generous female nature. The New Jerusalem in America will come into being by joining European cultural and historical traditions to the emptiness and blank historical background of the Nebraska plains.

A fictional counterpoint to the central plot of the creation of the land, "The Mulberry Tree" subplot illustrates the fate waiting the woman who lives primarily through emotion. Married to a sullen Bohemian farmer, Marie Tovesky has a romance with Emil Bergson, Alexandra's youngest brother. Her husband kills both upon his discovery of the pair in their first sexual embrace. Coming as it does, after Alexandra's creation of the farm, this violent resolution of the romance contrasts with the disciplined comradeship Alexandra shares with Carl. Destined to live through and for emotion and sexuality, Marie possesses the dangerous romantic attributes antithetical to those of the creative woman who gives her life to a communal commitment, whether domestic or artistic. Because of her passionate feminine nature, Marie swims in the stream of emotion, whereas Alexandra attempts to dam that stream, to shape its course. Marie remains trapped in her own short lifetime, having neither children to mourn her nor country or art to commemorate her. Immoderate emotion proves destructive both to the woman and the community, a circumstance that holds constant from *O Pioneers!* onward.

In *O Pioneers!* Cather shows the female body and creative vision devoted to the founding of a motherland through use of energies and acceptance of roles that the American literary community customarily associates with the writing of the male. Alexandra is the decision maker, the financial manager, and, most importantly, the visionary founder of the homeland. She triumphs, not only through energy and strength of vision—the hallmarks of the heroic American male individual—but also through her abiding love and her intuitive identification with the earth's life cycle, qualities culturally and historically identified with the feminine. As O'Brien argues, Cather humanizes the central American myth by adding the body and spirit that create a culture on a bare land. Moreover, she gives that American homeland a longer emotional history than actual fact warrants by connecting the immigrant daughter with the goddesses of the ancient epics. The book echoes with the time-honored myths which, as C. Kerenyi asserts, keep their vitality by mingling with each other, combining in ever new mythological narratives (*Science of Mythology*, 11). Such observations remind us that Cather's use of male myth is suggestive, as it is in the work of the other authors here. The addition of the woman's community enriches the myth, deepening it through the domestic arts and the evocation of the female creative source. Female nurture succeeds in making a civilization where male conquest fails.

In *The Song of the Lark*, Cather depicts another heroic protagonist, Thea Kronborg, who renounces marriage and biological maternity; she instead devotes her feminine creativity to the community of art. That maternity and birth are nonetheless at the center of the narrative is shown by the connection of Thea to her own mother and to the ancient Indian mothers. A *Künstlerroman*, *The Song of the Lark* details Thea Kronborg's life from the discovery of her talent, to her coming of age as singer, to her arrival as daughter of the kingdom of art.

As earlier works suggest, Cather felt America neglected the creativity of the immigrant woman's heritage. As a contrast, she shows the type of women produced by the popular culture of market capitalism. To illustrate the contrast between the two groups of women, Cather offers two female characters, Anna Kronborg and Lily Fisher, bringing the qualities of the heroic Mrs. Kronborg and her daughter Thea into sharp relief. The first, Thea's own sister, repudiates Swedish elements of her family as "foreign" and "old fashioned." She objects strongly to Thea's singing with the Mexican laborers and their families, for example, as an embarrassing activity. Thea's musical rival, Lily Fisher, also shows the emptiness of the American girl and her "art" as opposed to the woman-child Thea. All pink and white, Lily with her blond curls looks "exactly like the beautiful children on the soap calendars." Lily easily bests the serious, dignified Thea at Moonstone musicales by combining dramatic recitations and sentimental songs such as "Rock of Ages" and "Home, Sweet Home." Soap calendars, sentimental songs, and romantic novels form the American town's notions of art and beauty, in which women as children or mannequins move gingerly, safely asexual representations of womanhood, available to purchase and amenable to guidance. The diminished child-woman of the Baptist choir represents the feminine ideal, because she poses none of the threat and power of the formidable female sexual potential already apparent in Thea.

In contrast to safe, male-controlled femininity, Cather creates the vital womanliness of Mrs. Kronborg and Thea. For the first time, Cather celebrates the direct contribution of the mother to the feminine generations; she indicates the restoration of the lineage by creating Mrs. Kronborg as a double of her daughter. Both mother and daughter hold the same tie to their native earth, and they share the same blood, memories, and physical appearance. In the singular case of the female artist Thea, the mother's example advances, but does not shape, the daughter's art. Slote identifies the connection of female body and creativity throughout Cather's writing: "[Cather] conceived of the performer's own body and passion as the literal instrument of her art and used metaphors of quickening, awakening; the creation of art, in both the artist and the receiver, is described in terms of conception, birth, and growth" (*Kingdom*, 48). Without Mrs. Kronborg's generous and wise care, her daughter's art would be lost. Immigrant women like Mrs. Lee and Mrs. Kronborg, and later Mrs. Harling of *My Ántonia*, fill woman's traditional homemaking roles and create a setting that makes possible the emergence of the daughter's own personality and creativity. Cather ties female art, public and domestic, by observing that the old-fashioned farmer's wife shares a kinship with the prima donna. Their creativity comes from their physical labors in service to a communal goal. Moreover, they both have the deep joy in human experience that expands the power of the individual, the creative farm woman having, in Cather's opinion, "all the appreciation of the beautiful bodies of her children, of the odor and harmony of her kitchen, of the real creative joy of all her activities which marks the great artist."[8]

"Lost" women like Clara Vavrika, Marie Tovesky, Myra Driscoll, and Lucy Gayheart not only have no living mothers, but these precautionary characters also stake their happiness on male-female love, as deadly a bond in Cather as in Jewett. Women like Thea who renounce their personal lives to the discipline of art achieve an immortality that parallels the continuity of the family and the woman's community by moving beyond the confines of the aging body and the passing emotions. By her characterization, Cather suggests that significant art by women comes directly from the female body and spirit. To Cather, the sacrifice of the individual life represents the central paradox of her art and perhaps her own life—that the artist woman must consecrate her female identity, body and spirit, to the creation of a community of art and thereby to gain immortality.

Her biographers agree that Cather created a protagonist who deals with the author's own immediate concerns for the only time in her career. Although Thea the singer is drawn from the Wagnerian soprano Olive Fremstad, Thea the artist gains her intensity from Cather's own experiences. Thea's childhood comes from Cather's own; the singer's commitment to art grows out of her creator's dedication to literature. Elizabeth Sergeant records the strength of Cather's identification with her protagonist, noting that Thea had shared many of the author's characteristics and experiences (Sergeant, 137). *The Song of the Lark*, then, represents one of those novels in which the protagonist embodies the artist's fictional statement of deeply felt personal experience and belief. Two writers of the same generation, Cather and Glasgow, indicate their intense connections to two female protagonists in identical terms: Cather holds a "close inner" tie to Thea and Glasgow writes of the connection between her protagonist Dorinda Oakley of *Barren Ground* and herself as being that of a "living nerve." In the austerity of the personalities they draw in Thea Kronborg and Dorinda Oakley, the two writers show the social demands placed on the woman who would take a central role in modern America. These particular works deal with the author's perceptions of her own identity as self-conscious artist. (Others in this group: Jewett's *A Country Doctor* and *The Country of the Pointed Firs*, Glasgow's *Barren Ground* and *Vein of Iron*, Porter's "Old Mortality," "Pale Horse, Pale Rider," and *The Old*

Order, Welty's *The Optimist's Daughter*, and Cather's own "The Bohemian Girl" and *O Pioneers!*)

Cather thought long about the problem of female identity, specifically her relation as artist to the Nebraska farmwomen of her youth.
As Sergeant observed, *The Song of the Lark* depicts the passion driving
the artist-woman's decision to move away from "the instinctive woman's lot of marriage and children" to experience the second birth
achieved by a connection with her own female self, body, spirit, and
memories (Sergeant, 134). The importance of maternity and birth in
The Song of the Lark is often overlooked because of the glory of Thea's
individual artistic epiphany. As O'Brien notes, Cather's earlier com-
mentaries on female opera singers reveal a set of metaphoric equiva-
lences clustered around the standard pattern of male creativity, "sword/
penis/pen/male/artist," but by her reviews of the 1890s Cather began
to make new associations that center on female creativity: "vessel/
womb/throat/voice/woman/artist" (*Emerging Voice*, 171). In "The Joy
of Nelly Deane," "The Bohemian Girl," and *O Pioneers!*, Cather had
begun to discover connections between the art of the domestic woman
and that of the autonomous female achiever. The novel frees her for
an easier acceptance of woman's art, whether folk or self-conscious,
which culminates in the fully realized female pastoral of *My Ántonia*.
The domestic mother immerses herself in the inevitable cycle of life;
the artist daughter has no such peace. Ray Kennedy's observation suggests the difference between the two women, as he remarks that Mrs.
Kronborg's face, so similar to her daughter's, had the same dignity, but
that her aspect was "calm and satisfied" whereas Thea's was "intense
and questioning." He concludes that they have "a large kind of look"
and that both carry "their heads like Indian women, with a kind of
noble unconsciousness" (121). This passage groups together the creative women of the narrative, Mrs. Kronborg, the Ancient Mothers,
and *their* artist-daughter Thea. All live beyond the self and the passing
fashion, moving their bodies with calm purpose, unlike the "town
girls" Ray sees who handle their bodies like puppets, "always nodding
and jerking . . . insinuating with their heads" (121–22).

In this novel, Cather connects the two female creations through
Thea's two births. The first section of the narrative concerns itself almost as much with Mrs. Kronborg as with Thea herself. (The mother
is named only "Mrs. Kronborg," an underlining of her maternal, com-

munal identity.) The two women appear together, the mother emerging as a fully realized character. I am indebted to Linda Pannill's observation that the child Thea struggles for breath as Mrs. Kronborg struggles to give birth; the two physical births, the womb and the throat, are thus linked from the novel's first scene. Thea and her mother show the calm, stubborn, culturally conservative personality of the female creator of the homeland. Cather explicitly unites the female generations, mother's and daughter's strength increasing by contact with each other. Mrs. Kronborg gives birth to her daughter's physical and cultural self, but Thea herself must take the received female heritage and go beyond to her second birth.

When Thea returns to Moonstone for the final time, she realizes that she and her mother have chosen different fates. As her train pulls out of the depot, Thea, like her creator, knows she cannot return to live with her kin and her earth. In contrast to Clara Vavrika's instinctive hesitation and her own first homesickness, Thea realizes she has permanently lost contact with her people, especially her mother. She must leave, yet never does either character or creator leave her prairies behind. Fred Ottenburg tells Thea that she has never lost the values that fit the Moonstone scale, which has given her the perspective, the background enriching her art. Thea is preparing to give birth to Kronborg, the woman artist who finds her strength from her female family. As she prepares to leave for her first major role, Thea observes that one had to be born again to be an artist. Fred replies, "Exactly. And when I see you again I shall not see you, but your daughter" (378). Both of her music teachers speak of her talent in terms of a second birth; Wunsch tells Thea that every artist "makes himself born," and Thea quotes Harsanyi that to become an artist "one had to be born again" (378). The birth of her second self takes Thea out of her ongoing membership in the woman's local community to the eternal community of art.

On Dr. Archie's last visit to Mrs. Kronborg, which begins the "Kronborg" section, the dying woman sums up the cost of maternity. She raises her children to make their way in the world; thus she understands Thea's absence. As she talks of her daughter, the doctor notes "a fierce, defiant kind of pride he had heard often in Thea's voice" (407). As Mrs. Kronborg lies on her deathbed, Kronborg is born. And, in truth, an important part of Thea dies at this point; the death of her mother, so like Thea physically, signifies the final rejection of customary feminine roles by Kronborg. It signals the accession to the maternal power and memories by the artist daughter. The mother dies, the artist is born, as Thea's art expresses the female lineage. Dr. Archie, who serves as one of the "queenly" woman's pallbearers, muses that he felt almost as if he had helped bury the daughter "[t]he handsome head in the coffin seemed to him much more really Thea than did the radiant young woman in the picture" (408). Mrs. Kronborg's death signifies the death of the daughter Thea.

With the birth of the soul, the artistic voice that is Kronborg, the female body in its biological, personal sense is transcended. In writing of the Persephone figure, C. Kerenyi notes that "The maiden of primordial mythology may have harboured the cares and sorrows of motherhood in her nature, but the patient earthly endurance of the absolute mother is wholly lacking to her" (*Science of Mythology*, 136). In this narrative, Cather follows this pattern, Mrs. Kronborg's death making explicit the centrality of the themes of maternity and birth in *The Song of the Lark*. Although she dies without Thea, Mrs. Kronborg and her daughter will never separate because of the tie of family and shared experience; they carry each other in the same female flesh, memories, and emotions. In her second birth, Kronborg gives birth to her mother, to her people; she brings them to the "outside."

In the 1932 edition of *The Song of the Lark*, Cather notes in the preface that the personal Thea falls away, leaving behind the "imperishable daughter of music." Kronborg's everyday life is subject to all the regulations of the modern social order, concert dates and "dull business detail" and all the functionaries of that business: "But the free creature, who retains her youth and beauty and warm imagination, is kept shut up in the closet, along with the scores and wigs" (iii). In sum, the woman artist drains passion, personal life, birthing labor, all creative manifestations of her female personality into an artistic discipline. Cather's alter ego Thea instinctively understands that, when she goes to Germany to start her career, she will no longer be Thea, but will become the elemental force Kronborg. Although Kronborg must leave the mother's home to learn the language of her male teachers in the public world, she realizes and is realized by the home place and its tradition.

In case we readers have not understood her thematic intent, Cather further underlines Thea's connection with the mother women and their arts. Her artistic epiphany comes from the consonance she discovers with the Indian Mothers, who created jars in the shape of the matrix, the very shape of the contours of her mouth and throat as she sings. She finds a vessel to transform the future, to bring art into the world. The female generative power thus creates the alternate art of life.[9] In the symbolism of the jars, the cave, and the river, Cather comes to the archetypal symbols of the mother and transformation, subsuming the personal and encountering the mythic. In forming and decorating their vessels, the women potters integrated womanhood and creativity, nature and culture, body and spirit, as the singer's own voice does. Like the opera singer, whose strength comes from the cave and the stream, the Indian women use the primary materials of nature, earth and water, to make containers whose form, like Thea's throat, echoed the shape of the womb.[10]

Cather depicts Thea's connection to the ancient women as she literally follows their footsteps, feeling herself arising reborn from the "accustomed dust" of the trail. Finally she transforms into those Mothers, walks as they walked, physically, spiritually connected to them as she feels the "weight of an Indian baby hanging to her back as she climbs" (302). As those Naive American mothers of that lost women's community carried on their daily creative domestic tasks—bearing their children, carrying water in decorated pots—they destroyed the barriers of time and language, a process suggesting the dynamic of ritual. The art of these ancient women reached out to Thea, the daughter of art, bringing her to her female heritage, serving as midwives to her second birth. The meaning of their message to Thea comes clear when the artist sees a soaring eagle, the triumph of art broken free from the body, as she lifts above the shards of "their desire," above the glittering stream of time, as the relationship of her art to those Mothers becomes clear. They will attend her second birth. From their bodies and their domestic lives and through her individual artistic intelligence and her own body, Thea readies her self as artist to emerge in the ritualistic birth from the cave and her own baptism of her creation, Kronborg. The long-dead women of the oral community touch Thea across the boundaries of life and death, passing the gift of female creativity. Unlike the "stupid women," those who live for the day, those mother-artists achieve a sort of immortality by giving birth and adding art to domestic tasks. The metaphor of the jar not only suggests the shape of the womb and Thea's throat but also illustrates the integration of art with domestic tradition. Thea's recovery of her female history resolves Cather's own conflict between gender and art, the conflict shown in her early masculine persona and denigration of women's writing.

The present interpretation integrates another puzzling ending; the last section showing Tillie's life in Moonstone illustrates how prairie, family, and art intersect for Cather, who again uses the water imagery of the stream of time: "[Tillie's stories about Kronborg] give them something to talk about and to conjecture about, cut off as they are from the restless currents of the world" (490). Even though her quest takes her away from the home of her childhood and the homely tasks of the mothers, the coda indicates that Thea gives back to her native earth and her female family the cultural gifts that she has received from them. Individual female artistry filtered through the woman's community enrich the whole of the American society. As Cather concludes, Thea's doings "bring to the old, memories, and to the young, dreams" (490). By this ending Cather makes explicit the communal origins of individual art. In contrast to male stories of achievement, Thea's triumph comes from her contact with the earth and from her immersion in the lore and creativity of first her personal mother and finally that of the Native American Mothers and artisans.

In *O Pioneers!* Cather asserts that the individual woman's creative energies must flow from a shared cultural tradition to be enduring; in *The Song of the Lark* the author knowingly amplifies this belief to include the concepts of time and art. Art captures emotion, vision, the hidden daily life of a people—"the flash of arrested motion." The great aesthetic creations dam the stream of time so that the isolated individual set in time can be joined to the great community of art. In *The Song of the Lark*, Cather shows the voice flying free, released from the matrix of the throat, as the daughter emerges from the womb, as the eagle flies above Thea's cave. By use of this conventional imagery, which is coupled with an evocation of creative maternity, Cather links woman's history with the individual artist-woman. Commenting on the didactic intent of the narrative, E. K. Brown explains Cather's epiphany in Panther Canyon as the "lengthening of one's past as an American, especially if one were a Western American, an enlarging of one's frame of reference" (130). *The Song of the Lark* shows Cather using the female body itself as the source and model of creativity amidst the mirroring maternal landscape that Ellen Moers details in *Literary Women* (297). Even more significant, however, is Cather's insistence on the importance of reaching individually and collectively toward a female model of creativity, of connecting with the strength of the domestic tradition, and of tying that female creative myth to the American earth and history. Like Jewett, Cather insists on woman's contribution to the founding of the American homeland.

Music is, of course, a central metaphor of the novel, Cather indicating her yearning toward the emotionally freighted mother-daughter communication, which resembles the bonding emotion of the local language. Cather wrote about the problem of language, an even greater challenge to communication than music: "To keep an idea living, intact, tinged with all its original feeling, its original mood, preserving in it all the ecstasy which attended its birth, . . . that is the greatest of all the gifts of the gods" (*Kingdom*, 9). Richard Gianonne addresses Cather's problem in transcribing the community's oral transmissions to the printed page, noting that her efforts to bring the experience of the lyric, the public performance, to fiction, which had become trapped in the evolved literary conventions of the naturalistic novel's written descriptions. The critic continues that Cather sought to bond the members of the scattered society through the novel, "working against the prevailing emulation of technology that threatened to make the novel a laboratory experiment. Cather answered the need of the novel by bringing words back to their origins as spoken things" ("The Human Voice," 48–49). Cather not only seeks to unite her readers as listeners, but also as "see-ers," as true members of the American home place. With recourse to both active vision and hearing, she hopes to re-create the communal emotions of religious ritual in a secular age—her consistent interest in religious themes underlines this intent. She reaches toward the high seriousness of the ancient peoples' art, which was integrated fully into daily life, but she insists on woman as the creative source of life and art.

With this work, Cather realized intellectually and emotionally her connection with the women of her childhood. She would henceforth write from reflection and memory rather than from admiration and aspiration. The author herself would try to capture the essence of life through the words first formed in her immigrant neighbors' kitchens, as Thea tries to capture it through musical notes, as the Indian women tried to capture it in the design of water jars. She felt the connection between women of different times and experience; her own work issued from the matrix. The generations rejoin, but Thea's contribution to her family's history, as Cather's will be, lies in the qualities of her soul shaped by the maternal heritage and expressed through her songs, her roles, and her example. As O'Brien argues, she achieved integration of gender and art with *The Song of the Lark;* she now had the confidence as a writing woman to reach toward an imaginative construction of the home place. In returning to this communal mode, she prepares us for the language of *My Ántonia* where Cather's own authority as female artist overrides the trite assumptions of the unreliable male narrator.

In *My Ántonia* the creative power of protagonist Ántonia Shimerda contrasts with the impulse to romanticism of the narrator, Jim Burden. Like other women in this discussion, Cather acknowledges the American tendency to devalue women because of their biological contribution to the continuation of the communal tasks of maternity and society, and she reverses it dramatically in *My Ántonia.* The woman creates life, art, and civilization itself from her body and from her example.

By reaching toward the home place, Cather asserts her own power as writing daughter. At the beginning, we hear Cather's own authorial voice, warning us that the narrative that follows is *Jim's* Ántonia. The reader cannot assume that his perceptions are shared by the author, but we also know that she as female daughter-artist to Ántonia's Demeter has created the home place. Cather's art is the aperture capturing Ántonia's image, even though the male's empty romanticizing language clouds the conflict, drudgery, and violence of frontier life. Jim learns the classical and biblical legends, discerning the parallels between the ancient mothers and the immigrant girls and allowing Cather to underline their eternal nature. Like Jewett's Captain Littlepage, however, he continually makes their stories "literary," arranging them into traditional paternalistic myth. Blanche Gelfant comments that throughout his narrative of the Blind D'Arnault visit, Jim is unaware of his condescending characterization. Similarly, Gelfant notes the aura of romantic fiction Jim creates around the labor of the Danish laundresses, the horror of Peter's and Pavel's flight from the wolves, and Mr. Shimerda's suicide. Gelfant notes, "He has the insistent need—and the strategy—to turn away from the very material he presents" ("Reaping Hook," 114–15).

How then does the novel arise above Jim's romanticizing of experience? Just as Jewett's female narrator overcomes the tyranny of male theories of authorship, Cather's creativity, her use of the local language, is informed and informs Ántonia's labors. Ántonia's participation in sexuality and birth through emblematic scenes—the plow before the sun, the fruit cave, the hired girls dancing, the killing of the great snake, the immigrant woman on the page—these pictorial, evocative passages contrast female creativity with male language. Further, to link Nebraska with time and tradition in *My Ántonia*, Cather relies on symbolic motifs from Virgil's *Georgics* and the Bible, which we understand through her art more fully than does the childlike Jim Burden (Rosowski, *Voyage Perilous*, Stouck, *Cather's Imagination*). The setting itself recalls the natural rhythms of the ancient epics, which record the founding of the old civilizations: a vast ocean of a land, moving and shifting with "wine-dark" grasses. As unmarked as the sea, the land waits expectantly for the human hand both to shape and celebrate it.

But by his entanglement in the legalistic language of the urban center, Jim forfeits his part in Ántonia's task of creating an American homeland. Cather shows that Jim as a modern American has difficulty in progressing from childhood even as she contrasts Ántonia's movement through the stages of life. Cut off from woman's creativity (Ántonia), the American culture, represented by Jim Burden, has evolved into a sterile, mechanized society. Jim, and by implication the American civilization, cannot therefore create any enduring artifacts or relationships.

Part of the problem of critical interpretation of *My Ántonia* comes from Cather's attempt in her own modern fiction to re-create the feelings engendered by the communal language. To assertions that *My Ántonia* was not a novel, Cather retorted that she had never said it was. She was trying to evoke a spirit, a feeling of continuity and seriousness.

All art should be evaluated not by abstract critical measures and definitions but by its ability to evoke an ever-present and inexhaustible emotional memory:

> Whatever is felt upon the page without being specifically named there—that, one might say, is created. It is the unexplainable presence of the thing not named, of the overtone divined by the ear but not heard by it, the verbal mood, the emotional aura of the fact or the thing or the deed, that gives high quality to the novel or the drama, as well as to poetry itself. (*Not Under Forty*, 50)

As readers, we can see that Cather seems to be constructing her own woman's "ritual" through her literary commitment, just as the mother constructs her homeland. Ann Romines notes the importance of domestic arts in shaping the content of Cather's work; Cather reinvests the daily tasks with symbolic meaning constructed from biblical, classical, and natural symbols. Cather, as Fryer and Gianonne note, eschews the linear narrative typical of the modern novel. While promising to express the divine in the human, the narrative, like ritual, never compromises by resorting to explanation. Ritual ends in silence and contemplation: so too Cather ends by inviting us to "feel" the history of the woman and the land—here meaning Ántonia, not the artistic creator, Cather. She lifts Ántonia out of time. Through this strategy, with its intimations of communal context as source for individual art, Cather subverts the elaborated language of the rationalized social structures and the progressive morality of the entrepreneur and the plainsman. She rejects the American penchant to cast off the past, to leave behind the community and the present in favor of an ever-expanding future. Cather insists on the eternal present of ritual, which unites art, author, and readers in a community. The beginning of the novel, then, prepares the reader for the story of the two creations, the fleeing passions of the home place and the captured emotion of Cather's art, both of which bring Nebraska—the ideal, the idea, of America—into being.

The life of the new settlers in the raw land appears through the classic view of melancholy recollection, Cather first re-creating the pastoral interlude of youth and discovery. The next section shows the coming of age of both Ántonia and the land, for they are always connected as with a living, feeling intelligence. Until she lives with Mrs.

Harling, Antonia creates herself, undertaking tasks considered masculine. (This point should not overemphasized, given the exigent demands of harvest and sowing, and their import to the whole family's
existence on the farm of that period.) In contrast to Alexandra, who
consecrates the creative female energy of her body to the direct, physical creation of the homeland, however, Ántonia devotes her emotions
and fruitfulness to creating her own family and following her own domestic traditions. She is a "mother of a race," the matrix of civilization,
the source of art and custom.

Without contact with the female principle, which Ántonia and the
homeland represent, the artist becomes one of the culturally impoverished salon hangers-on like Mrs. Burden's circle, and the man becomes like the poor failures of Lena's apartment. In contrast to Ántonia, it is said of Lena Lingard, "She's the only person I know who
never gets any older" (302). She becomes the perfect romantic ideal,
the corresponding female to the male individual. Like that ideal, she
too defeats aging, refusing the cycles of life and death that Ántonia
embodies. At the same time, Lena draws creativity to extinction as a
series of men disappears into individual passion, drowning in the
stream.

The central episode of the novel, the vision of the plow against the
sun, illustrates Cather's transcendence of her limited male narrator.
As Jim Burden picnics with the immigrant girls on the prairie, the
group discuss the discovery of a Cordovan sword in a furrow of a
nearby field. The men of Spain did not come to the Plains to found a
homeland, but instead to plunder; like the money lenders and the railroad men, they are destined to disappear from the land. They leave
only their rusty swords in a furrow. As Ántonia reminds Jim of her own
father's sorrow in the New World, the prophetic vision of the plow
before the setting sun appears to the group: "Magnified across the distance by the horizontal light, it stood out against the sun, was exactly
contained within the circle of the disk; the handles, the tongue, the
share—black against the molten red. There it was, heroic in size, a
picture writing on the sun" (245). Through this pictographic vision,
Cather contrasts the exploitative, invasive quest of the male conquistadores with the female creation of the peaceful homeland arising
from the work of her protagonist. Insisting on the addition of woman's
creative efforts in shaping of culture, Cather challenges the ideals of

the dominant male material achiever. She creates instead the local wise woman's community, shaped by the labor and vision of both sexes. As Jennifer Bailey writes, Cather's attempt to reclaim the landscape integrates the raw land with the settlement, creating a homeland (405). Instead of calculation, Cather depicts nurture, instead of conquest, partnership. The New American Jerusalem emerges through Ántonia's labors, thus both re-creating the ancient pastoral ideal and achieving the Jeffersonian promise in the raw earth. Jehovah's promise is the basis for the vision:

> And he shall judge among many people, and rebuke strong nations afar off; and they shall beat their swords into plowshares, and their spears into pruning-hooks: nation shall not lift up a sword against nation, neither shall they learn war any more. But they shall sit every man under his vine and under his fig tree; and none shall make them afraid: for the mouth of the LORD of hosts hath spoken it. (Micah 4: 3–4)

These verses must be viewed not only in the context of Ántonia's creative mission, but also against the background of World War I. Like Gilman, Cather connects men in the narrative with war and conquest, women with fertility and care. The last part of the biblical verse prepares the reader for Ántonia's female creative task, almost exactly anticipating the last scene of the novel, which shows the battered, aged Ántonia and her large family sheltered by their vines and fruit trees at the end of a disappearing road. Lest we mistake the intent of that ending, Cather shows the children running out of the "fruit cave" into the sunlight, "a veritable explosion of life." Combined with the final pictorial vision of the novel, this prophecy suggests a particularly poignant outlook on the part of the author, since it shows a vision of special promise for the New World. The fields darken, the plow shrinks, the sun sets—all suggesting the disappearance of Ántonia's home. Like the sea route to Jewett's Dunnet Landing, like the map to Naylor's Willow Springs, like the climb to Welty's "up home," the path back is lost, Ántonia's American home existing in the female pastoral "somewhere."

Women as powerful, creative figures in their own right move from the center of her novels until *Shadows on the Rock* set in early Quebec, a pattern of characterization that parallels her gloomy assessment of contemporary America. *My Mortal Enemy* contrasts in tone and theme with *My Ántonia*. Woodress characterizes the novel as "the bitterest piece of fiction she wrote" (*Life and Art*, 213). Her heroine, Myra Driscoll, possesses a spiritual potential that dwarfs those around her, yet, unlike Cather's earlier prairie heroines, in the artificial urban setting she finds no task equal to the stature of her character and imagination. Symbolizing the diminished possibilities for female heroism, Myra is only a little taller than the short narrator. An orphan, adopted and raised by her uncle, Myra repudiates her religion and her Irish background, leaving her Illinois home when she elopes with Oswald Henshawe. This is the other side of the romantic "legend" of which Nils dreamed in "The Bohemian Girl"; Aunt Lydia still talks of Myra's romantic exit from her uncle's house, "leaving a great fortune behind her." Part I details Myra's romance, her marriage, and her life in New York when she is forty-five-years old; Part II occurs ten years later. Myra and her husband are living in a boarding house in a Western city.

After she leaves her hometown, Myra devotes herself as a patroness of "romance" and "art" in her rented apartment in New York. Seen through the eyes of the then-young, provincial narrator Nellie Birdseye, Myra's life has seemingly overcome the laws of nature. Outside the warmth of the apartment, vendors sell violets in December while willing hands sweep snow from the strollers' paths. The country girl observes, "Here, I felt, winter brought no desolation; it was tamed, like a polar bear led on a leash by a beautiful lady" (*Mortal Enemy*, 25). Material artifice is expensively maintained in the face of physical reality. As befits the artificial setting, all of Myra's friends are stage people, who live through personality, offering a reprise of scenes and themes of Mrs. Burden's circle in *My Ántonia*.

Having given up so much of her own inherited and personal identity for her marriage, Myra demands that her marriage replace all those connections—family, religion, homeland—that she has sloughed off for her great romance. Marcus Klein writes that Myra's problem lies in her emotional largeness and her lack of any field of action beyond her compulsive grand romantic passion ("Introduction," xix). In contrast with Alexandra's nurture of the Nebraska plains, Ántonia's building of a civilization, or Thea's creation of immortal art, Myra's life is a kaleidoscope of fashion, gossip, and amusements.

At the end of her life, aged, poverty-stricken, and ignored by her former friends, Myra yearns for silence instead of clever talk; she rejects the betraying male romantic language as she seeks solace in the natural world, gazing out across the Pacific. She turns back to her abandoned Irish identity, becoming more and more like her long-dead uncle. Gaelic phrases come to her out of her communal, not personal, past. Her husband and her friends bring her bitterness: "I have been true in friendship; I have faithfully nursed others in sickness. . . . Why must I die like this, alone with my mortal enemy?" (95). "Mortal," of course, because Oswald has stolen her life through their marriage. Played on the small stages of a succession of rented rooms, their romance has in fact robbed them of both their lives. Myra's passionate romance leads to an individual life that ultimately has no larger meaning than its effect on the immediate present. Myra has no claim on immortality because the romance, the fashion, and the celebrity that occupies the women of her New York circle demand only the externals of femininity: the youth, the beauty, and the ornamental consumption of goods.

In a far-flung regimented society, the generative power of woman, manifested by the care and creation of a family, community, or art, has no purpose. Thwarted, this emotional and physical drive turns into a malevolent force, withering all within its reach. Myra tells her young friend that love is both embrace and battle, and that this intensity wears itself out: "If there are children, that feeling goes through natural changes. But when it remains so personal . . . something gives way in one" (88–89). Myra Driscoll Henshawe realizes finally that the individual possesses an instinctive identity that more urgently demands expression as death approaches: "We think we are so individual and so misunderstood when we are young; but the nature our strain of blood carries is inside there, waiting, like our skeleton" (82). With this novel, Cather like Glasgow insists that the individual is always, body and spirit, a member of a group centered around the female source. With no grounding in a tradition, with no commitment beyond her own happiness, the human being is lost and alone. Myra has no child, no loving neighbors or friends, no church or landscape, no one group identity that places her life within a larger history, lending shape and scale to individual existence.

This is, however, a precautionary tale. Oswald persists in holding to the vision of his youthful romance, dismissing Myra's pain through his persistent romanticizing of their experience. In this, he resembles such male dreamers as Jim Burden, Nils Ericson, and Ray Kennedy. The "daughter" Nellie, however, never forgets the cost of romance. In later years, whenever she glimpses "the bright beginning of a love story," Myra's terrible cry comes to her. Here too the "mother" holds a lesson.

The late book, *Shadows on the Rock* (1931), offers a reprise to the themes found in *My Ántonia*. Brown early noticed that both the "prairie" novels and *Shadows on the Rock* depict the evolution from tired Old Europe to the growing New World. The time and the setting, Quebec in 1697–1713, is, however, far removed in time, place, religion, and culture from Cather's Nebraska. More importantly, it is a "town" novel, Cather abandoning the American landscape that is at the center of her most successful novels. Despite its optimistic conclusion, the novel forms a natural succession to the dark *My Mortal Enemy*. She can no longer imagine the home place as a communal example to America.

In this narrative, Cather returns to the female-centered Nativity, of "The Joy of Nelly Deane," the Old World patriarchy of injustice, rank, and pain is healed by the New World women's community. To emphasize her role as source for the whole culture, Cecile brings forth the new man, not the new land. Her four sons stand tall beside her; her husband returns again and again to her civilized center. She is bringing up the Canadians of the future with her blend of the old ways and her acceptance of new conditions. In the midst of the American Depression and her own personal dislocations, Cather could no longer envision such a creation on Nebraska soil. Like Porter's early writing on Indian Mexico, Cather moves the maternal home away from America and away from the American earth. As Rosowski argues, the novel installs a type of the Virgin Mary through Cather's protagonist ("Magnificat"). Instead of the actively creative American Ántonia, the founder is the safely dead, virginal handmaiden who is elevated by her connection with the paternal tradition.[11]

The serenity of *Shadows on the Rock*, however, empowered Cather to address directly memories of her heritage. In 1931, she produced a book of short stories, *Obscure Destinies*. The characterization of "Old Mrs. Harris" is Cather's own childhood memories of her Grandmother Boak, her mother Mary Virginia Boak Cather, and herself (Woodress, *Life and Art*, 239). At the end of the short story, the grandmother, slips out of life, the mother Victoria is expecting another baby, and the daughter Vickie prepares to pursue her fate away from her land and family. Cather makes the connection between the female lineage and its daughter, stressing the similarities of their life cycles (190). She needed no Kronborg to serve as the mask and the score for her life as she sings the forgotten lives of those women who generously give their care and their histories to the earth and to those who follow.

For these male authorities all converge upon
the modest axiom that while man desires more
than woman, woman desires only more of man.
—Preface,
They Stooped to Folly

"I am a Virginian in every drop of blood and
pulse of my heart."
—"The Dynamic Past,"
Reasonable Doubts

4.

Building on Barren Ground

ELLEN GLASGOW

SET APART from the national literary center, Ellen Glasgow spun out
her "social history of Virginia" from the family home at One West
Main, Richmond. Throughout her career, Glasgow's work contained
vivid portraits of women's lives in Virginia: from that of Betty Ambler
in *The Battle-Ground* (1902), set in the years from 1850–1865, to
those of Roy Timberlake and Kate Oliver in *Beyond Defeat* (1966),
which carries the female characters' lives to the eve of World War II.

Born the eighth of ten children to an upper-middle-class family in
Richmond, Glasgow found the contrast between the male vocational
world and the female relational sphere an especially compelling one
not only, like the other writers, because of her gender but also because
of her immediate perceptions of the troubled relationship of her parents. Trapped in an unsympathetic marriage to industrialist Francis
Glasgow, her mother, Anne Jane Gholson Glasgow, a "perfect flower
of the Tidewater," suffered a severe depression and later died during
Glasgow's youth. Glasgow portrays her father, a stern Scots Presbyte-

rian, as the very embodiment of Weber's Protestant Ethic. He appears as a hypocritical and unsympathetic male parent in Glasgow's autobiography, *The Woman Within* (1954). On a conscious level she acknowledges only the female parentage, insisting that she inherited nothing from her father, save the "color of my eyes and a share in a trust fund" (16). The characterization of her novels, however, suggests that Glasgow carries a half-conscious ambivalence toward her parentage. The modern protagonists who survive in her works share the "vein of iron," the Scots Presbyterian background of industrialist Francis Glasgow, whereas the female characters, most often mothers who suffer and perish, show the old Virginia communal Cavalier background of her own mother.

In choosing to reject and criticize the Presbyterianism of her father's lineage, Glasgow reflects in her own life the trend toward secularization of the larger society, which Jackson Lears details in *No Place of Grace*. After her mother's death, in her grief Glasgow undertook a course of study with her brother-in-law that included such male intellectuals as Kant, Nietzsche, and "all the German scientists I had heard mentioned" as well as Darwin and Huxley, because she sought "truth that was concrete and indestructible" (*Woman Within*, 91, 89). She accepted science and philosophy as her new religion, which would lead her out of the old Southern "garden of the chattel" (to use Lewis Simpson's felicitous characterization), which submerged all of society to the law of the white patriarch. Glasgow believed instead in a benevolent social evolution; thus she accepted the concept of an inherited character, which determines the individual's fate.[1] Without such strictures as patriarchal law and religion, the human being and thus society could live free of the oppression and unhappiness so visible in the sensitive child's own family.

Given her belief in nature rather than nurture, Glasgow needed to rationalize her place as a writer and an intellectual with her gender. For if all humans inherited their character, must there be an inherently female character, one incompatible with mental and imaginative creativity? Yet, triggered by an editor's advice to "go back to the South and have some babies," Glasgow realized that she lacked what appeared to be a natural female instinct (*Woman Within*, 108). Her self-characterization parallels those of the individualistic female achievers in the early works of Jewett and Cather: "At that age I suspected, and later I discovered, that the maternal instinct, sacred or profane, was left out of me when I was designed" (108). Glasgow sets up an explicitly either/or opposition: professional achievement/maternity, much as Cather does in *The Song of the Lark* and Jewett does in *A Woman Doctor*. To Glasgow, writing seemingly destroys the possibility of biological motherhood—and vice versa; this dichotomy underlies the characterization of Dorinda Oakley in *Barren Ground* and appears as well in the autonomous intellectual or artistic female protagonists found in Jewett, Cather, Porter, and Welty as well as Kate Chopin and Edith Wharton. Once again she was faced with the familiar female dilemma: how could she create a woman protagonist who reflected her gender and yet triumphed in the competitive society, given the communal roles to which women were traditionally ascribed? How could she accomplish self-conscious literary art, given the handicaps of female gender? Glasgow must initially claim for herself the "male" intellect, thereby distancing herself from those "natural" properties found in the mass of womanhood.

At the time Glasgow came into her own as an author, her native state had suffered an economic and cultural eclipse; Virginia did not participate in the Southern "industrial evolution." Many of the descendants of the former leaders of the country and the region looked backward to the antebellum glory days. One product Virginia still produced in great numbers was the romantic historical novel, liberally spiced with nostalgic dashes of local color. Those books, as well as the Bible, had formed much of Ellen Glasgow's early approved reading.[2] She came to believe that the South needed to be purged of the myths of heroism generated by patriarchal dominance and the supporting "evasive idealism" of female subordination. The industrializing New South, however, offered no solution. State and gender, both victimized, were equally and similarly dominated, in her opinion, by the male-controlled industrial order, symbolized in her work by New York City. She accepted in many of her novels a paradigm of experience that depended on a simplistic dichotomy derived from the "conflict of types" between the background and personalities of her father and mother. Her early novels, therefore, accepted the progressive, cause-effect narrative. In her "social history," fictional circumstance is divided into conflicting halves of experience, which underlie descriptions of artifacts and places as well as groups and individuals:

Puritan	Cavalier
Francis Glasgow	Anne Jane Gholson
male-female	weakness, femininity
Scotch-Irish	English
growth	decadence
practicality	generosity
discipline	indulgence
health	illness
realism	idealism
"good people"	"good families"
survivor	victim
strength	weakness
emotional restraint	emotional expressiveness
physical	spiritual

The dialectic pattern, which J. R. Raper considers reflective of Glasgow's personal development, appears repeatedly in the novels written from 1913 to 1935, as she searched for the synthesis in art and life (*Without Shelter*, 12). Her division betrays an inherent preference for the "male" side of the equation, the qualities in fact that define the dominant male individual. Glasgow accepted the male model of achievement as a way to overcome the victimization she associated with her mother and maternity itself.

Glasgow's first books, *The Descendant* (1897), *Phases of an Inferior Planet* (1898), and *The Voice of the People* (1900), as Linda Wagner notes, focus on the male protagonist.[3] Their content reflects contemporary intellectual trends. In *The Voice of the People*, however, she returns from New York City to Virginia, symbolically embracing, as her own, the history of state and sex.

From her third novel *Virginia* (1913) to the posthumously published *Beyond Defeat* (1966), Glasgow longs for the woman-centered home despite her initial intellectual inclination toward competitive individualism. Repeatedly, she stresses that the male leadership has never allowed women significant roles in American public life, nor has it taken women's relationships with each other seriously. In fact, the works of her most productive years go further than merely protesting injustice toward her gender: she identifies economic, sexual, and racial exploitation as arising from the social domination of wealthy white males. She insists that all are inevitable results of male-controlled hierarchies, which exist in *both* Old and New South. Despite her education in the old Virginia social order, with its privileging of the upper-class white male, Glasgow began an examination of the intersection of race, economic, and gender privilege. For example, Glasgow portrays the sexual exploitation of black women in the relationships of Cyrus Treadwell and Mandy, Old Mr. Greylock and his women servants, and George Birdsong and Memoria; in the casual destruction of a young black man's life to save the spoiled "youth in the machine," Stanley Timberlake, she reveals the human costs of racial and gender prejudice. In one passage, Glasgow exposes, in an otherwise sympathetic characterization, Mrs. Pendleton's evasive blindness to the close connection between racial and gender oppression: "She had known where the slave auction stood, without realizing in the least that men and women were sold there" (*Virginia*, 67). In Cyrus Treadwell's repudiation of Mandy and their doomed son and in his cruelty to his weak wife, Glasgow insists that the New South will not in fact offer any more justice. With Cyrus, naked financial power forces the subordination of all women in a parallel to the manner in which it coerces the obedience of his workers and the homage of the townspeople. Despite her remaining prejudice, Glasgow grows from the condescension toward her black characters in *Virginia* and, to a lesser degree in *Barren Ground*, to the deeper understanding of the human tragedy of the young man's unjust ruin in *In This Our Life*. In addition, she shows the lingering consequences of the Old South's oppressive society in *Barren Ground* by her description of the Greylocks' decaying plantation and the drunken patriarch. In her portrayal of the poor white classes of Virginia in *Barren Ground, The Voice of the People,* and *The Miller of Old Church*, she demonstrates the results of economic exploitation and restricted access to education, even though, as with the black characters, her portrayals reflect her cultural background.

Her characterization and plots suggest that Glasgow at first desires a sort of Jeffersonian egalitarian community based on the individual working in concert with the Virginia earth, but just before her death, she turns to the home place. Like Cather, she praises the female pastoral as the ideal model of human civilization, because it mediates between the threatening forest and its native inhabitants of the American pioneer past and the emerging Depression cities, New York or Richmond, always given the fictional name "Queenborough" in Glasgow's novels, and their idle men and ungendered "happiness hunters."

Glasgow enters the period of her greatest artistic mastery with *Virginia* (1913). The novel shares two fictional patterns with the works to follow. First, the choice of the name "Virginia" indicates Glasgow's intention to detail not only the career of a woman, but also the situation of her state. Both protagonist and state suffer the consequences of destructive, willed blindness—the "evasive idealism"—before the reality of the material fact. Second, *Virginia* shows the dialectic pattern through three major sections of the novel, "The Dream," "The Reality," and "The Adjustment." "The Dream," the thesis, illustrates the foundation for the myth of Southern Womanhood through the education and courtship of the protagonist, Virginia Pendleton; this section concludes with Virginia's marriage. "The Reality," the antithesis, shows the destruction of Virginia's personality as she immerses her identity dependently and obsessively in those of her husband and children. Like McIntosh's Grace Elliott, she lives only for "love," that is, a life immersed in immoderate emotionalism. "The Adjustment," the synthesis, indicates the consequences of Jinny's self-abnegation in a pragmatic, competitive social setting. Frederick McDowell delineates the archetypal dimensions of the novel, noting that, despite her charm, Jinny is more admired as symbol of abstract ideal than loved in reality (104). The reverberations of cultural myth, however, compel the reader's interest even when the somewhat static character herself does not.

As Cather found her "home pasture" in *O Pioneers!*, Glasgow found her life's work with *Virginia* as she returned to her native state for her fictional settings. She had regained her own cultural background, but she could not yet focus her novel because she had not resolved her "conflict of types," which is, I believe, a code for resolving her own female identity with her professional career. In fact, according to the respective research of Oliver Steele and Wagner, Glasgow was conflicted in the plan of the book as to whether she should have twin protagonists who reflected her parental heritage or whether she should portray the changes between two generations of women.

Two characters identified with her parents indicate the clash between the "aristocratic" old order and the industrial social structure:

the "flower" of Dinwiddie, Virginia Pendleton, and the "iron tower," Cyrus Treadwell. Spending two days a week on Wall Street and re-shaping the village of Dinwiddie to his will, despite its hate and be-cause of its fear, Cyrus acts as the figure of the impinging national industrial leadership. Glasgow notes the emergence of this dominant economic individual as the symbol of the social order: "The simple awe of financial success, which occupies in the American mind the vacant space of the monarchical cult, had already begun to generate the myth of greatness around Cyrus" (24). In researching Glasgow's early notes for *Virginia*, Steele discovered that she originally intended Cyrus to be an "almost allegorical embodiment" of commerce's evils. As Steele notes, Cyrus's ascent was to parallel Jinny's fall (271). The two figures contend for Dinwiddie: "The smoke of factories was already succeed-ing the smoke of the battlefields, and out of the ashes of a vanquished idealism the spirit of commercial materialism was born" (*Virginia*, 13).

From the first pages, Glasgow sets up another contrast between two women, the friends Jinny Pendleton and Susan Treadwell, Cyrus's daughter, who represents the rationality of her father leavened with womanly concern and care. Virginia, the "feminine ideal of the ages," and Susan, the new woman born out of industrialism, are contrasted in their attitudes toward woman's responsibilities.[4] Working with Glas-gow's early notes for *Virginia*, Wagner discovered that the author had intended to have twin protagonists, Virginia and Sarah Jane Treadwell (later renamed Susan). The two women led similar conventionally feminine lives, yet Glasgow intended Sarah Jane, as Wagner describes her, to be a model of the first wave of feminists who arose out of the woman's caretaking roles. One chapter was to be titled "The Wisdom of Sarah Jane," who is characterized as "the softened intellectual." She is "the actual"; Virginia is "the ideal." In a later set of notes, Sarah Jane has been renamed Sue, and Glasgow explains that, whereas Vir-ginia was exhausted at middle age, Susan, with six children, had none-theless kept her vitality and her civic and personal interests.

Glasgow stresses Susan's emotional discipline, contrasting her ap-pearance and attitudes with those of the paternalistic Southern ideals of womanhood: "She looked out upon the world with level, dispassion-ate eyes, in which there was none of Virginia's uncritical, emotional softness" (29). Glasgow makes the familiar contrast of the plain inde-pendent woman with the beguiling heroine of male desire, paralleling the characterizations of *Two Lives*, "The Foreigner," "The Bohemian Girl," "Old Mortality," *The Old Order, O Pioneers!*, and *My Mortal Enemy*. Susan's independence gives rise to a freely shared strength that supports those she loves and shapes limited circumstance by the "force of an energetic and capable mind" rather than by relying on the dependent charm of Jinny. Not content to live only as biological female or as self-abnegating mother, but equally sure that she does not wish to relinquish these experiences, Susan's strength comes out of her rational femininity. At the end of Virginia's story, as at the beginning, her female friend Susan supports her throughout her marriage and impending divorce.

As is the case with many protagonists created by these authors, Susan's parents offer no example or support for her. Mrs. Treadwell is a whining, weeping upper-class woman, for whom Susan must function as a parent, the daughter giving up college and timely marriage. Glasgow produces a horde of dying wives and mothers: Belinda Treadwell, Jinny Pendleton, Mrs. Pendleton, Eudora Oakley, Geneva Ellgood Greylock, Mary Evelyn Fincastle, Eva Birdsong, and Lavinia Fitzroy Timberlake, offering a succession of daughters and friends pitiful examples of victimization. Not only can Susan expect no support from her mother, but Cyrus refuses to pay for her education beyond the circumscribed Dinwiddie limits. Because of these parents, Susan has been forced to form her own life, much as the author herself felt she had done and as women's heroines and protagonists have done. Never is Glasgow's aphorism, "Character is fate," more true than in the career of this daughter of the New South.

Susan represents Glasgow's first attempt to imagine a female heroine who arises out of the social relationships of the industrializing South and her own intellectual theories of modernism. But Susan must bring herself up by her own psychic and intellectual bootstraps; there is no model for female steadfastness, for even women as loyal as Jinny give their central care to husband and children.

Having created her New Southern Woman but finding nothing in the social context to expand her influence, Glasgow turned back to Jinny's life. As Jinny views the older female generation, she imagines with the optimism of her youthful beauty "that she herself was predestined for something more wonderful than they ever dreamed of" (52). She sees no connection with their tired bodies and spirits and her own youthful vitality. In contrast to the Treadwells, Jinny's parents support their daughter to the point of considerable self-sacrifice. They both instill an outdated paternalistic pattern for marriage and family life in Jinny, thus ensuring that their daughter will be sacrificed to a man and his children. Ironically, Mrs. Pendleton serves as one of the few devoted protagonists' mothers in this discussion, suggesting the lack of positive maternal examples within the social order. Her minister father, too, supports and embodies the old Southern code—again, the female author's suspicion of male-controlled religion, however benevolent. Shaped as she is by Dinwiddie's traditions, Virginia expects that her husband and children will reward her with their lifelong devotion; they, however, leave her alone at midlife except for her son's melodramatic return, a failure of Glasgow's fictional will.

Writing of the desired balance of self-denial and self-assertion for the heroine in domestic fiction, Nina Baym offers a clear distinction: "Although committed to an ethic of social love, the authors differentiated it from self-love and linked love to wisdom, responsibility, rationality, and self-command" (*Woman's Fiction*, 25). Like earlier negative women's characters, Virginia evidences the lack of emotional balance that has proved so disastrous for the female protagonist from the domestic novel onward; as Anne Goodwyn Jones notes, all of her family have been ruined by "love." Immoderate emotion and romantic illusion invariably signal a coming tragedy in these women authors: "That one emotion [love] represented not only her sole opportunity of joy, it constituted as well her single field of activity" (148). As Gilman understood, Glasgow's heroine is shaped to male desire and those of *his* family. Watching the women whirl by her in their white dresses at a dance, the girl Jinny suddenly has a moment's insight, realizing that all share the fate of waiting for an invitation to join the dance of romance as they all "merged into one, and this was the face of all womanhood" (153). The scene anticipates Ellen Fairchild's epiphany in Welty's *Delta Wedding* as the courtship dance warns of the dangers of romantic fantasy.

In *Virginia* Glasgow moved to a new level of artistry. She shifted further away from the rationalized intellectualization of her apprentice novels. At its best, the novel engenders the characteristic impact of masterful self-conscious fiction. Further, Glasgow points toward a new ideal of women's friendships opposed to either the ruthless pragmatism of Cyrus Treadwell and the restless modernism of Jinny's husband and children or the ineffectual paternalism of Jinny's parents. As Jones demonstrates, Dinwiddie divides even more sharply along gender than class or racial lines. Miss Willy Whitlow, the seamstress, joins together the women of the community with her gossip, Glasgow using the metaphor of sewing. Miss Willy's sewing circle, however, has only the cast-off scraps of its members' lives to shape its patterns; the stories, unlike those of the female wise woman, offer no patterns for female strength and community. Although Glasgow was moving toward the community of women, she still found it hard to escape from the shadow of the "iron tower" of Treadwell, who inevitably triumphed over the maternally influenced character of Jinny Pendleton. The mature Glasgow understood that neither antebellum patriarchal Virginia nor the impersonal male-controlled New South offered any patterns for female achievement: "The world still clung to the belief that the business of humanity was confined to the preservation of the institutions which existed in the present moment of history" (14). Glasgow identified the most fundamental of these as male-controlled marriage and maternity.

But this final synthesis remained undeveloped. After *Virginia* Glasgow suffered a failure of imagination, and as before she sought a sustaining pattern of belief. She moved from biology to psychology for inspiration, influenced strongly by the ideas of Carl G. Jung. Raper discusses the appeal of Jungian psychology to Glasgow, concluding that its literary approach drew her, especially the emphasis on "the supernatural and mythic elements," which Jung considered as preserving the "forgotten language" of humanity (*Sunken Garden*, 77).[5] The Jungian influence remained as Glasgow blended the elements of the maternal archetype with feminism, a pattern of belief that culminates in the portrayal of Grandmother Fincastle in *Vein of Iron* and Kate Oliver of *In This Our Life* and *Beyond Defeat*. It would allow her to come to a more hopeful synthesis.

Barren Ground (1925) concludes for a time Glasgow's search for a heroine who transcends gender and economic exploitation. She wrote of her artistic and emotional satisfaction with its composition: "My book is a realistic picture of the poor class of farmers in Virginia—a study of poverty and endurance—a kind of epic plan with a single figure expressing the life and civilization in which she lives" (*Letters*, 69). As with *The Song of the Lark* and *Country of the Pointed Firs, Barren*

Ground centers on a character who faces the conflict between gender and authorship. As in Cather's *O Pioneers!*, Glasgow depicts the creation of a farm, thus blending male role and female motif. Here one female individual displays the personality attributes of the material achiever, which Glasgow previously associated with her father.

Raper explicitly contrasts Henry Nash Smith's "Garden of the World," the West-drawing American vision that tempts the individual away from the social order into nature, and the formal garden, which represents the old Southern "garden of the chattel," with the garden of civilization, a model described by Thomas Huxley in the Romanes Lecture of 1893. The Garden of the World evidences much of the expansiveness of the heroic individual, who writes his vision on a blank, supine, and female nature. Raper suggests that Glasgow accepted a "model of agrarian freedom much closer to Jefferson's ideal than the rose garden" (*Without Shelter*, 12). The formal garden, Raper observes, suggests decadence, an excess of artifice rather than organic growth; therefore, Glasgow associates this garden with the old paternalistic Southern aristocracy. Raper's astute analysis deepens with the addition of Cather's feminism. A difference must be drawn between the formal garden, which represents the upper-class ideal such as Eva's neglected garden in *The Sheltered Life*, and the female garden of civilization such as Kate Oliver's pastoral Hunter's fare in *Beyond Defeat*. Gwen Nagel observed that Jewett's New England women's gardens also stand as a contrast to the Garden of the World. In both Jewett and Cather, then, the woman's garden challenges the male desire for expansion and conquest toward the West and death. The woman as farmer brings a special understanding because of the consonance in rhythms of soil and cycles of her body. In her desire to mold nature and to expand her holdings, however, Dorinda's farm corresponds to the Garden of the World as Glasgow adapts the male cultural model to her protagonist, but with Kate Oliver's Hunter's Fare, she combines Jeffersonian and feminist beliefs.

With Dorinda, Glasgow creates a larger-than-life protagonist, who struggles to free herself from a dependent need for male love and social approval, claiming for her heroine the outlines of the male social leadership. In the 1933 preface to *Barren Ground*, Glasgow makes explicit her intent to portray an eternal female story: "But Dorinda, though she had been close to me for ten years before I began her story, is universal" (vi). Identifying the problems inherent in the woman writer's adaptation of the traditionally male quest, Mary C. Anderson asks, "How is the female hero to define her own progress into self-consciousness and self-determination without alienating herself from her biology?" (385). Again the woman writer must deal with the troublesome female body to face the male social order and the male model of creativity. The movement away from the female family and history toward the male quest poses a problem for the woman artist, which Glasgow confronts in *Barren Ground;* the quest proves particularly perilous for the writing woman in the American social order. The protagonist achieves freedom from anxiety of patriarchal influence by denying the elements in her life that she considers "feminine," proclaiming herself different from other women, accepting the rationalization of the dominant discourse, and demanding complete control of female body and human emotion. This will be especially apparent in Glasgow's portrayal of Dorinda Oakley in *Barren Ground.* In *Feminism Without Illusion,* Elizabeth Fox-Genovese notes that Harriet Jacobs takes great pains in her narrative of a slave woman's life to differentiate her protagonist from the ordinary slave women (211); Maria McIntosh showed the same tendency in *Two Lives;* Sharon O'Brien has noted a parallel pattern in Willa Cather's early critical writing, one that is echoed in Cather's early heroines, and Sarah Sherman depicts Jewett's identification with her physician father. In all these personal and fictional portrayals, the anxiety of female authorship appears. Finding it impossible simultaneously to claim the authority demanded of the creative writer and to take onto herself the oppression suffered by her gender, the women writer protects herself by an initial insistence on her separation from group membership even more vehement than that of her male contemporaries.

Barren Ground represents an inversion of the terms of the dominant discourse: if the American male demands the excision of emotion from public life and denies support—financial as well as emotional—for woman's historic roles, women, entering the public arena, will illustrate the costs to men as well as to their own gender. To cut the cultural Gordian knot of achievement and gender, Glasgow turned to the rationalism and bodily control she associated with her industrialist father. She believed that those stern ascetic Presbyterian qualities, with special emphasis on bodily discipline and emotional repression, would enable the individual woman to survive, even triumph. Dorinda will eschew romantic contact altogether in *Barren Ground* after her first disastrous passionate love, sowing all her personality into the earth.

With this novel Glasgow believed that she had achieved her philosophy of life: "I knew that I had found a code of living that was sufficient for life or for death" (*Woman Within*, 271). Dorinda, like Glasgow, was born of "a union of opposites" (*Certain Measure*, 158). Glasgow insisted on the identification she had formed with her protagonist, Dorinda Oakley, relating that they "changed and developed together," connected by a "living nerve" (*Certain Measure*, 162–63). Like Sarah Orne Jewett's Nan Prince of *A Country Doctor* and Willa Cather's Alexandra Bergson of *O Pioneers!*, Ellen Glasgow's Dorinda Oakley behaves in her public and private life with austerity. All traces of positive virtues culturally considered feminine are banished: gentleness, sensitivity, and generosity. Compromise and good humor disappear in Dorinda's character, replaced by a dry irony. Dorinda achieves her victory through rationality and asceticism, winning a victory over instinct and emotion.

Tonette Bond points to Glasgow's depiction of Dorinda's self-realization in a pastoral setting as foretelling a rational New South, based on a merging of art and intellect; as Bond describes the shaping of the land to Dorinda's "subjective vision," the dynamic shares many parallels with the literary task of the heroic American individual. Cather and Glasgow reshape the pastoral to the needs and symbolism of the female individual. Like Cather's Alexandra, Glasgow's Dorinda redeems the land from paternal failures. Their fathers die, leaving their daughters, not their sons, to bring to life the American earth that quivers with the red and oranges of life's blood itself. Both achieve their redemption by dedicating their fecundity and their emotions to the earth, Alexandra consecrating her sexuality to the Spirit of the Divide, and Dorinda fighting the imperatives of her emotions and her body to create a land that gives back the basic female food of life, milk.

Like her male literary counterparts, Dorinda brings to fruition her own personal vision by struggling with the Virginia soil, even though the nurturing, self-abnegating care displayed by the farmer-woman is basically at odds with the myth of the frontiersman, as Richard Slotkin has observed. The farmer's submission to forces outside the individual is diametrically opposed to the rootless, relentless male adventurer, who shapes outer reality to his inner vision; Dorinda's vocation thus mirrors her situation as a woman in Glasgow's mind. Nonetheless, as I say, her expansiveness and calculation mark her farm as akin in many respects to the heroic individual's vision of the Garden of the World. Despite her intentions, Glasgow cannot keep the balance of her stated goals with Dorinda claiming many of the attributes of the free-standing male individual. Like Alexandra Bergson, Dorinda re-forms and revitalizes male failures. She will, as it were, become a purer Cyrus Treadwell, retaining the energy, calculation, and determination, refusing the meanness and active subjugation of dependents. The purification of her motives occurs through the coordination of scientific knowledge and technology with the Virginia earth, thus redeeming and defeating Francis Glasgow's iron factory. The author indicated the impetus behind the novel in *A Certain Measure*, writing that the woman would for once be the victor in Southern fiction. Dorinda's triumph, however, is achieved by isolation from any human who challenges her dominance of the environment.

Dorinda demands the right to shape her own life in a role socially defined as individual, competitive, and male; therefore her withdrawal entails an ongoing confrontation with the basic female instinct, as Glasgow sees it, toward motherhood and sexual fulfillment, which immerse the woman in dependence. Throughout the novel, Dorinda repeats a phrase that becomes the theme for her life: "I'm through with all that." "All that" is her physical and social life as a woman, sexual yielding, childbirth pain, and maternal care. Dorinda puts aside contact with adult males because, as the author indicated in *Virginia*, they all demand woman to flesh out their dream of the understanding and self-abnegating imaginative self. Most of the crucially important dream of the thistles deals with the durability of Dorinda's instinctual sexual attraction and its danger to her self-creation; nonetheless it begins and ends with the scent of pine and everlasting. Glasgow frames the dream with the evocation of Dorinda's parents, thus identifying the enduring influence of the family heritage, which subsumes sexual desire. Glasgow, then, shows her character's debts to her parents' history, refusing the easy literary casting-off from history available to the male heroic individual. As she wins the struggle against her female nature, Dorinda confronts the natural environment and shapes it to her will, albeit Glasgow insists that her success comes from an instinctive identification with the Virginia earth.

Like many literary protagonists created by these authors, Dorinda looks and *is* physically different from the women who are considered, like Jinny Pendleton, to be attractive and pleasing to men. As Wagner observes, Dorinda whose features are "too stern, too decisive," wears men's overalls until she triumphs, at which time she attends church in a dress (74). However, Dorinda's relationship to her servant Fluvanna resembles the relationship of other heroic individuals with their socially inferior shadow companions in American literature by men. Her relationship with her husband's children is, at best, problematic, and her relationship to their admirable but unromantic father Nathan is frankly driven by ambition. She detests the laziness and sexuality of her blond stepdaughter and finds her stepson's maturity threatening to her own prominence. The protagonist exists as will and calculation within an androgynous body.

Eudora Oakley, Dorinda's mother, offers an example of the fate awaiting the young girl who immerses herself in romance and maternity. As a young woman, Eudora dreamed of life as a missionary, but the death of her first love and her subsequent sexual attraction to a handsome poor white farmer, Josiah Oakley, condemned her to life of endless sacrifice for her dull husband and her loutish sons. Now known as Mrs. Oakley, Eudora's personality disappears into her role in this paternalistic social order, her life passing in an endless search for heavenly salvation and earthly cleanliness. Parodying domestic martyrdom as constituted in paternalistic marriage, she searches for dirt and disorder in her house and prays for deliverance. Defeated in spirit and body, she dies after perjuring herself to save her ne'er-do-well younger son from imprisonment. Social duty and biological instinct, which led her into a life of domestic servitude, bring her destruction.

Barren Ground continues to emphasize the destructive potential of sexual involvement for independent female accomplishment. Geneva Ellgood Greylock's madness, her mother's martyrdom, and Dorinda's pregnancy and emotional obsession all have their roots not in sexuality, but more precisely, in romantic illusion—in sum, giving over their identity to a man. Obsessive romanticism, a pathological process in Glasgow as in other women writers, sickens and kills the woman as surely as a consuming physical disease. Since Dorinda refuses martyrdom, her body and emotions will be ruthlessly disciplined to achieve independence. The need to save herself from victimization through either maternal or romantic "love" under male control, leads to this insight: "Mother love was a wonderful thing, she reflected, a wonderful and ruinous thing!" (250) She continues her musings by directly connecting her mother's victimization through maternity and her own through romance. She links Eudora Oakley's maternal martyrdom with her own abandonment by Jason, seeing both as events that occur to women because of the intersection of feminine emotion and biological instinct. Glasgow insists that Dorinda stands for the new professional woman who wins a place in the previously male leadership of achievement, yet in this passage, the author indicates that her protagonist triumphs because of differences from other ordinary women. The female body must be subjugated to intellect, just as the land itself be disciplined to restrict its own natural overgrowth of broom sedge. The movement of the book is reminiscent of the draining of the woman's life and creativity into communal achievement, which Cather portrayed in *The Song of the Lark*. As the Wagnerian roles gleam with life, Kronborg ages; as the Virginia soil blooms, Dorinda hardens.

The plot of *Barren Ground* is simple, almost melodramatic, yet the subject matter is of such stature, with time, symbolism, setting, and characterization so well integrated, that the novel serves as a harbinger of the Southern Literary Renaissance.[6] Glasgow's inability to reify the land marks off the female achiever from her male counterpart: "The wall dividing her individual consciousness from the consciousness of nature vanished with the thin drift of woodsmoke over the fields" (102). The struggle she undertakes with the land parallels her struggle with her own female "nature." Glasgow indicates the elemental struggle with natural forces to define a role for both woman and state. She implies, as do Cather and Jewett, that woman has an instinctive sympathetic understanding with the natural world that grants her an advantage over male farmers, a bond that arises in a great part from her female identity, but that this potential can only be achieved by the most stringent discipline. The Virginia natural environment acts as a chorus, underlining and commenting on the narrative of its own creation and Dorinda's own growth.

The titles of the three sections of the book, "Broomsedge," "Pine," and "Life-Everlasting," all native vegetation, measure the growth of both protagonist and state. In its orange color and stubborn ability to spring up on either abandoned or poorly cultivated ground, broom sedge represents both untilled earth and instinctive sexuality. In its sober endurance, the pine symbolizes the futile labor of her father and the passing of the land to Dorinda. (The pine identified with Dorinda's father grows in a graveyard.) In its spreading ghostly silver, life-everlasting represents Virginia's future as an agricultural state and Dorinda's spiritual transcendence over both broom sedge and pine, biology and reaction. In her research on Glasgow's notes for the novel, Wagner discovered that the author initially intended to divide the novel into five sections: "The End of Winter (Broomsedge)," "Spring (Pine)," "Summer (Life-Everlasting)," "Autumn," and "The Return of Winter" (*Beyond Convention,* 77). This violated her customary fictional practice, and the author ultimately reverted to her usual pattern. Wagner suggests that she saw the proposed plan to end upon a negative note, and thus she changed her fictional direction to emphasize the cyclical nature of Dorinda's achievement, thus reinforcing the cycles of nature and female body.

Within the intellectual and emotional framework demanded by success in the public sphere and in male activities, Glasgow finds it impossible to bring to fruition her ideal of the egalitarian community or to imagine any crucial social roles for women built on their histories. In the last account, despite the resonance of its symbolism, the beauty of its descriptions of nature, and the daring of its themes, *Barren Ground* mirrors the sublimation of the female body and the emotional regimentation she saw in the male leadership in New York. In this novel, Glasgow finds no place for women's families or equal friendship, accepting instead the values of rationalism, pragmatism, and rugged individualism as necessary for the salvation of gender and region, accepting the iron creed of Francis Glasgow and rewriting the male model as the "self-made" woman.

The writing of *Barren Ground* freed Glasgow for a time of comparatively carefree composition; Raper observes that she now "sloughed Dorinda from the core of her being" (*Sunken Garden,* 99). The next six years saw the composition and production of her Queenborough trilogy of manners. Until the comedies of manners, C. Hugh Holman argues that Glasgow's career had been one of self-involvement, either from her own personal history or with her philosophy ("April," 265). Out of the release granted by the composition of *Barren Ground,* however, she advanced to a higher level of artistry. In 1926 she published the first of the trilogy, *The Romantic Comedians*, a bagatelle that directs its witty irony at the upper-class Richmond male with sharp, if good-natured, humor. *They Stooped to Folly* (1929) shows a darker strain in its irony, whereas *The Sheltered Life* (1932), although still a comedy of manners, has pathos at its core.

They Stooped to Folly shows a broadening of focus. Within the modern urban setting, the author sees old communal relationships as problematic and offers no emerging vision of more equitable relations between the sexes. The scattered urban setting impels the young daughter figure Milly Burden to cry out that she is not looking for love, but "something worth loving!" (350). In her vain search, in the evocation of the mother as source of physical life and human memory, and in the intrusion of the larger world on Queenborough, *They Stooped to Folly* anticipates the fictional strands of the last novels, *Vein of Iron*, *In This Our Life*, and *Beyond Defeat*.

Presenting its action through twin observers—a middle-aged representative of Richmond's upper classes, Virginius Littlepage, and his virtuous wife, Victoria—Glasgow frames the narrative in the familiar tripartite construction that suggests the novel's progressive movement: "Mr. Littlepage," "Mrs. Littlepage," and "False Spring," in which the author asserts that there are no fresh starts for her male creation. Again, Glasgow shows that the male leadership defines no central roles for women within the society, but women's relationships with each other provide support through life's vicissitudes. Interestingly enough, Glasgow borrows the name of Jewett's literary sea captain to give to her own fanciful main male character, who spins his account of experience in the old Virginian upper classes. As a contrast to the deluded Virginius, Glasgow paints portraits of women who have been absent from male literature, older, homebound, and professional—in sum, middle-aged women who have passed beyond male-controlled romance and maternity like the Mothers of Herland. Victoria Littlepage, for example, offers a most difficult authorial challenge, the "good" wife and mother with few personal ambitions. Like Jinny Pendleton of *Virginia* and Eva Birdsong of *The Sheltered Life*, Victoria has been reified by her husband into Woman, although here the male emphasis is not on the romantic ideal but the opposite, the Wife, a sort of cultural Widow Douglas to her husband's Huck. Glasgow, however, takes the woman's perspective on the relationship. In the preface, Glasgow presents the neglect of female friendship as her literary theme.

She notes that seldom in modern literature has such a relationship been accorded a central place: "The novelist, since he is usually a man, has found the relationship to be deficient alike in the excitement of sex and the masculine drama of action" (*A Certain Measure*, 245). But she concludes that women are coming "to understand their interdependence as human beings" and, lacking a portrayal of this, literature fails to reach "complete life veracity" in its depiction of social reality (245).

In Glasgow's defense of the pureness and generosity of female friendships, which ends with a sarcastic allusion to Freud, the reader can experience the effects of the incursion of the dominant discourse into women's relationships with each other. The male-female bond is now of almost exclusive centrality in the dominant discourse, other relationships declared deviant or insignificant. When she was a girl, Victoria remembers that she imagined being swept off her feet, quite literally, into a romantic dream of a perfect future: "'Is it he? Is he coming at last?' Then, in her sleep, she was lifted by an arm like the wind, and borne away, with the wild horses, over the rustling broom-sedge, into a sunset that was like the fire at the heart of an opal" (151). But in her maturity, she realizes that there are no Lochinvars, and she takes on her duties as mother and as friend. Glasgow reasserts the importance of female relationships to the individual woman's life. Victoria attempts to shelter the two modern daughters, Milly Burden and her own child Mary Victoria, who is herself reborn; indeed, Victoria stands as sister, rival, and mother for the three generations of abandoned women "who stooped to folly" in the changing male-defined mores of Queenborough. Although Victoria is limited by her upper middle-class Queenborough upbringing—for example, too often accepting without question the verities of her youth—she has in the last account a clear emotional honesty. As she comes to the end of her life, Victoria compares the companionship found in her marriage with that found in her friendship with Louisa Goddard: "She had never, except for the few months of courtship, enjoyed him as naturally as she enjoyed Louisa. For more than fifty years Louisa had understood her more absolutely than any man can understand the woman he loves" (185). Unlike Jewett who was quite unself-conscious in portraying warm, emotional relationships between women, Glasgow explicitly protests the conclusions of the Freudian movement, which, in her view, classifies all relationships and touches and declares legitimate only those contained within a heterosexual romantic relationship.

Louisa shares central characteristics with Susan Pendleton of *Virginia;* both are sensible women who scorn the charming arts of the belle, and both bear the marks of a self-portrait. Louisa loves her friend's children and her husband as her own, serving as a dear aunt without any sense of possessiveness or jealousy. In her mature years—all three main characters are in their midfifties—she retains her varied intellectual and political interests and her unbounded vitality. Only at the end of the novel does the reader discover what Victoria never does, that the great love of Louisa's life has always been Virginius, indicating the greater weight Glasgow gives to female friendship over romantic and sexual attraction. In this, Louisa anticipates another unmarried teacher-woman, Miss Adele Courtland of Welty's *The Optimist's Daughter.* Both raise their friends' children as their own and understand that, whereas romantic passion passes, the female friendship endures.

Moving closer to the resolution of female gender and womanly achievement, Glasgow depicts Victoria as offering maternal support and understanding, if not always wisdom, and like the domestic heroines, Victoria still holds a living relationship with her own long-dead mother. As she slips toward death, Victoria realizes that the memory of her long marriage diminishes in importance. Like Kate Chopin's Edna Pontellier and Willa Cather's Myra Driscoll Henshawe, she goes back to her childhood as the darkness comes: "She was no longer worn and discarded by time. . . . She saw, through this rich darkness, the glimmering outline of her mother's head against the pale sunshine beyond the window" (180). With the reach back toward the mother as the source of emotion, imagination, and memory, Glasgow turns away from the attitudes of the heroic individual Dorinda toward the female source of life and language. The passage mirrors the visitation of Mrs. Tolland's mother at her daughter's death in Jewett's "The Foreigner," as the bonds between mother and daughter surmount the limitations of time.

They Stooped to Folly portrays the same tension underlying *Virginia.* The dynamics of the friendship between the limited Victoria and the practical Louisa parallels the relationship between Jinny and Susan; both Victoria and Jinny, despite their innate kindness, suffer because of their limited female education; both Louisa and Susan, despite—Glasgow would say because of—their inability to approach the

Southern feminine ideal, live generous and full lives. Here too the book strays between detached irony and emotional involvement. When Glasgow enters Victoria's mind, she evidences the same tone she uses to address the limits of thought found in Jinny and Mrs. Pendleton: "Though she was perfectly aware that a single fatal misstep may make a Magdalen, it required, she told herself, both a slip and a recovery to create a hussy" (235). Nonetheless, the passages on the women's friendship and on Victoria's dying dream indicate Glasgow's authorial involvement with all irony removed. At this point, Glasgow found no way to realize her expressed ideal of female friendship within the modern urban environment. She needed first to go back to her beginnings.

The theme that undergirds the last books, *Vein of Iron* (1935), *In This Our Life* (1941), and *Beyond Defeat* (1945), is the urgent need for human beings of goodwill—especially women but also socially powerless men and children—to join together to combat an encroaching mercenary environment administered by legions of Cyrus Treadwells. Glasgow indicated in an article that the New South faced three dangers: the exploitation of Southern workers by Northern moneymen, the destruction of manner by "mad" industrialism, and the surrender to the "forces of ignorance," by which she meant Fundamentalist religion (Godbold, 174).

In the Glasgow canon, *The Sheltered Life* serves the same authorial purpose as Cather's *My Mortal Enemy*, both novels showing the bitter death of the female personality through subjugation of all relationships and beliefs to a male-female emotional and marital bond, which the authors depict as sterile and deadly. Eva abandoned her "song," her own female language and connections, to marry the ironically named George Birdsong, "the least eligible of her suitors." After her flight to romance, Eva has surrendered to the existence of the ideal mannequin of Southern Womanhood. Eva's value is, like Wharton's Lily Bart, associated with her rarity, her superiority to other women; by men's desires and belief, she is lifted up and above her sisters, her reputation as a beauty supporting her "like a cross." Finally, Eva undergoes a hysterectomy, becoming, in Glasgow's Darwin-influenced terms, the perfect female mannequin, completely dependent on the male. Unlike positive, creative female figures in American women's writing from Jewett to Naylor, Eva herself never tends the garden: "The truth was that she knew little of flowers, and loved most the orchids and gardenias that came from florists and were grown only in hothouses" (44). Like Lily Bart of *The House of Mirth* or Welty's Wanda Fay Chisom of *The Optimist's Daughter*, Eva finds no creativity within herself; she must await the gift of the flower shaped like herself to male visions of the ideal.

With Eva's destruction, Glasgow finally found herself able to re-nounce romance completely. In earlier books, even such independent women as Dorinda Oakley and Gabriella Carr found themselves driven by reactions to the romantic relationship. With the second book of her trilogy Glasgow portrayed the female family and friendships as the abiding relationship in women's lives, and with the third she finally showed the male-female romance in its deadly possessiveness for both men and women. The pathos of destruction in *The Sheltered Life* pre-pares us for the changes found in her next book, *Vein of Iron* (1935), as Glasgow evokes the elder wise woman. After *Barren Ground*, Glas-gow slowly lost her belief in the individual material achiever as a model applicable for woman, body or soul. Her later novels indicate a change of outlook, as does the draining away of the flashes of irony that previously lightened the tone of even her bleakest novels. Glasgow again creates a character who depicts the author's view of experience for both woman and state; now, however, she incorporates the home place in her last novels.

Important alterations in the narrative circumstance signal that Glas-gow achieved a new philosophical and psychological synthesis. In line with those new beginnings, Glasgow left her long-time publisher Dou-bleday in favor of Harcourt, Brace, & Company (Godbold, 213–14). She made two significant changes in fictional strategy as well. Turning to interior monologue to carry the narrative, Glasgow relaxed the con-trol inherent in her usual authorial omniscience. Most significantly, for the first time in her major novels, the author abandons the tripartite structure, which, by its inner logic, implies a world under logical con-trol as the novel progresses toward closure. Instead, Glasgow uses a narrative that circles back in past and looks to the future, interjecting oral history and mysticism into its account. She rewrites the history of Virginia and, by implication, America, reinstating women's lives and rejoining the generations in her hidden valley.

In the preface to *Vein of Iron*, Glasgow brings together strands of the woman's fiction we have previously encountered. From her first words,

"Tucked away in some hidden recess of my memory . . ." she indicates a new depth of introspection, which reaches beyond strict fictional verisimilitude (*Certain Measure,* 165). Summoning the woman's emotional, connective language, Glasgow recollects that the seeds of the novel were germinating from her youth, planted in the child Ellen's imagination by the voice of her Aunt Rebecca Glasgow singing Scottish ballads or enlivening the Waverley novels by her readings, in which the old lady took all roles, alternating English and Scots accents. The male written literature came alive with the addition of the loving voice. Glasgow identifies the impetus her aunt's living narrative gave to her niece, the woman's language drawing toward the written language, but also teaching her disappointment in the printed narrative: "The glorious adventures seemed to grow stale and flatten out when I read them in cold and faded print, deprived of the magical tones of my Aunt Rebecca's voice" (*Certain Measure,* 166–67). "Magical," "thrilling," "glorious," the words of the efficacious ritual as the local language comes to life through the voice of the elder female generations. The preface names Aunt Rebecca, her father's sister, as the author of her niece's creativity, ironically from the same strain of blood that also brought the "age of the machine," represented by her industrialist father himself. After years of feeling herself an isolated artist, Glasgow discovered a connection to her father's Scottish ancestry, refusing the harshness of industrialism, building instead on the memories that her aunt conjured up.[7] Depression America needed Francis Glasgow's "vein of iron," but his daughter made his female family its caretakers. With *Vein of Iron,* Glasgow reaffirms the abiding influence of woman's lineage through the home place.

Although the present narrative has its setting in the Shenandoah Valley and Queenborough from 1901 to 1932, much of Glasgow's fictive interest centers on the circumstance of the classic American pioneer legend, here the coming of the first settlers from Ulster to the hidden valley, one of the customary settings of the home place. The narrative of the homeland, the small local community begins with the story of its male founder, the first Fincastle. Glasgow clearly intends her readers to associate John Fincastle's search with the Puritan "errand into the wilderness." Fincastle moves his people ever farther from Europe into the American wilderness, seeking to create the ideal godly community as he envisions it.[8] Each time the group makes a

settlement, his followers reveal their human failings. Like other protagonists of the mainstream canon, Fincastle renounces the fallen social world, withdrawing from the town he has founded. He spends the
last years of his life among the Indians and untouched nature, a white
page available to express the male individual's private vision. Unable
to ameliorate human cruelty by creating the just society, unable as well
to engage human evil, Fincastle retreats alone to his "virgin land."

By his retreat, Glasgow implicitly suggests that the male quest is an
abandonment of the social compact, an inhuman insistence on a tab-
ula rasa upon which to etch his own vision. The story is told to Ada by
the family matriarch, Grandmother Fincastle; indeed, *Vein of Iron* centers on the redemption of the fallen social world by woman's power of
regeneration. Glasgow reframes the literary, cultural narrative from a
woman's perspective, at the same time noting the cost to the native
people with whom the settlers come in contact. The narrative tells the
story often submerged within the tale of the heroic individual, who
cannot, Glasgow implies, create a lasting homeland because of his demand to step out of history and society in his quest for expansion of
the personality. At once, Glasgow demythologizes the frontier narrative, suggests the male inability to live in a world after the fall, and
establishes the woman as the enduring repository of society and its
history.

Woman's experience in the community contrasts with man's movement away from the social center; throughout Glasgow's later books
men appear as dreamers, incapable of forming the human home. Although Glasgow approves the morality of Ada's male ancestor, his
goodness, his vision, and his integrity, she undercuts this sympathy by
suggesting that the first American Fincastle, like the last, Ada's father,
engages in an abstract search for perfect truth and justice that progressively separates him from the rest of humanity. And Ada's husband in
his turn demands the support of the family for one scheme after another; the family survives the poverty of the Depression only when Ada
asserts herself as creator of the family. If Ada represents Glasgow's
own history rewritten, then John Fincastle, as Wagner suggests, offers
a picture of Glasgow herself as author, isolated and uncertain as to
her future reception. As an alternative to her lonely individualism,
Glasgow offers the accumulated wisdom of the Fincastle women and
their home.

Glasgow also re-creates the common fictional device of the absent or weak parents, which has been a staple in much woman's fiction in America. The protagonist's father, John Fincastle, has neither the ability nor the desire to serve as a traditional male protector for his daughter Ada. Like Eva Birdsong and Jinny Pendleton, Ada's hysterical mother, Mary Evelyn Fincastle, burns with the fever of the great romantic attachment. Holding the outlines of her mother's old Virginian tradition, Mary Evelyn has the grace, manner, and sensitivity unshared by the coarser Fincastles. Glasgow reaches again for her perceived conflict of types as the basis for her fiction.

And, as often happens in a Glasgow novel, female sexual expression leads to single motherhood. Raper notes that Ada is the first of Glasgow's women to bear an illegitimate child and face the community (*Sunken Garden*, 167). Glasgow depicts Ada as facing the biological potential of her female body. Eventually, she will accept her place in the Fincastle lineage. She understands the cost of her passionate sexuality in the Indian-haunted forest, a search outside community order, which leads to Grandmother's death. When Ada has her child out of wedlock, the old woman rises from her sickbed to help her granddaughter: "The steadfast life of the house, the strong fibers, the closely knit generations, had gathered above, around, underneath" (228). Ada replaces her as mother of the Fincastle family and keeper of the living family home, the Manse. She undergoes an epiphany as she connects with earlier generations, "This was the heritage they had left. She could lean back on their strength; she could recover that lost certainty of a continuing education" (404). The fortitude that the Fincastles leave her is something beyond, but inseparable from, the physical heritage. Glasgow tries to reunite emotion and rationality, body and spirit, love and work through the figure of Grandmother Fincastle.

After Grandmother's death, the Manse passes from the Fincastles, and the family moves to Depression Queenborough. Ada's life in Queenborough during World War I and the Depression offers the testing of her communal vision. Like earlier protagonist-daughters, she must be educated to succeed in carrying the female physical and spiritual heritage. Like Ántonia, Ada separates from her home place, the Manse and the valley, to appreciate the ties and virtues she has lost. If John Fincastle willingly turned from Grandmother's home and traditions, Ada, like female protagonists before her, has no choice. Through the reactions of the family, Glasgow portrays her fear that all enduring human ties dissolve in the modern city as Ada struggles to hold the family together. Children run unattended in packs. Strangely sexless girls, a "puny" breed, live sexual lives of no commitment and no consequence. In their boyish figures and casual personal relationships, these "happiness hunters" resemble the "town girls" of Cather's later books, the trivial storklike girls of Porter's urban setting, or the "third sex" of Gilman's writing.

Like Cather, Glasgow in her later career believes that the individual woman needs the shelter of tradition and the continuity of the generations to rescue her sexuality from male exploitation and failure. Exemplifying this changed authorial attitude, Grandmother Fincastle gives a model of fortitude to her granddaughter. The elder carries the life and the history of her family; like Cather's Ántonia, she is a rich mine of life who keeps the old customs and beliefs. Her female creativity and her stern, unbending faith allow Grandmother to understand the origins of life more profoundly than her philosopher son. Representing female creativity, this wise woman integrates spirit and body, past and present, emotion and will in one personality. In a central passage, Glasgow pictures the seer entering her spiritual realm, where history is born out of memory and labor:

> Suddenly, without warning, descended upon her a sleep that was not sleep as yet. Her eyes saw; her ears heard; and in her stiff fingers the needles did not slacken. But she was immersed in profound stillness; she rested upon an immovable rock. And about her could feel the pulse of the manse beating with that secret life which was as near to her as the life in her womb. All the generations which had been a part, and yet not a part, of that secret life. The solid roof overhead, the solid floor underfoot, the fears of the night without, the flames and the shadows of flames within, the murmurs that had no voices, the creepings that had no shape, were all mingled now. Weaving in and out of her body and soul, knitting her into the past as she knitted life into stockings, moved the familiar rhythms and pauses—now—of the house; and moved as a casual wave, as barely a minute's ebbing and flow, in the timeless surge of predestination. (41)

In *Vein of Iron*, Grandmother Fincastle appears as the archetypal female creator, the generative force that creates life and transmits the historical and physical female identity. The home *place* has an ongoing life that replenishes and receives the creativity of individual women.

Grandmother dies as Ada gives birth to her son. With the creation of this seer, Glasgow returns, as had Jewett, Gilman, and Cather before her, to a type of wise woman who weaves vitality and strength from her body and female essence, "her secret life." Grandmother Fincastle reaches forward and backward in time to knit together the fabric of the family along with the bright wool.

Juxtaposed with the magnificent character of Grandmother, her son John represents another type of heroism, the bravery of the isolated intellectual. In *A Certain Measure*, Glasgow identifies John Fincastle as representing the fate "of the philosopher in an era of science, of the scholar in a world of mechanical inventions" (171). In contrast to his mother, John has the gift of words; he, like Glasgow, works with ideas and language. Wagner sees Ada and her father as a splitting of Glasgow's dual identities of woman and writer (97). Certainly his rejection of the ministry for the loneliness of the unrecognized scholar parallels in the author's mind her own journey from orthodoxy to defiance. She saw his life like hers as centered on a search for ultimate meaning.

At his death, a vision comes to the old man which ends his search. A boy again, John accompanies his mother on a medical mission to aid poor mountain settlers. They ride higher and higher, deeper and deeper into the wilderness until they reach a cabin surrounded by charred stumps. As his mother enters the cabin, John feels a horrible premonition. The family of idiots pours from the cabin, surrounding the child, jeering, gibbering, screeching, and dancing. These fools of words separate him from his mother, leaving him terrified: "To escape from them, to run away, he must break through not only a throng, but a whole world of idiots" (399). John's loss of the old maternal faith dooms him to a vision of life that he, and Ellen Glasgow, finally share: a world of idiots, unable to communicate, moving to inner hungers, to some indefinable feeling of loss. Crazed disorder and tormenting instinct remain after the loss of the woman's healing care.

What remains, then, to the dying philosopher and to the disillusioned author? In his last vision John Fincastle breaks through the ring of leering faces and jabbering voices to the female source of life and identity. His first thought is of his great romantic love, Mary Evelyn, but as with Victoria Littlepage's last memory, this fades as John dreams back to his mother, musing that from his childhood to his death there has been only loneliness through the loss of that authentic language and female presence: "The sunset blazed on the broken windowpanes of the house, and the dark face—dark and stern and bright—watching beyond the panes was the face of his mother. 'It's time to go in,' he thought" (401). The creative female source represented by the mother abides as the true mediating force in a world ruled by instinct or impersonality. Like Victoria, the dying man finds woman to be the final reality, as he returns to the hidden life of his family.

The creative female source of language and emotion replaces God the Father and human language and philosophy as the humanity's ultimate home. The move from weak, maddened, or dead mothers, earlier a constant in Glasgow's fiction, to the larger-than-life wise woman represents a fundamental change. By ignoring her voice, the artist's life becomes a brutish exercise, literally a "tale told by an idiot."

From the beginning of her career to the end, through the self-identified characters and through autobiographical writings, Glasgow insisted on the essential emotional differences between independent female achievers, herself among them, and the rest of womankind. Like Cather, Glasgow seems always to have felt separate from other women in her psychic and physical makeup; nonetheless with the writing of *The Vein of Iron* Glasgow discovered her place in the history of her female family and accepted her identity as a woman. She also found a reality that transcended the individual life, ending the search she began in her father's devout Presbyterian home. In *Vein of Iron*, Glasgow turns back to a communal life, based on the woman as center of a reconstituted family within the home place. Wagner recounts that Glasgow changes her fictional direction with this book, making "plain that the novel is a story of a family rather than of a single character" (103). Wagner continues that, throughout Glasgow's earlier career, most characters succeed because they break with their families. Around Ada, the cruelty of fallen humanity represented by the idiot Toby and his tormenters remains or the impersonal life-in-death of the materialistic urban "happiness hunters" threatens; within the Manse, the home place views all with charity and disposes them in order and peace. Ada reclaims the manse of belief.

Given the identification that Glasgow felt for Ada, and given the change in her customary structure, *Vein of Iron* represents a significant departure (Godbold, 211). From the rational Darwinism and the progressive individual feminism of her early years, Glasgow moved toward the prophetic, mystical feminism of her last works. With the return to the Manse, Glasgow suggests a model for the establishment of social arrangements that more closely approximate her Jeffersonian beliefs. With the change from the rational, individualistic intellectual stance to her later communal, emotional belief, Glasgow indicates her intent to start anew by a number of significant markers. Furthermore, as with Jewett and Cather, Glasgow realizes her creativity as influenced by and carrying forth her female heritage, composed of physical identity, family memory, and woman's myth. Significantly, in her preface to the novel, Glasgow speaks of her books as her "children" and discusses the process of creation in terms of gestation and birth. She no longer needs to insist on her essential difference from the rest of womanhood.

Glasgow's last novels, *In This Our Life* (1941) and the posthumously published *Beyond Defeat: The Epilogue to an Era* (1966), continue the themes established by *Vein of Iron*. Glasgow had at last achieved a faith with which she could live and die. The first novel ends with Roy Timberlake, the young female protagonist, fleeing into a rainstorm as she cries for "something to hold by" in the chaos of Depression Queenborough. Concerned that her readers misunderstood her optimistic intent in the novel, the author used the last bit of her flagging strength to compose *Beyond Defeat* in 1942 and 1943, a narrative in which Roy gains peace by resting her faith on the reconstituted family of Kate Oliver's Hunter's Fare, her illegitimate son Timothy, her father Asa Timberlake, and her friend Craig Fleming (Godbold, 289). Raper argues—correctly, I believe—that the two novels should be published as one volume (*Sunken Garden*, 192).

In This Our Life suffers from Glasgow's malaise at portraying a Queenborough under the domination of a corrupt entrepreneur. William Fitzroy rules that social order just as Kate Oliver creates the contrasting female pastoral of Hunter's Fare. Glasgow juxtaposed the family created by male-controlled industrial Queenborough with that evolved from the female-centered agrarian home. Through his calculated use of power within human relationships, industrialist William Fitzroy drives the action of *In This Our Life*; his removal through death in *Beyond Defeat* establishes the triumph of the home place.

Asa Timberlake, a decent man, lives in a time and a place that rejects his loyalties and mocks his morality. Through a youthful romantic error, he finds himself tied to the unholy family of modern industrialism: rich Uncle William Fitzroy, Asa's whining invalid wife Lavinia (who is also Fitzroy's niece), and Lavinia's spoiled, blond daughter Stanley. Asa's qualities of character expose him to victimization, exiling him within his own family, now dominated by Fitzroy's immense figure. Like Cather and Jewett, Glasgow portrays the modern urban setting as one that treads on the lives of those at the bottom of society. Glasgow felt that the novel came to "a pause, not an end." *A Certain Measure* indicated her resolve to complete a sequel.

Roy fits the outlines of the independent woman, contrasting with the blond childish appeal of her sister Stanley. Roy bears more than a passing resemblance to Susan Treadwell and Dorinda Oakley in her forthrightness and lack of artifice, but men prefer the vacuous Stanley, characterized by Glasgow as a "soulless little pleasure-seeker" (*Certain Measure*, 259). Stanley destroys many lives to validate her power over others, killing a little girl with her speeding sports car, sending a young black man to prison for the crime, conducting an affair and eloping with Roy's husband, subsequently driving him to suicide with her material demands, and through all the emotional and physical violence escaping through her appeal to male vanity and power. Throughout the narrative, one man after another, young or old, seeks Stanley as the prize in the social competition, and one after another she uses and destroys them—all except the indestructible William Fitzroy. Stanley's career anticipates other "happiness hunters" in the women's writing of the middle twentieth century; Glasgow, however, cannot muster the distance of irony and wit as she had in her Queenborough trilogy. Glasgow writes of Stanley in the terms of the mannequin shaped to the outer world: "She embodies . . . the logical result of that modern materialism which destroys its own happiness. It was her father who said of her, 'I sometimes think she has no real existence apart from her effect upon other people'" (*Certain Measure*, 259). Like Wharton's avenging angel of material hunger and social notice, Undine Spragg of *The Custom of the Country*, Stanley is created—the passive is the appropriate voice—by male desire; like Undine, Glasgow's character also represents "the perfect result of the system." In truth, Stanley's negative energy makes *In This Our Life* a less successful book than the sequel.

Beyond Defeat was written in fifteen-minute writing sessions by the mortally ill author, yet, despite the difficulty of its composition, it serves as the summation of Glasgow's career. Critics such as Wagner and Raper have come to the defense of this book, which was often treated as an embarrassment by earlier critics. Far from being the defeated book of a dying author, the sequel looks forward serenely to the future and to the passing of the generations. In both books Kate Oliver appears as the elder wise woman, who partakes of the "natural harmony of air" (188). With her tall, full-bodied figure, Kate contrasts with the sexless, but sexual, girls of modern Queenborough, much as Cather's Alexandra, Thea, and Ántonia stand in contrast to the "town girls." Like Ada Fincastle, Kate gathers together a loving family from the artificial restless city which produces Ada's first family, with its materialistic, complaining wife and the vicious, vain daughter, Stanley, a family whose real founder and head is William Fitzroy. Describing Kate as the "Gaea-Rhea-Demeter figure of the two novels," Raper details the extrarational content of the last novel (*Sunken Garden*, 188). Through her powerful femininity, she creates a magnetic social center countering the centrifugal force of Fitzroy's materialism. From her first appearance in *In This Our Life*, Kate, like Ántonia Shimerda, embodies the harvest home, as Hunter's Fare becomes the home place for the rootless outcasts, as she transfigures the "whole world" with "the flushed air of October." Her smile is "as genial as autumn" and her "large, warm hand" is "burned as brown as the soil." As the lost modern man, Asa comes home to the female pastoral, experiencing "an excitement which was not joy alone, but a feeling of sanity, of rightness, and of a spirit replenished" (173). In her calm female strength and wisdom, in her connection to the Virginia earth, Kate offers an alternative to the feverish, temporary city ruled by the materialistic "father," its leader William Fitzroy. If his creation and bloated embodiment is the city, hers is Hunter's Fare, yet Craig Fleming tells Roy that is not the house that brings her completion and joy: "It is Kate" (*Beyond Defeat*, 110). Like the autumn she represents, Kate emanates with the glow that lights the coming dark. She fills all the womanly roles, and she shares with other creations—Jewett's Mrs. Todd, the nature goddess, Cather's Alexandra Bergson, the guardian of the land, and Porter's Aunt Eliza of "The Fig Tree," the mountainous seer, single nurturing sibyls all—the huge size of all outdoors. Like Mrs. Todd, Alexandra Bergson, and Naylor's Mama Day, Kate herself has no biological children. Instead she becomes the mother all these lost Queenborough inhabitants miss. For Asa, Kate fills the loss felt by

Asa for his long-dead mother; for Roy, Kate serves as the true mother she has never known, and for the third generation, Roy's son, she creates the loving maternal home missing in Queenborough. At Hunter's Fare, goodness, warmth, and abundance allow each person to develop the true individuality of uncoerced identity and evolved wisdom. Kate's re-formed family operates as a source of communal strength, resting on "something bigger than one person—or than two persons." The home within nature teaches Roy that her son belongs not only to her, but also to a human family and tradition. Roy at last discovers something good to hold by; all the outcasts of Fitzroy's materialistic city come together to be healed at Hunter's Fare, a place located in the pastoral distance: "Still ahead, and within sight, but just out of reach, and always a little father away, fading, but not ever disappearing, was freedom" (467).

Beyond Defeat achieves the serenity Glasgow sought throughout her career. The sequel shows the author's intent to create a new language, evoking spirituality, an expanded vision with the emotional impact of communal ritual. As Wagner observes, this novel concerns itself with Asa, the modern man, finding his way back to "roots, sources, and stability" (113). Therefore, the novel contains none of the legendary Glasgow wit and little appeal to intellectual systems as had her earlier works. Instead, like *Vein of Iron*, it displays an inward creativity. Like Jewett and Cather, Glasgow attempted to broaden the causal assumptions of the linear narrative and the elaborated language to embrace the network of relationships and associations that form the home place and require the solemnity of tradition. Accordingly, she draws scenes that resonate in the senses and the emotions as well as the intellect. Despite her grave illness during their composition, the novels hold some of the author's most moving, evocative descriptive passages:

> At Hunter's Fare, he knew, the wind from the river would have sprung up; colored leaves, blanched with moonlight, would hurtle over the grass to the house; the earthy scents of smoke and wood mold and cider would be strengthened by the fresh darkness. Inside the house, Kate would be lingering over her book (for books overflowed the tables and chairs and were piled up in corners), and Pat and Percy would have their run out-of-doors before they went on guard for the night. Peace is there, he thought, in that house, with that friendship. Love comes, love goes; but comradeship is woven of an indestructible element. (*In This Our Life*, 196)

Glasgow thus evokes companionship, not the possessiveness of romance, as the bond that brings together men and women and shapes the home place. She believes that shared interests, commitment, and respect offer the only basis for lasting love relationships between men and women. Like Cather's *My Ántonia* and *O Pioneers!* and Jewett's *The Country of the Pointed Firs*, *Beyond Defeat* depicts satisfaction in male and female relationships coming only after the disorders of youthful romantic illusion and sexuality have passed.

The passages at Hunter's Fare, both in *Beyond Defeat* and *In This Our Life*, like the other manifestations of the female pastoral, require a different critical approach from that customarily taken toward realistic fiction. Glasgow's approach in her later work eschews the earlier male-influenced dramatic narrative, progressing logically to closure. Raper assesses the intent of *Beyond Defeat* as that of "wisdom literature," which demands a different judgment from that rendered to realistic fiction. Raper correctly notes the novel's emphasis on "liturgical cadence" and "stress on vision" parallels the messages of Glasgow's beloved Marcus Aurelius, the *Bhagavad Gita*, and *The Enneads*. He concludes that its ritual structure unites it with literature that addresses the central dramas of existence such as the tragedies of Aeschylus or the tales of the medieval quest. He observes, "Like those works, it should be judged upon its style and vision" (191–92). As Raper understands, Glasgow hopes to achieve an emotion similar to that accompanying ritual, to bring the reader into Hunter's Fare, to grant the peace the author achieved in her last moments. Glasgow reaches for mythic reverberations through the incantatory phrases, the conventional descriptions, all marks of the attempt to bring the emotions of ritual to the modern prose narrative.

Glimpsing the eternity that had so occupied her since her father's compulsory prayers, Glasgow at last understood that the force that had created the natural world must be feminine. At the end of the lives of John Fincastle and Victoria Littlepage, we as readers saw the face of the mother transfigured into archetype, but Asa Timberlake returns to a representative figure who transcends the personal memory and reaches toward the concept of the home place. Unlike the thundering, jealous deity Glasgow put aside in her youth, Kate engenders feelings of love, of harvest, of reward. All the feelings of connectedness excluded by Queenborough's regulated life and its dead male leader

come to rest at Hunter's Face like the circling birds at the novel's opening. In re-creating the loving separate community with the rejoined
generations, the novel serves as Glasgow's valedictory. Glasgow believes that the loving community can best be created by the individual
woman through cooperation with the land, whereas the city leads to
mercenary social arrangements and the male-dominated family. She
found at last the language that allowed her to balance her womanly
identity with the profession of authorship. After the false spring of *Bar-*
ren Ground, Ellen Glasgow at last found her way home to the figure of
elder wise woman, Mother Autumn.

It may not have any particular meaning that
the place where I was born, the other place near
my grandmother's farm where I spent an important part of my childhood, and the very tribu-
tary of the Colorado river which ran beside the
house where I was born are not to be found on
any map I have seen.
                          —Katherine Anne Porter
                          "The Land That Is Nowhere"

5.

The Land That Is Nowhere

KATHERINE ANNE PORTER

LIKE HER PREDECESSORS, Porter feels compelled to claim her place
within the female generations; yet portrayal or even evaluation of her
communal past becomes increasingly problematic. She is affected by
the bureaucratization of the social order, which demands a more and
more specialized language, making it difficult to portray an ideal pastoral community. The refusal of Porter's Miranda to be recruited to
any ideological cause or received role reflects the suspicion of the writers previously discussed toward both nostalgia for an old patriarchal
order and optimism for male-controlled social organizations. The fear
of the female self's annihilation or oppression reflects her rejection of
the patriarchal past as well as a distrust of the massive regimented
social structures. In the last account, she escapes the trap of solipsism
through recourse to the home place, espousing at last an alternate reality in her narratives of the women's world of Sophia Jane, Nannie,
and Aunt Eliza.

The core of Porter's work evokes a stable woman's world presided over by a group of female seers, the Grandmother, Sophia Jane Rhea, her sister Eliza, and the former slave Nannie. Miranda Gay succeeds them as guardian of the family history. Porter distinguishes this imaginary women's realm from a nostalgic passive domestic past by having Grandmother assume power after the men die—the women's domain succeeds male authority. Moreover, Miranda's female artistic powers emerge after the death of sexual love with its attachment to patriarchal possession.

The works I will discuss are those that have as their protagonist Miranda and Mirandalike figures, as well as the early works, which show an idealized Mexican pre-Columbian Indian community headed by a mother goddess, a community of Porter's imagination that incorporates essential characteristics of the home place. The Mexican works represent an implicit criticism of woman's place in the modern America Porter fled, and the American works show Porter's semi-autobiographical figure Miranda emerging as witness to the brave new technological world. I will treat the Miranda stories originally found in *The Leaning Tower and Other Stories* in the order presented in *The Collected Stories* because this represents Porter's last published ordering of Miranda's experience. One of the seemingly unrelated stories will be examined, "The Jilting of Granny Weatherall," in which Porter first attempts to portray the elder wise woman.

To see the pattern of Porter's fiction, the reader should profitably approach the Miranda stories by considering the narratives as a unified set of tales sharing themes and metaphors seen through the eyes of one female observer.[1] S. H. Poss argues that the Miranda stories form a sort of bildungsroman because they "manifest that typical structure of the genre which may be described as a secular version of the medieval notion of life as a pilgrimage" (21). Taken together, the Miranda stories constitute a type of modern spiritual autobiography; again an American woman writer infuses her narrative with the sacred, didactic element. The fact that the author published the stories in different volumes in combination with other stories does not negate their thematic unity. In this, Porter advances the pattern seen in *The Golden Apples, O Pioneers!, My Ántonia, The Country of the Pointed Firs, Linden Hills,* and *The Women of Brewster Place.*

Porter's first published stories, contained in *Flowering Judas and Other Stories* (1935), have as their setting her "familiar country" Mexico. Her first published story, "Maria Concepción" (1922) attempts to submerge the authorial personality and experience completely in a narrative of Indian communal life, which contrasts sharply with the increasingly organized, technological American social structure portrayed in stories such as "Pale Horse, Pale Rider." Like Glasgow and Cather, Porter explored fictionally events that occurred in her own life; during those years Porter was also involved in an ambitious plan to bring Mexican folk art to the United States. Placed against the background of these works, Porter's search for the ideal oral community under the protection of a strong female deity becomes unmistakably clear. Her fascination with the Mexican goddesses emerges through her nonfictional writings of her time in Mexico, 1920–31, as Porter turned to her "discovery" of the female seer.

Written four months after her arrival in Mexico simultaneously with her composition of "Maria Concepción," "The Children of Xochitl," an unpublished sketch, shows Porter idealizing the pre-Columbian Indian experience. The manuscript, given the probable date of March 1921 by Thomas F. Walsh, presents the visit of a group of tourists to a village church dedicated to the Virgin Mary. An old man tells the visitors that Xochitl, "the Aztec goddess of the earth," is also patroness of the church and the village, blessing the community with her favor and protection. Xochitl creates a community of brothers and sisters and defeats the male Spanish conquerors attempts to usurp her authority. The old man concludes, "Xochitl feeds us!" The narrator interposes, "Thus the goddess who feeds the Indians is their mother, they her children." The active, female goddess remains in power, overcoming the passive virginal handmaiden of the male God.*

Throughout the Xochitl typescript, an anonymous article "Xochimilco," and her guidebook to the Mexican Popular Arts Exposition, Porter portrays an ideal preindustrial Mexico, an eternal pastoral

---

*Xochitl, misnamed by Porter, represents the Great Mother of the Aztecs. Erich Neumann identifies Coatlique, Tlazolteotl, and even the goddess of love, Xochiquetzal, as names of the Great Mother (182–208). This figure, like Porter's Xochitl, fertilizes the earth, but Neumann stresses her negative aspect as Terrible Mother, whereas Porter negates this. She may have changed the name to simplify it, or she may have gotten the facts wrong. Whatever the case, Porter evokes the growth or creative aspect of the Mother Goddess, and finds this emphasis essential to her vision of her New World home place.

homeland of abundance and "relaxed and unresisting permanence": "The inhabitants have invested their surroundings with their own deep and slow moving rhythm of life. . . . Their open markets are centers not only of commerce, but of social exchange" ("Popular Arts," 40). Over this idyllic landscape of tiny pueblos, Xochitl reigned in pre-Columbian times, and she preserved the equality of women, her earthly representatives. Women served as priestesses and held a major responsibility for the children's education: "Every evidence is that they enjoyed a clearly human equality in society utterly foreign to the ideals that governed the relations between men and women of the European and Asiatic races" ("Popular Arts," 26). Indian Mexico, as Porter saw it, passes arts, skills, and custom from mother to daughter, from father to son. The cyclical rhythms of planting and harvesting, of birth and death, the rituals and beliefs of the Indian religion, represented an ideal of female care and creativity. The communal order drew Porter into her love affair with Mexico as she fled an America she perceived as increasingly regimented. A comparison with Cather's supplanting of the conquistadores with Ántonia, Jewett's replacement of Captain Littlepage by Mrs. Todd, and Glasgow's succession of Kate Oliver over William Fitzroy reveals the shared underlying dynamic; male domination fails in winning the New World, whereas female care brings forth its true riches.

Through her early re-creation of the female pastoral in Indian Mexico, Porter strengthened herself for her artistic return to an American society that she considered under sway of the male expert, his machines, and his supporting bureaucratic institutions. That she intended her writings as a criticism of the modern industrial social structure becomes clear from her occasional writings. In a review of a book on Mexico by Diego Rivera and Bertram Wolfe, Porter offered perhaps her most pointed commentary on the threat to her ideal community, concluding that their study of progress through mechanization ends on a note "so rosy one would like to share it, but so vague one does not know where to begin."[2] For Porter, as for many other American writers since industrialization, the machine stands as representative of the impersonal modern state; a variety of associations cluster around it: male control, regimentation, unthinking power, inhumanity. In "Flowering Judas," for example, the handmade lace collars of Laura's maternal background contrast with the machine of Braggioni's revolution, and in "Pale Horse, Pale Rider," the machinery of Dr. Hildesheim's hospital overcomes the woman's body and soul with its efficiency. Porter balances her equation nicely: Man–woman; machine–humanity; rules–custom; spareness–abundance; efficiency–generosity; impersonality–humanity. Thus she suggests the continuing process of rationalization.

At the time of the Mexican writings, Porter did not allow herself to enter the emotional and intellectual turmoil entailed by the sorting of personal truth and legend; her earliest solution as a writer was to stay firmly in a culture and a time not her own. It is, therefore, fitting that the first fiction she wrote, "Maria Concepción," is deeply entrenched in an idealized Mexican past. "Maria Concepción" reflects and extends in a fictional form Porter's contemporary concerns over female role. As Jane DeMouy points out in *Katherine Anne Porter's Women*, the protagonist is a primal mother goddess who subsumes the sexual goddess Maria Rosa. DeMouy continues by noting a trinity of maternal corn goddess, a maiden—"the goddess of love's pleasure and sins"—and a flower prince. The mother goddess was also the destructive goddess "of the obsidian knife," who manifests the creative aspect of the Great Mother. (The concept of this trinity is relevant as well to the triangle of Alexandra, Marie, and Emil in Cather's *O Pioneers!*.)

"Maria Concepción" portrays an ideal woman's community centered around the female goddess. M. M. Liberman designates the protagonist an earth goddess who carries the history and the future of her ancient community. As befits the bounded community, no outside narrative voice intrudes; instead, the perspective is that of an omniscient author. The cyclical rhythms of growth, the rituals of Indian Catholicism imperfectly overlaying native belief, and the direct and immediate translation of emotion into action are juxtaposed by implication with the disbelieving, detached intellectual witness of the male American archaeologist Givens. He lives a secondhand existence examining the shards of the past female culture of Xochitl. In his habit of collecting and preserving past lives, Givens resembles such other male figures in American woman's writing as the young hunter in Sarah Orne Jewett's "A White Heron," Newland Archer in Wharton's *The Age of Innocence*, Lucius Harney in Wharton's *Summer*, Audubon in Welty's "A Still Moment," Van and his companions in *Herland*, Dr. Braithwaite in Naylor's *Linden Hills*, and Reema's boy in Naylor's *Mama Day*, all male representatives of scientific method and associational language.

Again the woman writer removes the sexual goddess, the woman devoted to a passionate romantic connection, from the history and physical continuity of the woman's community. The women of the community acquiesce in Maria Concepción's adoption of the dead woman's son as a right and natural restoration of the generations. From the wise woman Lupe to Maria Concepción herself, the women of the community work together to defeat the trespassing police of the outside order after Maria Rosa's murder. Even Juan resigns himself with comparative equanimity as he gives himself up to sleep and, by implication, death. The flower prince and princess vanish into death, having fulfilled their parts in the drama of ongoing life. The sexuality of Maria Rosa is engulfed by the mother goddess who commands life and death. She replaces Juan's wanderings in the Revolution with a place as protector of her family.

Porter's "Flowering Judas" (1930) shows the author moving away from her idealized oral community; the story thus evidences a growing suspicion of the author's decision to remain in Mexico during those early days of the Revolution. The emphasis shifts from the mother goddess to an isolated single American woman cut off from her land and time. With its recurring symbols of betrayal—Laura repeatedly refuses the sexuality implied by the roses and flowers offered to her—the narrative indicates Porter's suspicion of both Mexican revolutionary and detached female outsider. Even though Porter has identified other sources than her own personal experience as sources for the protagonist, several components of Laura's character, as Darlene Unrue argues, suggest her connection with the strongly autobiographical persona Miranda: both are emotionally controlled American women—detached, well-educated, single, who come from a Roman Catholic background. Moreover, both share a Southwestern background.

Like Porter herself, Laura came to help the Revolution.[3] Most significant for Porter's later fiction is the portrayal of Laura as a collector who shares no emotional bond or instinctual connection with the country and its people. Instead, like Givens, she has the desire to "possess" and classify Mexico as she "haunts the markets listening to the ballad singers," collecting the local color as did Porter herself (90). Like the corrupt, obese Braggioni, Laura too feeds on the Revolution, using its sacrifices for her own personal salvation, thus partaking of a false Eucharist. She stays in Mexico, dispensing lies and death, forcing belief in intellectual abstractions: "But she cannot help feeling that she

has been betrayed irreparably by the disunion between her way of living and her feeling of what life should be" (91). Laura's moment of
self-discovery comes to her against her will. Excuse by excuse, she
forges the chain binding her to her life in Mexico, but bit by bit her
own insights corrode it. But Laura has no place to go because "she can
no longer imagine herself living in another country, and there is no
pleasure in remembering her life before she came here" (93). Laura
wears the drab "uniform of an idea," suggesting the renunciation of
her gender and her own personal past. In this, as Donald Madden
writes, she is less capable of salvation into humanity than Braggioni,
who can still share human communion with his ill-treated wife. Dorothy Redden identifies the source of Laura's fear of "everything" as her
unwillingless to enter the realm of death but more importantly her
inability to choose life.

Like the self-made American man, Laura has shed history, family,
and past, but as a woman, without that past and those identities,
she cannot believe in the future. In Porter's fiction and nonfiction,
woman is, despite all denial, inescapably immersed in birth and death.
She must always address the fact of her woman's body, for, as DeMouy
remarks, "If a woman cannot control her body, she cannot control her
life" (117). Control, however, does not mean repression but rather understanding such as Miranda achieves at the end of *The Old Order*.
Unlike Maria Concepción, with whom she must be contrasted, Laura's
talisman is refusal: "No matter what this stranger says to her, nor what
her message to him, the very cells of her flesh reject knowledge and
kinship in one monotonous word. No. No. No" (97). Her last vision
forces upon Laura a recognition of her position "outside."

During the late 1920s, Porter began writing stories with American
settings. This discussion considers "The Jilting of Granny Weatherall"
(1929), the short story that gave Porter an early chance to deal with
her own woman's history. Much in the characterization of Granny
Weatherall anticipates the later stories of the grandmother of the Miranda stories, the aptly named Sophia. As DeMouy writes, the story
displays the components of the typical Porter story in its focus on the
matriarch, its examination of life and death, the collapsing of time into
dream and memory, and its emphasis on the protagonist's psychic
reality (45). Defeat of linear time by the expanding present of the
mother, her control over birth and death, and the betrayal of the woman

by romance mark the stories that have the Grandmother at the center of her own stable domestic universe. The American setting of the story indicates that Porter is resolving her relationship as a woman of the twentieth century to the women's world of her female family.

In her youth Ellen Weatherall imagines an ornamental life of received order granted by an adoring man's favor. When her fiancé George jilts her, frustrating those romantic dreams, her life seems ruined, but she finds her redemption through her husband John, who brings her to her full power through maternity. Like many another heroine, Ellen learns that "investing in the love of a man is ruination," in DeMouy's words, and that her true destiny is the creation of the matriarchal homeland (50).

Like Glasgow's Grandmother Fincastle of *Vein of Iron*, Cather's old grandmothers of "The Bohemian Girl," Naylor's Sapphira Wade of *Mama Day*, and Welty's Granny Vaughn of *Losing Battles*, the aptly named Granny Weatherall has accomplished marvels of female creation, food cooked and served, clothes cut and sewed, humans and animals nursed and healed, and gardens planted and harvested. And most of all, she has brought the children to life: "There they were, made out of her, and they couldn't get away from that" (83). She outlives both George and John and, like those elder wise women, takes on tasks traditionally considered as male—once she fenced in one hundred acres with one helper. As the old woman moves toward death, Porter shows the continuity of the generations through her living memory of her favorite daughter, Hapsy: "She seemed to herself to be Hapsy also, and the baby on Hapsy's arm was Hapsy and himself and herself, all at once" (85). At another point, Granny reflects that her dead husband would now be "a child beside her" (83). Daniel and Madeline Barnes suggest that Ellen may have been pregnant when she was jilted because of her preoccupation with childbirth. The female family continues with John as a sort of Joseph to Granny's maternity much as Anton Cuzak relates to Ántonia. Porter's holy family centers on the mother and her power over life and death. The linear nature of time, the progression of cause and effect, are collapsed into the vibrancy of an expanded present. The power of the father is absorbed into the timelessness of the matriarch, who offers a model of creativity for the society and for the writer herself.

The wise woman, whom John Edward Hardy identifies as a type of

Great Mother, truly "weathers all," creating a home place out of her body and her vision. Her ultimate betrayal comes from her handing her soul and her world over to undependable males, first her fiancé George, then her husband John, and finally the Father God. As the source of life, she is, after all, Hapsy and the baby and herself in both the living memory and the continuity of the flesh. Instead of Joyce's Molly Bloom or Faulkner's Eula Varner, male visions of the earth goddess, Porter, as well as earlier woman writers, created figures like Granny, a seer who transcends the passing of youthful loveliness and romantic dreams—the lure of courtship by the male—to undertake the creativity of active femininity and finally to ascend to a sort of female divinity, which challenges the distant male deity. Even as the dying Granny Weatherall awaits the Mystical Bridegroom, she herself has already created the human home and the female lineage from her own woman's body and her own woman's strength.

With the creation of Granny Weatherall, Porter was ready to put aside her Edenic Mexican community and face her own future. Harry Mooney ties Granny Weatherall with Miranda in her movement between states of being and her concern with her lost first love and also with Grandmother Sophia Jane in her position as stable center in a large family. These connections suggest that Porter was ready to face fictionally her own personal history.

"Hacienda" represents one of those watershed works in the writer's career, works like *The Country of the Pointed Firs, Vein of Iron, Mama Day,* and *The Song of the Lark,* which signal a fundamental change of direction for the artist. As such, it is written with the immediacy of reported experience; Givner notes that "it was the summation of all her feelings about Mexico" (239). The first-person narrator again shares important similarities with Porter herself and her alter ego Miranda: she is a single professional woman connected both with Mexico and the film industry. In her depiction of the fleeing narrator, the mannequinlike women, and the fading goddesses, Porter frees herself from her idealized Mexico.

Her position as outsider in Mexico extends to the narrator's sense of her own gender, like other female protagonists; DeMouy observes that the narrator is an androgynous outsider and concludes that having chosen art and independence, the narrator "finds that in so doing she eschews the right and natural proportions of a woman, that she cannot

have the easy familial role of the Mexican women around her" (99–
100). She is considered always, and only, a woman by the Mexicans,
but an androgynous professional colleague by all her coworkers. The
ambiguous state of her gender finds its reflection in the shifting sexuality of the actress Lolita and the childish "lady" of the hacienda, Doña
Julia. The climactic scene shows the narrator in the vat room, which
she has entered through Doña Julia's ruffle-filled bedroom with its
doll-covered bed. The women produced by modern Spanish Mexico
and its tradition of the patrón are repeatedly depicted as diminished,
distorted from the prim Virgin framed by "fly-blown paper flowers" to
the doll-like Julia with her ridiculous costumes. All the scent and gloss
does not hide the stink of the liquor: "A thick vapor through the heavy
drone of flies, sour, stale, like rotting milk and blood" (161). The fluids
of nature and of the mother have spoiled, like the rotting pears of
Welty's dying Morgana. Around the walls, but fading, there still remains a fresco showing an Indian girl who brought the divine liquor to
the emperor—she became a "half-goddess." The narrator continues,
"An old legend: maybe the oldest: something to do with man's con-
fused veneration for, and terror of, the fertility of women and vegetation" (165). Underneath the old Spanish culture, now the American
and Russian cultures—the invaders—the pre-Columbian memories
still glimmer dimly. But instead of the gift of the brown goddess, now
the pulque is produced for profit by machine. The pulque hacienda
shows the death of the goddess, the spoliation of her abundant generosity by the male leader and his supporting bureaucracies. Now
throughout Mexico "the Indians would drink the corpse-white liquor,
swallow forgetfulness and ease by the riverful, and the money would
flow silver-white into the government treasury" (168). The forgetfulness they swallow is the memory of the goddess Xochitl and of a village
square that integrated commercial and social exchange; the essential
fluids of maternal nurture turn rotten, a deadly, obscene communion
transubstantiated into money. At the end, the narrator flees the con-
tamination of the sustenance of life, even the air itself, in Mexico. Like
Laura, she has refused to make elemental choices: nationality, sexuality, and belief. Now she must choose.[4]

   After her worship of the Mexican life and goddesses, Porter turns to
an exploration of her own dual identities of woman and writer within
the American cultural context. A retreat to the order of an idealized

female community or a refuge in an organized system of rationality would not be granted to her alter ego Miranda. During 1935, according to DeMouy's chronology, Porter published the Miranda stories dealing with the blacks of her youth: "The Witness" and "The Last Leaf" and her own artistic development, "The Grave" and "The Circus"; she notes that the Sophia stories were published in 1936 and 1941. "The Fig Tree" was published in 1960 as the Miranda narrative achieved its final form. (The order of composition of the other stories of *The Old Order* is problematic, Joan Givner dating them from Porter's Paris years, probably in 1933 and 1934 [339]. Whatever the truth, Porter published them after the *Pale Horse* collection and places them after those stories in the final arrangement.) Her next collection of three long short stories, *Pale Horse, Pale Rider* (1939), composed of "Old Mortality," "Noon Wine," and "Pale Horse, Pale Rider," takes its settings and situations from Porter's own life, all having Miranda as protagonist or narrator. Like "Flowering Judas" and "Hacienda," the first, "Old Mortality," has the interplay of illusion and reality at its center as Miranda attempts to find her own time and language.* Several core themes have been suggested for the Miranda stories; I suggest the search for a language and a homeland true to the protagonist's female experience. Like the characters of earlier authors, Miranda achieves a measure of peace when she takes her place in the ongoing female community, a circumstance suggesting Porter's own resolution of female gender and individual art.

As "Old Morality" opens, Miranda is eight years old, an age, Porter tells the reader, that lives equally in the daily world of demanding, unpredictable relatives in stuffy living rooms and the literary realm of ethereal lords and damsels in glittering castles and enchanted forests. Miranda and her older sister Maria do not doubt "either Death or the Devil riding at the stirrups of the grim knight" (a foreshadowing of the race that begins "Pale Horse, Pale Rider"), any more than they question the facts of their daily life (178). Porter contrasts the children's innocent view of literature as "real," as having effects on daily life, with

---

*The name "Miranda" suggests her long, wondering vision. First, there is the reference to the character from *The Tempest*; second, in Spanish, the word itself means a vantage point. *Mirar*, the infinitive from which Miranda comes, means "to see." Thus, Porter designates Miranda as her "see-er" or by extension seer.

the male elders' classification of false, ornamental graveside doggerel as "poetry."

Three generations of women carry the weight of the action in "Old Mortality," the Grandmother, her daughter Amy, and her cousin Eva Parrington, and her granddaughter and our witness, Miranda. Amy, Eva, and Miranda are continually present in actuality or in memory. Amy illustrates the costs of the old paternalistic order to the female rebel, Eva represents progressive individualistic feminism, and Miranda remains the observing emerging female consciousness who must find her own way.

In "Old Mortality" the Grandmother's stories have no light to shed on Miranda's emerging history. The Grandmother is a diminished, almost background figure, mediating ineffectually between her rebellious daughter and the world of men. The Grandmother does not here even own her significant first name, Sophia. Miranda remembers her periodic rummaging among and weeping over the old ball gowns and trinkets of a remembered romantic past, which has left behind only "[s]uch dowdy little wreaths and necklaces" (175). These ornaments expose the reality underlying the romanticism of female experience with the male family—instead of the diamonds and emeralds of legend, the reality of paste and sequins. Miranda here evidences barely concealed contempt at the inability of the female family—dead mother, weakened grandmother—to protect Amy and herself and Maria from the death-making myths of the men of the family, especially Gabriel and her father Harry. Foremost among those stories is the romance of Amy and Gabriel, his pursuit of her and her early death was a story in the young girls' minds to rival those of the great romantic tales, the *Vita Nuova*, Spenser, and Poe, but the two, gazing at the stiff portraits, also associate the stories "with dead things." Porter signals her fear of falsified female experience, a repeated note in her work, which indirectly addresses doubts over her own practice of literature within a male tradition.

Like her female predecessors, Porter illustrates the danger of sexuality to the individual woman in Part I, in which the living present time of Maria and Miranda (1902) becomes secondary, less alive, compared to the legend of Amy's romance (1885).

The danger in this narrative comes not from female misbehavior, but from male possessiveness of both woman and language, from Gabriel, Amy's suitor, and from Harry, Miranda's father, also Amy's brother and Sophia's son. The first words introduce the readers to the sexual rebel, forever subdued into feminine decorum: "She sat thus, forever in the pose of being photographed, a motionless image in her dark walnut frame" (173). Throughout the narrative, Amy refuses the customary female sexual and maternal roles of paternalistic Southern society. Amy is imprisoned in death by the mold of Southern Womanhood much as Glasgow's Eva Birdsong was in life. Judging all women's appearance "severely," the social order in "Old Mortality" objectifies woman fully as much as does the emerging modern era in "Pale Horse, Pale Rider."

In her father's attitude toward his daughters, we perceive the making of a belle by the men of the family. He holds them on his knee if their appearance meets his approval but pushes them away if they do not, " 'Go away, you're disgusting,' he would say, in a matter-of-fact voice" (184). The girls already assess each other's "points" of appearance in harsh terms learned from the men. The judgment of the male relatives shapes the events of the women's lives, even in rebellion. Miranda's disastrous elopement arises from her desire to be a figure of romance, although she knows she cannot compare with Amy's adventures and beauty.

Dance appears again as the central episode in a young woman's life, bringing her first to sexuality and ultimately to death. Here Amy meets and, almost certainly, embarks on a sexual escapade with Raymond, the dashing visitor from New Orleans. Through the dances—which Porter presents as neither the romantic dramas of Grandmother's memories nor the sexual marketplaces of Eva's diatribe—Amy, like Grace Elliott, Ántonia Shimerda, Ellen Fairchild, and Jinny Pendleton, is immersed in female social and biological roles. For Amy, this forced immersion will bring her to death through her inability to place her sexuality into any rewarding social context. Here the men shape the woman's reality; in *The Old Order* the Grandmother, Nannie, and Aunt Eliza, here a figure of fun, emerge as strong figures of creativity.

In "Old Mortality," the young woman knows well her place in male romantic legends as well as the limits of feminine rebellion. When she returns gravely ill with a relapse of tuberculosis after a flight on horseback to the Mexican border with her brothers—a flight caused by her brother's ignoble shooting of a man in defense of her "honor"—Amy laughs and says, "And if I am to be the heroine of this novel, why shouldn't I make the most of it?" (189). She understands, as does the adult Miranda, that the men of the family conspire in writing—and thus controlling—the family history. Through this, Porter obliquely criticizes portrayals of women in male fiction.

After witnessing the death in childbirth of her sister-in-law, Maria's and Miranda's mother, Amy suspects, given her poor health, that she too will die if she marries—her hemorrhaging suggests the blood of menstruation and childbirth, a connection Eva makes explicit in her narrative. Having refused Gabriel so many times, Amy abruptly demands they marry before Mardi Gras, because after Lent "may be too late." Cousin Eva, at least, suggests that pregnancy impels Amy into her marriage. When she plans her wedding dress, Amy will not wear white or a veil, despite her mother's urging, saying, "I shall wear mourning if I like . . . it is *my* funeral, you know" (182). As she runs to the wedding carriage waiting in the "gray cold," Amy wears the color of Porter's woman in-between, gray, with a splash of dark (blood) red feathers. Amy dies of an overdose of sedatives, which she takes while her nurse sleeps. The nurse's note to the Grandmother sums up Amy's life simply and with understanding: "She suffered a good deal and now she is at rest. She could not get well, but she might have lived longer" (193).

Unable to submerge her sexuality into a creative commitment, whether community, art, or land, as do such heroines as Dorinda Oakley, Ántonia Shimerda, or Almira Todd, Amy's individual personality suffers obliteration. DeMouy calls Amy "the ultimate portrait of a woman in suspension" and marks the ambivalence of her death. Porter, however, does not draw the rebellious woman passing from the communal history. Instead, in this critical portrayal of female roles within the paternal family, Porter portrays a series of young women— Isabel, cousin Amy, Eva, Maria, and Miranda—as victimized by the legend of the dead woman who becomes the object of family hagiography. Thus Amy dies twice at the hands of the men of the family, who capture woman's experience in the romances of their own lives. In an implicit contrast to the simple, but resonant, words of the nurse's note, Gabriel's graveyard poetry reveals a falsification, an almost willful misunderstanding, of Amy both in life and death, calling her "a singing angel." As trapped as Amy was in life by the perimeters of male desire, her imprisonment is even more final in death. The accepted story of the romance is Gabriel's, not Amy's, as male language overcomes female experience, again a reference to the nature of Porter's artistic commitment.

Gabriel's romance is presented by Porter through floral imagery; the floral tribute he offers Amy is an enameled rose with paste dewdrops; if he sends live flowers, they arrive dead when the Grandmother's rose garden is in full bloom. Porter contrasts Gabriel's possessive romantic falsification of experience with the vitality and substance of the Grandmother's garden. This imagery reinforces the falsity of male myth with the reality of female creativity, however muted in this narrative.

The child suffers from the patriarchal command of language, which demands she deny the reality of her own observations. Miranda notices that Amy looks like no angel she's seen in her picture books. She discovers that her questions about Amy's singing ability, which really addresses the relation of physical reality to emotion, are considered foolish by her father, because the verse is a "poem," an oblique commentary on the propagandistic function "literature" assumes for the male family.

Cousin Eva Parrington's opposite approach, however, offers little example for Miranda; Eva's attempts to transcend her female body, never allowing what she calls woman's "physical handicaps" to impede her fight for suffrage. She represents the demands of the rationalizing social order for erasure of female body as the cost for entrance in the public competition. In "Part III: 1912," Miranda at eighteen is returning home for the first time after her precipitous elopement. On the train she meets Eva, who is also coming back for Gabriel's funeral. As they begin to talk, Miranda remembers the legend of Amy's romance that has formed her own life. A "blot" on the family romances, the ill-favored Eva is an unmarried, dedicated schoolteacher, who has refused assimilation into male legend. Despite her will, Eva too has been molded by the male legends, unable to replace the still-strong family ties, however hated, with any other human relationship of intensity. Eva describes Amy's career far differently than the family does. Amy's glowing cheeks signaled tuberculosis; her romantic death, a suicide over a pregnancy conceived from a man other than Gabriel: "It was all smothered under pretty names, but that's all it was, sex" (216). Phrased as it is in the scientific, rationalized terms of the social structure, Eva's account distorts the meaning of Amy's life almost as much as Gabriel's romantic poetry. And Miranda's mother is as reified as Amy by Eva's casual answer to Miranda's query: "Your mother was a saint." Eva concludes that "the whole hideous institution [of family] should be wiped from the face of the earth" (217). Like the Grandmother, and unlike the men in the story, Eva herself cannot be lightly dismissed; she has suffered ridicule and imprisonment for her beliefs in women's rights. Eva is a figure of gallantry, far braver than Miranda's father, who flees to Mexico to avoid the consequences of Gabriel's affair of honor. Like Chopin's Mademoiselle Reisz, Cather's Kronborg, Glasgow's Dorinda Oakley before her, and Welty's Miss Eckhart of "June Recital" after her, Porter's Eva Parrington displays the all-consuming commitment that destroys the personal life.

As Eva walks away with Harry, both safe in a shared history, Miranda asks, "Where are my own people and my own time?" What language is adequate to tell her own experience as a woman free from male-imposed myths? John Hardy asks the question that defines Miranda's position at the end of the story: "But if the vote for women and the 'realism' of the new psychology of sex cannot provide the bases for new social institutions to accommodate the vital human impulses that the old forms threaten to stifle, then what can?" (*Katherine Anne Porter*, 32). Miranda now understands the flaw of old patriarchal romantic myth, and she guesses that the new rationalized body of science is in its way equally false to female experience. But, having glimpsed the limitations imposed on women by both patterns of belief, she has at yet no story that offers the truth of her own existence as a woman. Nonetheless, Miranda has full and childish confidence, as the adult narrator indicates, that she will break away from a woman's history that she fears is captive either to male romantic myth or to scientific rationalistic examination. She will find her own individual story written in her own distinctive language. Her leave-taking involves tearing herself out of a web of family relationships and communal language and rejecting impersonal biological explanations and associational language. Even though "Old Mortality" shows Miranda rejecting her Southern family as false and confining, yet the last sentence undercuts her youthful optimism in the liberation of individualism: "At least I can know the truth about what happens to me, she assured herself silently, making a promise to herself, in her hopefulness, her ignorance" (221). At this time, language seems to Miranda to be the key; if she can only get to *her* own language, *her* own time, *her* own place, she will be free.

Having declared her independence, Miranda, like Thea, wants to sleep one more time within the home of the family, in her childhood bed. To the woman writer, the house, with the meaning of *home*, assumes a far greater place in shaping the woman's identity. In Welty's *Delta Wedding* and *The Optimist's Daughter*, in Glasgow's *Vein of Iron*, in Cather's *Shadows on the Rock*, in Naylor's *Mama Day* and *Linden Hills*, the physical house itself, as in "Old Mortality" and "Pale Horse, Pale Rider," actually becomes the ultimate reality, serving as a physical center for the woman's history.[5] Thea Kronborg's final leave-taking from her maternal home, in fact, illustrates her assumption of her place in the community of art. The two "Miranda" novellas in *Pale Horse, Pale Rider* are connected by the lying down and rising up of the woman Miranda from the girl's bed in her old room.

"Pale Horse, Pale Rider" begins with Miranda's race with the Pale Rider to the bridge. She chooses not Grandmother's horse Fiddler or Amy's horse Miss Lucy, but Graylie, the horse of Miranda's emblematic color. Graylie, like Miranda, is not afraid of bridges. In her delirium, brought on by the war plague,—the figurative demoralization, the dis-ease, which has as its metaphor the flu pandemic—Miranda knows she must leave the shelter of the communal home that she wants, foolishly, to possess without the encumbering ties of relationships. Miranda succeeds in making her crossing to her own individual professional life as a newspaper reporter in a modern city, living in a small rented woman's space in a boardinghouse. No longer functioning in the traditional roles of daughter and wife, Miranda now claims the vocational identity of writer and the emotional passion of lover. Against the symbols of the spreading social structures, the war and the plague, Miranda must find her own way in the vocational competition. Noting Miranda's disillusionment with romantic love in "Old Mortality," Rosemary Hennessy concludes that Miranda will have to reject romance in order to reach back to her own memories. As other writers indicate, passion separates the individual woman from the women's community.

In Porter's female community, the Grandmother, the maternal ideal, controls life and death; in the bureaucratic social order of "Pale Horse,

Pale Rider," it is the machinery of the sterile hospital under the male leader. The novella portrays Miranda's time in purgatory within the modern technological society and indicates her road out. As she earlier saw the falsity of Gabriel's pursuit of Amy, now Miranda sees the failure of communication between individuals before the reality of the always demanding impersonal social structures. Repeatedly, Miranda shows the inability of an increasingly pervasive public language to express human reality, and Porter suggests the coercive potential of that language to force emotion into its prescribed channels. When the two Liberty Bond salesmen demand her contribution to the war effort as a token of her patriotism, Miranda thinks, "desperately silent," "'Suppose I said to hell with this filthy war? Suppose I asked that little thug, why aren't you rotting in Belleau Wood?'" (273). Again, when another volunteer questions their work in the hospital and Miranda agrees, both back away for fear of lack of "patriotism," an indication of the separation between women caused by the coercive national bureaucracies that put the young women's perky cheerleader sexuality at service of war morale. Finally, when Adam and she listen to a hackneyed patriotic speech before the third act of a play, Miranda thinks, "Did you mention Adam? If you didn't I'm not interested. What about Adam, you little pig?" (293). She knows that her own profession of reporter, an especially apt one, is "too dizzy for words." Lovers too find language separating, not joining, them as Porter contrasts the silent lovers' "dumb show" in a public place, a café, with the prattling account of the attempted seduction that serves as its accompaniment. Adam and Miranda also barricade themselves against the reality of death and war by banter similar in tone to the speech Paul Fussell calls "British phlegm" in *The Great War and Modern Memory* (21). Just before she crosses back over to death and leaves Adam, Miranda sees clearly the loneliness and fear of the citizens of her deadly society, which offers no connection between people except the specious "patriotic" language of an expanding public life: "There must be many of them here who think as I do, and we dare not say a word to each other of our desperation. . . . Does anybody here believe the things we say to each other?" (291). Twice, with the woman volunteer and with her colleague Towney, Miranda starts to communicate with other women, but then, out of fear, they retreat to the male language of "patriotism." In contrast, Porter shows the lovers singing a song remembered from childhood, which, unlike the empty public rhetoric, truly foretells the fate of Adam and Miranda.

In Miranda's encounters with the pragmatic workplace—the expanding vocational sector of the Great War society—she finds herself lacking in the necessary priorities for success in the rationalized working place. She and Towney suffer demotion to the "woman's beat" because of their refusal to print a torrid scandal after the pleas of the young girl's mother and a subsequent "scoop" by a rival newspaper. Refusing to expose other human beings, all of whom are women, to an anonymous, sensation-seeking mass readership for her own advancement, Miranda cannot separate the emotional consequences from the impersonal vocational setting. She ignores her male colleague's advice to flatter the famous performers; instead she makes trouble for herself by her honest drama criticism.

For his part, her lover, a true "American Adam," represents the potential of an earlier Edenic America, one closer to nature—again the female writer pictures the soil as a lover or, alternately, a partner rather than a resource for material exploitation. Described repeatedly in terms of unspoiled, unfallen nature, Adam has the coloring of the sunburnt American earth: "He really did look, Miranda thought, like a fine healthy apple this morning" (280). Again: "He was wearing his new uniform, and he was all olive and tan and tawny, hay colored and sand colored from hair to boots" (278). In a reverse of the male pattern as outlined by Annette Kolodny, Porter shows her American earth as a beloved familiar being rather than an adversary, often female, waiting for conquest. Miranda shares an attitude toward the natural world much like that of Alexandra in *O Pioneers!* and Kate Oliver in *Beyond Defeat*. Porter creates a modern America which has been tempted by a romance with its machines: "He loved airplanes too, all sorts of machinery, things carved out of wood and stone" (285). Like the classic American man of action created by male writers such as Ernest Hemingway, Adam has no patience with literature, repository of imagination and emotion; instead he seeks books of fact, "textbooks on engineering" (285). Hardy considers Adam as a representative of that natural innocence at the center of so much of the national literature, yet in his intense interest in technology, the machine, he suggests the increasingly mechanized nature of American life, an abiding concern of these writers. Miranda believes she can lead Adam back to his essential humanity as she brings him away from machines into nature, leaving the car, escaping the noise and smells of the urban setting for the beauty of the mountains. High above the city, Adam and Miranda suspect that the vista is illusory: "No doubt, Miranda said, quite apocryphal—'We need not believe it, but it is fine poetry'" (285). Again Porter questions the efficaciousness of literature in her contemporary society. In "Pale Horse, Pale Rider" the romantic retreat is, as it was in Glasgow, Jewett, and Cather, an illusion. Here the interlude occurs not in the present, but in memory, broken by the telephone's mechanical ringing, which summons Miranda back to work and, by implication, the vocational setting.

The modern bureaucracy controls life and death, time itself. The witnessing woman finds no institutions to counter the dominance of the clock as she finds herself alone in an impersonal regimented world. The family is a memory, sexuality serves to lead men to the death of the war machine, and the hospital machine drags Miranda back to a sterile life without Adam and without the Grandmother. Hardy names the villain of the story, the captured, measured time and the banal urban language of the "political and economic society" (81). Falling to the delirium of the war plague, Miranda leaves the modern vocational setting of newsroom, the bureaucracies of the hospital and army, for another level of primordial existence, where experience dwells in an ominous jungle of savagery. The vision of brutal riotous nature contrasts with the dream of mechanized horror of the hospital, a place of "pallid white fog" that conceals "all terror and weariness," that repairs "all the wrung faces and twisted backs and broken feet," a place where the nurses' hands are tarantulas, and a place where Dr. Hildesheim poisons the pure water of the well of her natural American home place.

Her back to the granite walls of her reclaimed living memory of her female family, Miranda finds the courage to seize and release, to control, the "angry point of life." She comes through to the serene rapture of immediate emotional connection; she lives with her family again, all accidents of the physical life and all falsities of paternal myth burned away into ineffable "prodigal warmth" of a vision of all the "living she had known," "pure identities," "alone, but not solitary" (311). She intuits that continuity and order occur only in "the fictions of memory," in Schwartz's pithy phrase. Miranda understands that although she has crossed the bridge from her childhood, her truth, the only heaven she will know, is the restored membership in the circle of love and responsibility of the first home, freed from paternalistic control. But this woman's home cannot live with either the savagery of mechanized war and the sterility of the hospital or with the brutality of instinctual nature. Porter indicates that her woman's experience will not yield to linear analysis; it comes to her through evocative wisdom, rather than deductive thought. She occupies the American "middle landscape," which is really a "no man's land."

Miranda turns back to life, to fetch her lover and restore her American Adam to the home place within an Eden of peace and content, but when she returns, she finds that the procedures of the technological structure have betrayed her. She has been seduced back to life as the woman volunteers seduce men to death. Adam is dead; his death hidden from her by the hospital personnel. She lives on a gray world, dressed in gray, with stockings "without clocks," wearing a perfume called "Bois d'Hiver." Betrayed by her own romantic passion and the hospital's efficiency, separated from her own female past, she awakes to the sounds of her Armistice, the singing of bedridden old women, the safely captured "mothers" who flute "My country 'tis of thee." The American innocence that would have allowed Miranda to build a home has been destroyed by the "old tomcats" who devour their kittens, leaving sterile female "patients," safely confined, to sing their ironic patriotic songs.

In "Pale Horse, Pale Rider," Porter presents even more bleakly than her literary predecessors the defeat of woman by the complex and impersonal social structures under male leadership. At every point in the narrative, women are put at the service of the war machine and its specious patriotism. Further, the language of the dominant discourse is depicted as separating them from each other, demanding their sexuality, their labor, their loyalty be given to the war, and the plague that symbolizes its effects. When they come through, they will, like Miranda, like the weakly grateful old ladies, be cured of their womanliness.

In the last account, Miranda cannot bring Adam—America—away from the machine and out of the war and disease. But the narrative suggests a further positive evolution in Porter's vision. In its final arrangement in *The Collected Stories*, Porter shows Miranda taking the Grandmother's place, starting with "Pale Horse, Pale Rider," becoming through the fictions of memory a mediator between both states of existence. Because in Porter's work, death mingles with birth, the female artist who would claim the solitary life of the creative artist can take her place in writing of those extremities through identification with the female spirit—not a Muse, for Adam is dead, but the wise woman, the Grandmother. The Grandmother, as Hennessy notes, is a model for female heroism to Miranda.

In the interrelated Miranda stories collected in *The Leaning Tower and Other Stories* (1944), Porter discovers that Miranda can move between the imaginary visions and the material existence because of her place in the female lineage inherited through Grandmother Sophia, an emotional and physical connection that she realizes in "The Grave." I will use the final arrangement as seen in the *Collected Stories,* in which the whole cycle is retitled "The Old Order," the title story renamed "The Journey," and "The Fig Tree" added to the book. These stories conclude the Miranda cycle and depict Miranda's expansion of models of female creativity through her education by Aunt Eliza. Much has been made of Porter's lack of fictional production, most forcibly by Givner—I believe this is misplaced.[6] The coming together of the stories as a whole and the writing of "Portrait: Old South" in *The Days Before* in 1952 shows Porter's artistic evolution as Miranda takes her place as a woman in her own time and in her own female history. Each of these groupings from short story to story cycle to separate book represents a coalescence of Porter's thoughts on the relationship of women to each other and to the large-scale bureaucratic and technological social order.

In "Old Mortality," the grandmother and the granddaughter share no common ground, looking at each other across an unbridgeable chasm. At the end of the cycle, the grandmother's memories and forms become one with the artist granddaughter's own vibrant memory and sympathetic understanding, a process Porter depicts as ritualistic: although the form of a ritual like the Eucharist changes with every occurrence, its substance does not. Like the earlier authors, Porter discovered the need to place her own female experience within a woman's context transcending the purely personal. As they appear in *The Collected Stories of Katherine Anne Porter* (1965), the short stories appear in this order: "The Source," "The Journey," "The Witness," "The Circus," "The Last Leaf," "The Fig Tree," and "The Grave." In all of the stories, Sophia—again, the name is significant—is present as a living force, even though she is physically dead during the present action of two of the stories, "The Last Leaf" and "The Grave." The earliest of the stories published were those centered on the black servants, "The Witness" and "The Last Leaf," followed by those dealing with Miranda as a child, "The Grave" and "The Circus." The "Grandmother" stories and "The Fig Tree" were among the last works Porter published as she worked back from Miranda to the female family.

"The Source" portrays the Grandmother as an archetypal figure much like Glasgow's Grandmother Fincastle of *Vein of Iron.* DeMouy deems her "not only a person but a symbol of her world," a type of Great Mother (120). A brave, stubborn woman who brings civilized decorum to a succession of homes, the Grandmother illustrates the fate of the forgotten wives of the pioneers, showing Sophia's frustration before the feckless wandering of the men in her family. With the death of the fathers, Sophia Jane and Nannie at last can create their own shared realm. Porter rewrites American history, as have Cather, Jewett, and Glasgow, to include the mother's contribution to the creation of the American homeland. The old woman's insistence on ceremony and propriety here seems less the querulousness of jealous old age and more an attempt to bring civilized feminine order to one American backwoods settlement after another. As she says, "I have planted five orchards in three States, and now I see only one tree in bloom" (*The Old Order* 322). She offers her grandchildren, especially Miranda, the only permanence "in a world that seemed otherwise without fixed authority or refuge" (324).

Like such maternal demigoddesses as Gilman's Mothers, Grandmother Fincastle, Kate Oliver, Ántonia Shimerda, Cecile Auclair, and Granny Weatherall, Sophia in "The Source" appears dispensing food and justice, setting house, farm buildings, and gardens right, minding and mending children's manners, and finally dusting and ordering the library. Hers is a life filled with labor until the end of "The Journey," where she drops dead after having caused a fifty-foot adobe wall to be moved on her son's farm. DeMouy identifies her divinity as that of the cyclical goddesses of agricultural fertility such as Demeter.

In anticipation of the last story of Miranda's artistic epiphany, the Grandmother too yearns for the ease of fabled, pampered femininity, the life that the romantic illusion has taught them to expect as a female birthright: "She always imagined herself as walking at leisure in the

shade of the orchards watching the peaches ripen; she spoke with long-
ing of clipping the rosebushes, or of tying up the trellised honeysuckle
with her own hands" (321). Instead of leisure, however, Sophia finds
hard physical labor and adjudication of family and community squab-
bles. In reality, her long life has been a rear-guard action against the
reckless, controlling world of the male leadership, the world that
brings slavery in her time and will bring the Great War in her granddaughter's age. Like Ellen Weatherall, her husband passes away after
she bears her children and undertakes her life's work.

As a former slave and a woman, Nannie, Sophia's servant and companion, has been subject to men too and, even more, to the white race,
but in "The Last Leaf" we see Nannie sitting in front of her cabin:
"But she was no longer the faithful old servant Nannie, a freed slave;
she was an aged Bantu woman of independent means, sitting on the
steps, breathing the free air" (349), her face the "eyeless mask" of the
female seer. Like Sophia and like Myra Driscoll, she comes into her
authentic identity through her maternal group as she faces death. Unrue writes that Nannie's face becomes the mask of ritual looking back
at her people's past, whereas DeMouy considers Sophia and Nannie as
"two halves of one universal female experience" (123). That Porter
held racist views of blacks, especially in her old age, cannot be denied,
and here Porter elides the realities of slavery. Nonetheless, the figure
of Nannie possesses dignity and wisdom, which transcend Porter's
conscious attitudes, and she becomes a cocreator of the home place in
"The Old Order," an essential collector of woman's memories and narrator of women's stories.

Like the female literary artist, the wise woman preserves and lovingly commemorates the plain tools of the pioneer past, through her
work and example molding the artifacts of the past into a homeland
and a history. Furthermore, in Sophia's relationship with Nannie, her
former slave, the two women overcome the limitations imposed on
them both by an unjust male-controlled hierarchical social order. The
personal tie of shared female experience reorders the dominant individual—shadow companion relationship appearing in so much American male literature. The bond between the two women is stronger than
that of mistress-servant, longer than life, for it is the bond between
women who have come through numerous childbirths, nursed and

nurtured each other's babies, and buried each other's dead, often in defiance of the male-defined rules that seek to separate them. In "The Journey," the two women sit together, like Fates, guarding the present, and putting the future into a pattern of continuity and stability: "Even the future seemed like something gone and done with when they spoke of it. It did not seem an extension of their past, but a repetition of it" (327). As they stitch their past and their future into recognizable patterns, they appear as the shapers of the human history, again an appearance of sewing as the metaphor for the creation of a civilization and art out of the shared communal memory and imagination. Both Nannie and Sophia appear as sources of creativity, as they weave their stories over the great universe, the tasks of the day mingle with thoughts of the eternity they will pass together and again sewing, especially quilting becomes emblematic of the woman's language, "often a scrap of silk under their hands would start them on long trains of family reminiscences" (328). Sewing serves as the metaphoric tie between the literature produced by artist-woman and the domestic arts produced by the woman's community.

In *The Old Order*, Porter discovers her connection with the female family, its history and people, a tradition that the younger Miranda so confidently rejected in "Old Mortality." Throughout the Grandmother stories, the tie between the independent Miranda of the other novellas and the Sophia of the old order grows. With "The Circus," the center of the cycle shifts from Sophia to Miranda as "the old order gives way to the new." However painfully, Grandmother reconstructed her home and replanted her garden, extending the pioneer experience beyond the dominant individual; in contrast, Miranda has no received role, no home really. With the Grandmother's death, the Old Order passes, leaving Miranda with the memories and the traditions but no accustomed social matrix in which to continue those patterns. Each of the Miranda stories shows the girl preparing to define her womanhood in a way that grants her continuity of experience. In "The Circus" we as readers understand that Miranda sees her world more clearly, its shams and casual cruelties, than the scoffing members of the family around her; only Grandmother observes sagely to Miranda's unheeding father that the past extends into the future, that there is a consequential history to which she is heiress. Charles Kaplan connects

Sophia's prophetic statement with the ending of "The Grave" as an acknowledgment of the power of immediate emotional memory both women share.

The next story, "The Fig Tree," presents a competing demigoddess, Aunt Eliza, who is literally a giant figure. As she appears briefly in "Old Mortality," Porter describes her as "one solid pyramidal monument from floor to neck" who is so much a part of the outdoors that she "quite squeezed through doors" (174). William Nance deems Eliza a nature goddess, who grants Miranda an alternate conscious route to Sophia's domesticity, one that passes the doors of life and death as closely as that of her sister. DeMouy marks Eliza as the teacher, who challenges the authority of the Grandmother. This sibyl brings Miranda's intellect into another world, the knowledge of which eventually will allow Miranda to be our observing, detached witness, our seer. Appropriately, the Grandmother takes little part in the central action of the story. Lest the reader escape the symbolism of Eliza as seer, Porter describes her as almost an extension of the Texas earth around her, as monumental as the mountains or the dust storms. She succeeds Adam in the Miranda story cycle as the representation of the native earth. Filling the door with her great frame, Aunt Eliza looms "like a mountain" with "iron-colored" hair, "snuff-colored" eyes and skirts," and when she sits, she appears to be "sitting solidly on herself" (359). With her telescope, her microscope, and her burning glass, Eliza grants Miranda new perspectives on life and death. In Nance's opinion, her vision is represented by those optical implements that grant the woman the magic of extended sight, access to previously forbidden (male) worlds.

The story centers on Miranda's fear that she may have buried a chick alive; Eliza shows the child that the "weep, weep" Miranda fears is the cry of the buried chick pursuing her is merely the call of the tree frogs. Eliza gives Miranda an alternate explanatory paradigm that counters the false male stories that entrapped the young women in the assumptions of paternalistic old order, just as Sophia and Nannie give her the stability and creativity to counter the mechanized bureaucratic institutions. Finally, the reader understands how Miranda got her name. As the children and the mountain-woman climb a ladder to look at the stars, Miranda calls out "in pure rapture" that recalls the central scene in "Pale Horse, Pale Rider":

"Oh, it's like another world!"

"Why, of course, child," said Great-Aunt Eliza, in her growling voice, but kindly, "other worlds, a million other worlds."

"Like this one?" asked Miranda, timidly.

"Nobody knows, child. . . ."

"Nobody knows, nobody knows," Miranda sang to a tune in her head, and when the others walked on, she was so dazzled with joy she fell back by herself. (361)

With this discovery, the cycle anticipates its conclusion; Miranda finds her brave new world. She discovers that the Old Order and even the Grandmother do not offer her the only definition of womanhood. As the child Miranda sings to herself, dropping away from Eliza, dazzled by the knowledge that her childhood world is only one of millions, the intellectual shape of the narrating consciousness comes clear—past and future join. Miranda gains the ability to rise out of herself, to break the prison of modern isolation. Miranda comes into her own creativity by learning from both the women of the old order and the new social structures, women who demonstrate that both those experiences may be purged of male definition and control. The women of the Old Order have each in their turn proved mothers to Miranda, the spinster Eliza and the seer Nannie rivaling even Sophia in influence.

"The Grave" expands Miranda's knowledge into a female context and at last connects her Grandmother's experience with her own, portraying Miranda's coming of age as a creator and the passing of the Old Order. Now the Grandmother is dead and the motherless family is considered to be "running down with the Grandmother no longer there to hold it together" (365). Miranda discovers her female identity, its connections to the interrelated boundaries of life and death, and Miranda's own awareness of the eternal presence of the now-dead Sophia. As the narrative begins, Miranda and her brother Paul, out hunting, are playing on the grave of their long-dead grandfather, abandoned through the "constancy and possessiveness of his widow" as Sophia carries along her dead with her living as she conducts her rootless American life. Although Constance Rooke and Bruce Wallis view the setting as a fallen Eden, it seems more likely in light of Porter's other fictional motifs that the garden is the neglected American nature after the loss of the female seer. The circumstance also reprises the figure of the woman's garden, which has appeared repeatedly in Gilman, Glasgow, Wharton, and Cather. Without access to the home place, the children are abandoned, left to wander without guide among the intertwining boundaries of life and death. Like Miranda, Sophia too had no fixed home in the restless American frontier of her life, but she nonetheless forged bonds of continuity and connection amidst temporality.

As the children play on the graves, the tomboy Miranda uncovers a small silver dove, poised for flight, a perfectly shaped familiar symbol of transcendence of time and the body, while Paul in his turn discovers a gold wedding band, a seamless emblem of loving interdependence. They trade, the boy giving the girl the ring, the girl ceding to him the dove. The symbol of artistic flight appeals less to Miranda than the ring, which turns her against her tomboy garb. Her first impulse is to return to the house, bathe, and put on her sister's violet talcum powder. Then she will "put on the thinnest, most becoming dress she owned, with a big sash, and sit in a wicker chair under the trees" (365). Like Sophia in "The Journey," Miranda at first wants to sink into the promise of romantic femininity. For the moment she forgets the lessons of Great-Aunt Eliza for the ease of woman's life in the family legends, foreshadowing Miranda's later elopement. But even as she dreams, almost turning back to the house and the lawn from the field and nature, Paul shoots a female rabbit. In skinning the animal, the children see that the bloated belly contains unborn baby rabbits, perfectly formed. Suddenly, Miranda understands emotionally, profoundly, that she herself is female. Even as the now-dead grandmother had tended and moved her graves and brought the family to life, the granddaughter stands in line to bring forth the living family and to bury her dead. In a knowledge deeper than words, than rationality, Miranda senses that she is "learning what she had to know" (367), an intuitive knowledge of her inherited place in the family scheme of things, in contrast to her rational observations of the farm animals' mating and, it should be added, in contrast to the male legends of "Old Mortality." Now she has the felt knowledge, which deepens the deductive reasoning and objective observations of Aunt Eliza.

The universal, elemental nature of the event completely obliterates Miranda's romantic dreams of dresses and leisure, as earlier Sophia and Granny Weatherall turned from feminine ease to active creation, as later the death of Adam will erase forever the appeal of the sentimental secondhand tales of Amy's romantic death. Birth and death are at the same time ephemeral and eternal, interwoven, as are the fates of the dead baby creatures buried in the womb of their mother, as Miranda herself was and is contained and contains the influence, the memory, and the female body of her dead Grandmother. The ring, a token of male adoration, is transformed into an emblem of female infinity, its pledge of immortality through female procreative potential, tied forever in memory to the individual artistic creativity promised by the dove.

At the end of the story, twenty years later, Miranda stands in an Indian marketplace in Mexico, the sort of marketplace, in fact, she previously idealized in her fiction. Alone, away from home, away from her mother tongue, Miranda has chosen, we know, to reject the traditional female legacy of the ring, the tasks and female relationships represented by Sophia and Nannie. Instead she has reached for the promise of the dove, which, as a girl child, she so quickly, almost instinctively handed to her brother. She believes she has broken that golden circle, that female connection, by her flight to Mexico. The circle of the ring is now rejoined. A vendor holds up a tray of dyed sugar animals, baby chicks, birds, and rabbits, and suddenly the scents of the Mexican market bring her home; they were like "the mingled sweetness and corruption she had smelled that other day in the empty cemetery at home" (367). At first, the smells and the associations flicker in recollection with the abandoned grave, a suggestion of Porter's recurring Saturn–Eucharist motif, which is central in "Flowering Judas." Then Miranda feels the "dreadful vision" of reality fade as the immediacy of her artistic emotional memory brings back the mingled hope and innocence of her "brother whose childhood face she had forgotten" and the joy of the silver dove, which is now hers. In the midst of the decay and death of fallen Mexico, the child's face appears, beckoning the wanderer back to her Grandmother's home.

Like Jim Burden's image of the immigrant girl on the Latin page in *My Ántonia*, Miranda's experience sums up the meaning of the author's work and the protagonist's life in an image that redeems the experience distorted in the flood of language. Like emblematic scenes in earlier authors, the last moment strives to say more than the specialized, linear language can summon; Porter hopes, like the women artists before her, to summon the present emotion of ritual and immediate experience. Under the force of that pictographic memory, past and future collapse together, and the family is rejoined beyond the limits of death and life.

With the closing of the Old Order cycle, Katherine Anne Porter joined with the Grandmother and reconciled her profession with her gender. The home place lives and continues through the reclaimed language of the individual woman. Porter has shown the modern American social order falling into decadence by the passing of the mother. The young Adam, after all, suffers not martyrdom, like the Mexican flower prince, for renewal through blood, but mere extinction through the sickness of the war flu. With the neglect of woman's contribution, the death of the son becomes pointless, for the American land is not renewed. At the end, Miranda herself is subsumed into the mother, and the home place is renewed through the daughter's memories and the woman's language. Through her coming of age, she reclaims the power of creation. Whereas her Grandmother labored physically, Miranda, like Cather's Kronborg, will express her maternal heritage at the same time that she gains her strength as an artist from her maternal tradition. In the last of the Miranda stories, Porter helps us to to understand that the Old Order still lives.

Recipes, in the first place, had to be imparted—
there was something oracular in the transac-
tion—and however often they were made after
that by others, they kept their right names.
I make Mrs. Mosal's White Fruitcake every
Christmas, having got it from my mother, who
got it from Mrs. Mosal, and I often think to
make a friend's fine recipe is to celebrate her
once more, and in that cheeriest, most aromatic
of places to celebrate in, the home kitchen.
                    —"The Flavor of Jackson"
                        The Eye of the Story

[My mother] was teaching me one more, almost her last, lesson; emotions do not grow old.
I knew I would feel as she did, and I do.
                    —*One Writer's Beginnings*

6.

The Oldest Root Sometimes Blooms Most

EUDORA WELTY

EUDORA WELTY ONCE WROTE that Austen's family chronicles "give
their testimony to Jane Austen's ardent belief—which our century's
city dwellers find odd—that the unit of everything worth knowing in
life is in the family" ("The Radiance of Jane Austen," *The Eye of the
Story,* 7). In this passage, Welty implicitly states her own authorial
creed. Her writing has focused on the fate of the female family and the
woman's community in the face of an encroaching urbanized, technological, and bureaucratized modernism, a theme finessed by the fairy
tale *The Robber Bridegroom* (1942), but dominant in *Delta Wedding*

(1946), *Losing Battles* (1970), and *The Optimist's Daughter* (1972), and her short story collection, *The Golden Apples* (1949).

For Welty, the home retains its place at the center of her autobiographical account, *One Writer's Beginnings*. Welty remembers herself as the beloved oldest daughter of two loving parents.[1] Her memories recall a world sharply divided between the impressive public world of her Northern-born executive father and the sheltering domestic sphere of her West Virginia-born mother. The three lectures that compose *One Writer's Beginnings* (1984) move forward from "Listening" to "Learning to See" to "Finding a Voice," as the author traces her progress from the passive girl child to the mature master of woman's language. "Listening" begins with the child's first memories: the voice of her mother. Her first "literary" memories are of her mother Chestina reading stories aloud while mother and daughter shared their days; the child thus connected literature with the mother's voice rather than with the printed page. As happened with Glasgow, the concept of the book as object contradicts Welty's experiences in Chestina's kitchen: "It had been startling and disappointing to me to find out that story books had been written by *people*, that books were not natural wonders, coming up of themselves like grass" (5). From her mother's stories, her memory moves out to other women's voices; she realizes that she "had to grow up and learn to listen for the unspoken as well as the spoken" (15).

The child next passes to the authority of the principal of Davis School, Miss Duling. Offering young Eudora an alternate model of womanhood, Miss Duling inspires the author's "perhaps inordinate number of schoolteacher characters" (23). Early in her life the author seizes upon two models of female achievement, the mother and the unmarried schoolteacher, models who appear in her novels from *The Golden Apples* to *The Optimist's Daughter*. Mother and teacher find their reconciliation at last in her re-creation of the home place in *The Optimist's Daughter*.

Throughout the autobiography Welty contrasts the public business world of her father, Christian Welty, the optimist who believed in a rationalized, progressive future, with the private domestic sphere of her mother, the pessimist whose "mind was a mass of associations," connecting past and future in a continuous, expanding present (19). Her father is characterized as "stable, reticent, self-contained, willing to be patient if need be, and, in all *he* said, factual" (53). In contrast to Chestina's kitchen and its traditional housewifely tools, Christian Welty's library table holds the scientifically created instruments of extended sight: maps, telescope, camera, magnifying glass, kaleidoscope, and gyroscope. He replaces Chestina Welty's somewhat flawed singing with a Victrola, the mother's voice replaced by a more perfect machine. Michael Kreyling notes that Christian Welty is a checker of train schedules, a measurer of time ("Subject and Object," 634). Leavened though they are with his love and solicitous care, his daughter's memories of her father identify him with the measured, the mechanical, and the factual, the qualities associated with the great public modern world.

Throughout her work, Welty defines and contrasts the maternal language—physical, oral—with the paternal language—abstract, written; in many respects these two languages parallel the communal and associational languages. As a reader and a writer, Welty finds that her early experience of literature as an oral medium continues into her maturity: "There has never been a line I didn't *hear*" (*One Writer's Beginnings*, 12, emphasis Welty's). Welty's maternal or local language suggests its orality with short sentences, ample use of conjunctions bridging disparate elements, commands and questions—all forms demanding response and interaction. Robert Heilman cites these stylistic tendencies in Welty's work: short, simply constructed sentences, generous use of coordination, little recourse to analytical, logical argument, very few abstract nouns, and ample use of dialogue, exclamations, expletives, colloquial language, and compact syntax.

Discussion of a particular passage will best illustrate Welty's use of language and metaphor to suggest the connectedness of experience in the woman's local neighborhood. She introduces a symphony blending the sounds of the human voice with those of nature and home in *Losing Battles*, as she connects the song of a mockingbird with the voices of the family on the porch at Granny Vaughn's birthday celebration. As the passage continues, the author ties the natural world of the mockingbird with the sounds of homely items and wild and domestic creatures, "some like pans clashing on the stove, some like chains dropping into buckets, some like pigeons in the barn, some like roosters in the morning, some like the evening song of katydids, making a chorus"

(27). Having linked natural and domestic worlds, Welty now introduces the dialogue that carries the greater part of her narrative:

> "Well, crops was laid by one more year. Time for the children to all be swallowed up in school," Uncle Percy's thready voice had already begun. "We can be sure that Granny Vaughn had started 'em off good, praying over 'em good and long at the table, and they all left good and merry, fresh, clean, and bright. Jack's on his best behavior. Drove 'em off to the school bus, got 'em all there a-shrieking. . . . That's from Etoyle."
>
> "But it don't take Ella Fay long!" prompted Aunt Nancy.
>
> "Crammed in at her desk, she took a strong a strong notion for candy," Uncle Percy quavered. "So when the new teacher looked the other way, she's across the road and into the store after it."
>
> "And shame once more on a big girl like that," said Miss Lexie.
>
> "Well, wouldn't you have liked the same?" Uncle Noah Webster teased. "A little something sweet to hold in your cheek, Lexie?"
>
> "Not I."
>
> Aunt Nanny winked at the porchful. "The first day I had to go back to Banner School, I'd get a gnawing and a craving for the same thing!"
>
> "And been switched for it!" they cheered. "By a good right arm!"
>
> "It didn't take Ella Fay but one good jump across a dry mudhole to the store. And old Curly Stovall's just waiting."
>
> "Stovall? Wait a minute, slow down, halt," interrupted Aunt Cleo.
>
> "You're a Stovall," several guessed.
>
> "Wrong. I was married to one, the first time round," she said. . . . "It's a whole roaring horde of 'em still there" (27–28).

So the passage continues, the family history spun out by familiar voices, connections made between the family gathered there, the natural world mingling through birds and butterflies with the tasks of the celebration. Moreover, the porch is an especially apt setting, standing as it does between nature and domestic space. The conversation is shorthand, shared history and future assumed—"That's from Etoyle," for example, names the source for the account of the children's arrival at school. Speech is kept within the local context; the metaphors too are local, referring to and tying together the domestic life and the natural environment. Clearly, speech here not only communicates a story—in the case of well-loved stories the facts are almost secondary—but it also reinforces the relationships of the group. This local language is the language of the lifelong neighbor, the mother, the sister, understood by intonation, by look, shaped by emotions. Welty's skill is such that we as outsiders are brought into this language, partaking of the context for the length of the narrative.

Moreover in *Losing Battles* and other works, Welty celebrates the connectedness of human existence through the abundant use of similes, the sparsity of punctuation, and the borrowing of myth from several traditions. J. A. Bryant, Jr., John F. Fleischauer, Harriet Pollack, and Patricia Yaeger have written on Welty's distinctive use of language; the characteristics they detail suggest that Welty re-creates the female family within the American neighborhood by retaining several linguistic attributes suggestive of the bounded community. As Fleischauer notes the characteristics of Welty's styles, the similarities emerge: the expletives indicative of colloquial speech, her figures of speech, which tie the object at hand with unexpected objects of the natural world or the home, a lack of logical connectives, an emphasis on feelings rather than facts, specificity of place, the use of myth, and the single perspective's persistent unreliability. Welty's prose achieves its coherence from symbolic patterns and parallel structures rather than rational linearity and abstract ideas.

In contrast, the associational language of abstraction, of the citizen, of the father, of the legalistic optimists (and Miss Julia Mortimer), in its disregard of human emotions and natural realities renders its followers comic in Welty's writing. Significantly, the communications of Christian Welty, Judge McKelva, George Fairchild, Judge Moody, and, to a lesser extent, Miss Julia are best represented by the written word. These are people who in their attempt to control the social and natural environments by impersonal rules often disregard the forces of nature and the power of human emotion. They are tied to the father's language, and the mother's world stands as a reproach to their rigidity in the books in which they appear.

Welty reinforces her use of language by centering the four novels in this discussion on family rituals: *Delta Wedding* on the nuptials of the daughter of a plantation family; the funeral of Miss Katie Rainey and the June recital of *The Golden Apples;* the ninetieth birthday celebration of Granny Vaughn and the funeral of Miss Julia Mortimer in *Losing Battles,* and the funeral of Judge McKelva in *The Optimist's Daughter.* As we the readers and outsiders view these women-controlled ritual events, Welty simultaneously educates us in the ways of the community and exposes our distance from it by withholding circumstances implicitly understood by its members. The natural world is enlivened, often anthropomorphized, drawn in living connection to the elder woman's house, joining the natural and domestic worlds. J. A. Bryant relates the "recovery of the confident narrator" with Welty's emphasis on community and communal language in *Losing Battles*, noting that we feel that "all things are connected, or at least connectable" (68). The sense of connectedness extends to everyday reality and wonderful events, united with ease in many of Welty's books. Through the confluence of myth, ritual, communal language, and a strong sense of the visual, Welty hopes to imbue literature with the immediacy and power, the ability to unite scattered social order, formerly exerted by religion. From her first book of stories, *The Curtain of Green* and her first novel, the fairy tale *The Robber Bridegroom*, Welty has striven to transcend the bounds of the actual, to join the reader in a universal loving community. In "Love and Separateness in Eudora Welty," Robert Penn Warren wrote that Welty defeats our expectations of normality to achieve her fictional goals, observing that her logic is "not quite the logic by which we live, or think we live, our ordinary daylight lives" (157). Welty achieves her immediate emotion, the communal awe, without recourse to religious symbolism, preferring instead to use fairy tale and myth to underlie her language usage; she early discovered that the reverence she holds "for the holiness of life is not ever likely to be entirely at home in organized religion" (*Beginnings*, 33).

In such works as *Losing Battles, The Optimist's Daughter, The Golden Apples, The Wide Net,* and *Delta Wedding* as well as the autobiographical *One Writer's Beginnings,* Welty opposes the woman-centered, most often pastoral, home to both the dangers of the undomesticated natural world and to the incursions of corrupt, man-made modernisms: to the Yazoo River—called by the Indians the River of Death—and to the railroad (here, as in Cather, a negative entity), the penitentiary (a dustbin for the legal system), and the beauty parlor (gathering place for Welty's "town girls," barren female consumers given over to fashion and gossip). These harsh environments allow neither the feminine emotion nor the female sexuality full and safe expression. The forest and the swamp hide the marauding, wandering males of *The Robber Bridegroom*—"At the Landing," or "Sir Rabbit"—whereas the town forces the woman into the outlines of the barren spiteful female caricatures of "Why I Live at the P.O." or "The Petrified Man."

The godlike males in her work, King MacLain, Jack Renfro, and Denis and George Fairchild, in contrast to the women, move out of the community, paralleling the journey away from society of the heroic American individual as well the hero of the classic quest. All, as well as other important male figures such as Judge Moody and Judge McKelva, have been involved with the law as practitioner or victim. As the machinery of the invading woodsmen represents the technology, the legal definitions represent the associational language of the impersonal outside social order. The more immersed in the legal system the man, the less emotional insight, the more "optimistic."

Delta Wedding (1946) shows the isolated agricultural home place with woman's traditional roles of mother and bride intact at the instant just before these possibilities threaten to dissolve into the larger, national social organization; in many respects Welty is torn between nostalgia of the type seen in the portrayal of ideal past communities in Porter and Cather and the creation of an ongoing home place. Set in the Delta, beginning on September 10, 1923, a year Welty chose because it "was uneventful," allowing her "to concentrate on the people without undue outside influences" (Bunting, *Conversations*, 50). The time of year suggests Welty's dual meaning—for Welty characteristically doubles experience—harvest, yes, but also the approach of death.

The narrative action centers on the conventional celebration of renewed familial order, a wedding of the daughter of the family. The Fairchilds of Shellmound plantation live in a fluid continuum of past and future, life and death, all members of the family being present, immediately, emotionally. The framing witness of the novel, nine-year-old orphaned niece Laura McRaven quickly realizes that her mother remains more of a Fairchild in death than she, an urban outsider, does in life. Welty invests Shellmound and its inhabitants with a sense of timelessness: "Laura from her earliest memory had heard how they 'never seemed to change at all,'" but the family changes on the "inside"—that is, the individual members in their changing relationships hold "iridescent life" (15). To indicate Shellmound's harmony, the music of the piano underscores the action, the bridesmaid player unseen like the female narrator herself. Identifying pastoral elements in the novel, John Hardy points to the lack of introspection, which shows forth the communal, ritual intent, identifying the music of the unseen piano as "a figure of the author's omnipresence" ("Region and Symbol," 406).

Houses here serve as the repository for the female family's history; each recipe in the kitchen, each rose in the garden, each custom and anecdote of the family history bears a woman's name and celebrates and reinforces the family. As Madelon Sprengnether notes, women "hold all the narrative threads" and "maintain the social fabric of the family" (127). Joseph Childers offers a parallel observation that "the women are the Homers who control the narrative" (246). Aunt Mac and Aunt Shannon, for example, take small part in the central action of the narrative, yet in their widowhood they raised all the seven children of the previous generation, and "if anything should, God prevent it, happen to Ellen now, [Aunt Mac] was prepared to do it again" (67). The Fairchild women have held the land and run the household perhaps since Indian times. Robbie Reid muses, "It was as if the women had exacted the place, the land, for something—for something they had had to give" (145). As with previous writers, Welty rewrites *her* American history, the narrative of the woman's home.

Throughout the novel, sunny Shellmound has a reverse underworld, which suggests the buried forces of the fields and river—death, male violence, and uncontained sexuality. The dual fictional world of Eudora Welty operates on the contrast of sunlight and shadow, thus, the Demeter figure Ellen Fairchild has her opposite, the mother of secrets, the unchangeable sorceress Partheny. Suzanne Marrs connects these two women through their shared immersion in the extrarational, "Partheny's faith in the magical serves as an emblem of Ellen's intuitions" (700). The seer, who first appears coming out of a trance, is "taller than a man," "midnight-blue" in complexion with a midnight-blue dress, and on her head a white cap like a "crown" (128). Above all, she has the timelessness that marks her divinity. Partheny and Aunt Studney, also a wise woman, are by no means minor characters because they reveal the magic and mystery attending the rites of renewal. Without the permission and active help of these two female seers, Shellmound cannot renew itself. Aunt Studney, for example, brings the magic sack of bees that bless Marmion with fertility and renewal as Dabney prepares to start life in darkened, deserted Marmion, and the matriarch Partheny comes out of her trance as the wedding nears to bake the aphrodisiac black patticake for the groom and to affirm that the un-confined sexuality represented by the lost garnet pin is safely banished.

Along with outsiders Laura and Robbie, Ellen Fairchild, the Vir-ginia-born mother of *Delta Wedding*, introduces us to the daylight, public face of the Shellmound's world of women. Her perspective brings the reader closer to the center, because Ellen, unlike the city child Laura, the mad Virgie, and the black seers, occupies the dual position of insider and outsider in Shellmound. Sensitive and frail, Ellen nonetheless repeatedly summons the strength to gather in the orphans and the misfits who come to the borders of her life at the plantation. Abandoned by her own mother, who returned without ex-planation three years later, Ellen seeks, like many another earlier women protagonist, to re-create the woman's community out of the devastation wrought by war and natural catastrophe. Serving as the keeper of the gates of Shellmound, Ellen announces Laura's accep-tance into the family with the same certainty with which she seeks to reconcile Robbie Reid and to understand George Fairchild.

As the careers of the other mother-women have suggested in these writers' works, passionate sexual involvement is sacrificed to insure the stability of the domestic order. The symbolic motif for this renuncia-tion is the loss of the garnet brooch given to Ellen during courtship. Early in the novel, she dreams of sitting under a cypress tree and see-ing the lost brooch "shining in the leaves like fire." She "knelt down and took her pin back" as she is drawn to the emotion of that intense time (65). The romantic dream comes as a warning of sexual disorder, although Ellen converts it to a pleasant bedtime story for her child. Finally lost in the Yazoo River by Laura, the flash of sexuality buried in the River of Death, the brooch finds its reflection in the red glass buttons flashing on the dress of the runaway girl, the archetypal daughter who "sheds" beauty, who meets Ellen in undomesticated na-ture. Refusing Ellen's help and shrugging off her warnings of dangers in the woods—in Welty the province of rampant male sexuality—the lost girl refuses to enter the woman's community and continues her flight to Memphis. The girl's subsequent sexual encounter with George, her later death, and Ellen's inability to shelter her suggest the power of passionate, uncommitted sexuality to destroy Shellmound.

The glow of sexuality in the pin reflects the flames of the night lamp, an article identified with the women of the family as long as old Aunt

Primrose can remember. Strangely, the lamp shows a fire destroying a small town, its people, and the natural world itself, [it] "was all on fire, even to the motion of the fire, which came from the candle flame drawing" (46). The vestal virgin aunts, Jim Allen and Primrose, give Dabney this ambiguous wedding gift, which depicts the community's destruction by desire, but which warms, not consumes, as long as the lamp around the flame, the sheath of womanly order and female art, remains intact. Passion is contained, yet endlessly recurring through the simple domestic object, which glows with history, with controlled emotion. Significantly, Welty chooses to depict the effect of art with the same female-identified article in her essay, "Place in Fiction" in *The Eye of the Story.* Welty here implies the wholeness found in the ritualistic woman's utterance, observing that the lamp when lighted "is the combination of internal and external, glowing at the imagination as one; and so is the good novel" (120).

Continuing that interior and exterior existence lie so close and so inseparable, Welty ties the ongoing female domestic community with the community of art in fictional narrative and critical essay through the figure of this particular lamp. Both forms of creativity, contained within each other and aligned in Welty's imagination, blaze with emotion controlled and defined by creativity. Art defeats time and death through its endless repetition, as the woman's domestic tradition achieves its immortality by its time-honored usage, granting to the vicissitudes of the individual life an order that both shelters and shapes. Furthermore, through the linking of interior and exterior, Welty summons the physical presence of the word found in ritual and in women's writing as well as the joining of female body and spirit.

In common with other women authors, the female garden becomes the symbol for feminine order and care. Welty shows the pregnant Ellen bidding good-bye to her garden as her daughter leaves with Troy on her wedding trip. The scene of the garden just before harvest holds key elements of other wise women at home in their natural creations: Glasgow's Kate Oliver and Hunter's Fare; Cather's Ántonia and her farm; Gilman's Mothers and Herland; Porter's Granny Weatherall and her home; Porter's Miss Sophia Jane and her farm land, Naylor's Miranda and Willow Springs, Jewett's Mrs. Todd and her New England garden, and Welty's own Miss Katie Rainey and her renunciation of the natural world. Daughter gone, captured by the field god, the wise woman surveys the natural world and prepares it for its rest: caterpillar nets to be burned, chrysanthemums to tie up, dead iris leaves to be removed, dahlias to separate, and hyacinth bulbs to be separated and spread. She thinks of her care to children and to the garden in equal terms: "What would happen to everything if she were not here to watch it. . . . Of all the things she would leave undone, she hated leaving the garden untended—sometimes as much as leaving Bluet or Battle" (226). The bees buzz, a conventional symbol of fertility; the butterfly flutters, in Welty a symbol of temporality; and the birds fly, an image of the creative spirit. As with Porter's "The Grave," the mingled images of birth, growth, decay, and death swirl around Ellen, indicating her position as the female creator. Sprengnether writes that the cyclical narrative replicates the circle of mourning and celebration of the Demeter–Kore myth, which, in its turn, connects to the cycle of life both in nature and in humanity. By consistent use of the imagery and its accompanying myth, Welty imbues Ellen, "the mother of all the world," with eternal power of renewal; she, like her fictional sisters, guards the rites of life and death. The mingling of birth and death calls forth the ritual emotions, as abstract, linear thought is confounded.

Louise Westling identifies other circumstances around Ellen that suggest the reshaping of the Demeter myth: she considers Dabney as a Kore figure about to be stolen by the outsider-field god Troy Flavin; the coconut cake baked by Ellen and its counterpart, the magic patti-cake baked by Partheny; the ritual journey by bride and attendants to the grove where the virgin aunts relate the history of the women's home; the encounter of archetypal mother and daughter; a trip to the underworld; the blessing by bees, and finally, the pastoral motif and the wedding itself all serve as underpinnings of myth ("Demeter and Kore," 103). Shellmound's eternal, ritualistic nature, Dorothy Griffin maintains, is indicated as well by the circular images in *Delta Wedding:* the circle of the heavens, the earth itself, the cycle of pregnancy, and the circles the family forms in play (107).

The dance of romance represents the most important of these circular patterns, the cycle of life. With the wedding of her daughter, Ellen has the momentary fear that the progression of life and death has no purpose, that, in sum, the life of the woman, especially the mother, is a senseless biological round. Like Jinny in Glasgow's *Virginia*, Ellen watches the young women whirling in the courtship dance with their partners in a climactic scene. She notes with fear that the painted faces of the women, the smooth faces of the men are indistinguishable. With horror, she realizes, "It was too the season of changeless weather, of the changeless world, in a land without hill or valley. How could she know anything of her own daughters, how find them, like this?" (221). The dance spins the women into marriages, taking the daughters away to the husband's realm. Unable to find her own children, Ellen has a moment of fear that she may never find her daughters again. Ellen experiences for a moment separation from her family, the precursor of age and death. But then her own small daughter breaks from the circle—partnerless, running, joyous, restored to her in her "iridescent life"—and Ellen knows that contained within the "lamp," the flame of passion flickers; passing life is contained in the women's world of Shellmound. Like light in a prism, the women separate into individuals, "more different and further apart than the stars" (221). Welty insists, like early writers, that the woman's community, far from insisting on conformity, enhances the particular identities of each of its daughters.

The end of *Delta Wedding* shows the daughter restored to the Fairchilds and the mother achieving an understanding that brings her maternal passion into loving communion with the natural world, defeating the flow of the deadly Yazoo River. Ellen sums up the essence of her womanliness, the natural environment echoing the emotional, imaginative inner world: "The repeating fields, the repeating cycles of seasons and her own life—there was something in the monotony itself that was beautiful, rewarding—perhaps to what was womanly in her. . . . The wheels rolled, but nothing changed. Only the heartbeat played its little drum" (240).

Welty juxtaposes the circular motion of the wagon's turning wheels—a figure for the cycle of nature, endlessly repeating its motion—with the beating of the heart, a metaphor for the passing, limited human life. The natural cycle, in which Ellen immerses herself as mother of the "world," offers consolation for the fact of death. In this sense of the recurring eternal, Welty enters into the communal sense that underlies ritual, and correspondingly the language takes on the repetitive, incantatory nature of ritual utterance. In the authors discussed here, time is depicted as cyclical rather than linear; all important experience is not to be found in the goal but in the journey.

Here Ellen of traditional past is opposed initially by Robbie Reid of the urban future. Ellen derives her identity from her cycle of birth, nurture, memory, and death; Robbie Reid lives through romance and material acquisition. Admittedly, Robbie Reid has the positive aspects in her portrayal that foreshadow her possible redemption from Memphis and its measures of worth. The daughter of a general store owner and a schoolteacher (always a positive signal in Welty's writing), she has shaped her life by herself outside the domestic world. Nonetheless, as we first see her, Robbie Reid evidences a preponderance of negative features, joining her to a sisterhood of similar characters in Welty's work, among them Wanda Fay Chisom of *The Optimist's Daughter* and Bonnie Dee Peacock of *The Ponder Heart*. Robbie Reid, if not a sister, is certainly a cousin of such slight figures. These women share many characteristics with Glasgow's "happiness hunters," Cather's town girls, and Porter's city girls of the cafés and streets. All lack the rich, strong, but disciplined emotional life, the sexuality contained within the time-honored house, the commitment to future generations of women, and the store of memory seen in the positive women protagonists and most fully exemplified by the wise woman. Their identities come from the male with whom they are joined by romance or material advantage. Robbie Reid's reason for existence, quite simply, comes from her relationship to George, just as he himself, until the visit to Shellmound, derives his identity from his law practice in Memphis.

The description of living space is a strong indicator of female character in Welty, as Griffin has detailed in a discussion of house architecture in *Delta Wedding*. Welty, as well as Naylor, Jewett, Cather, Glasgow, and Porter, uses living space as the crucial indicator of feminine character. In contrast to the house at Shellmound, where all the furniture is identified with a particular individual female ancestor, Robbie Reid's small apartment has no hand-me-downs, nothing with a history; instead she admires her carefully matched furniture's newness. She wants a Moorish couch with cushions such as that upon which Alice Ayres had reclined in a movie. Like earlier portrayals of urban girls and women, she finds her ideas formed by the communications of the mass society of the great cities. Unlike Shellmound's old books and peeling paint, Robbie's apartment furnishings are "matched," "expensive," "new," and "shiny." Anthony Bukoski characterizes Welty's successful houses as projecting "rootedness," that is, identification with a particular place which, even though under siege by modernity, still maintains an integral family past and forecasts "present and future stability" (326).

Despite her childhood in the Delta, Robbie Reid displays her new-found alienation with Shellmound's rural setting by her inappropriate fashionable clothing, for example, her tottering, out-of-place high heels and wool tam-o'-shanter. Now a confirmed urban dweller whose so-called life-style is in fact her life, she has repudiated her status as neighbor. She instinctively hates the communal Fairchild clan, leaving George when he endangers his life to save the demented child Maureen from an oncoming train. "George Fairchild, you didn't do this for me!" Robbie Reid's cry highlights the nature of her complaint. She expects, as do Cather's Clara Vavrika and Myra Henshawe, Porter's youthful Granny Weatherall and Sophia Jane, and Glasgow's Eva Birdsong, that her husband justify her life by complete devotion only to her. With her idea of possession of one individual by another, of an easily achieved, endlessly romantic bliss, Robbie Reid has no idea of commitment to a shared history, whatever the rubs of personality and the strike of fate. As Welty has remarked of Wanda Fay, she has no family, no homeland, no memory, and thus no female history. By the end of the novel, however, Robbie Reid indicates she may accept Ellen's invitation to join Shellmound and make a new home at The Grove, the Edenic home from which the two strains of Fairchilds, Shellmound and Marmion, sprang. The mother Ellen succeeds, we are led to believe, in bringing the couple back home, rejoining the circle.[2]

For a moment in this book, September 1923, the forces of family and place enjoy the last blaze of an Indian summer—the orphan Laura learns her place in the Fairchild history, the wedding of Dabney and Troy goes forward, Ellen is expecting another child, and Robbie Reid and George intend to return. This novel shows community and individual in a delicate balance—the feeling is of a bright late summer day. In keeping with Welty's belief that the home and the province contain all the great human dramas, the massive social changes of America between the two World Wars appear in the form of family events: the wedding of the family's daughter to an employee of Shellmound—even more significantly, the plantation overseer; the departure of George Fairchild, one of the owner-brothers, to practice law in

Memphis; the death of Denis, another of the brothers, in World War I; and finally the refusal of young Laura McRaven to join the family after her education in its history and its ritual. Even the devotion and the care of the "mother of all the world," the protection of the natural world, and the refusal of the family to admit time, uncommitted sexuality, and death into Shellmound do not seem, at first thought, able to create a safe home for the Delta wedding and the community in which it takes place. With Welty, however, all experience is doubled. John A. Allen considers Denis and George, each in his turn, to be Dionysus figures, sacrificed as they are to the renewal the women's community. In the end, George's return, the revitalization of the abandoned home Marmion, and, above all, the underpinnings of the Demeter myth leave open the question of the decay of the timeless community: this novel refuses to be tied to pure material reality and confined within historical time. Welty restores to her narrative the mystery and magic that give passing emotion and experience its vitality. The girls and women of *Delta Wedding* understand that the cycle of life always repeats. At the end of the novel, Laura murmurs, "My secret is . . . I've been in Marmion afore ye. I've seen it all afore. It's all happened afore" (241). She spreads wide her arms, enclosing nature, Ellen, the pregnant Robbie Reid, the bride Dabney, the artist-watcher Shelley, and her own restored past in a benedictory embrace. We as readers have reached our point of revelation; we feel that Shellmound and Ellen have an eternal, emotional reality that even the encroachments of Memphis cannot destroy. The tranquil woman's world of Shellmound, in the last account, seems like Herland and Hunter's Fare and Ántonia's farm to exist in the endless time of the female artist's memory.

In *The Golden Apples* (1949), Welty details the passing of the personal community of neighbors and families through the encroachments of the impersonal social order of citizens and experts. The changes found in this evolution bring Welty to the height of her powers; she herself names *The Golden Apples* as "closest to my heart of all my books" (Bunting, *Conversations*, 42). A group of seven interrelated short stories sharing character, plot, and setting, the cycle spans the crucial half century from the beginning of the twentieth century to the mid-1940s in the small communities of Morgana and MacLain, Mississippi.[3] Here we see the mother's garden connected with the kitchens and the hearths of Morgana in a continuous flow. At the beginning of the cycle, Welty portrays daily life as having the seamlessness of classic narrative, the constancy of the eternal. Kreyling indicates that this sense of unity in *The Golden Apples* builds on the connection between myth and the living Mississippi landscape (*Achievement*, 78). The vines and flowers of Miss Katie become as much a part of the living space for the characters as their houses.

In "Shower of Gold," Miss Katie relates the story of King MacLain and his wife, Miss Snowdie. Welty establishes King as the magical, sexual god-made-human. Unable to commit himself to home and to a single woman, King, like other American male protagonists, very quickly goes "west," to the deadly blank land of the future, leading the townspeople to search for his body in the Yazoo. His miraculous comings and goings, his implied death and resurrection, his association with gold, his many children with a variety of young women, and his undeniable attraction for Miss Katie Rainey point to King as the archetypal male. At the same time, of course, he suggests the westering American adventurer.

Miss Katie's Demeter finds its opposite in King MacLain's Zeus, forming the balancing halves of experience that give the community within nature its organic creative energy. At her funeral, King remembers her as the young "Katie Blazes," whom he later enthroned by the road. Occasionally, King's outside exploits drift back to enter Morgana's mythology; even then Miss Katie dismisses as irrelevant the stories of King's male heroism outside her domain: "They might mean something—might not" (10). Julia Demmins and Daniel Curley caution the reader against seeing King as an absolute male god, because his power is limited when confronted by the balancing, and opposing, mysterious female realm (130). Miss Katie in her strength can dismiss the outside world: "Time goes like a dream no matter how hard you run, and all the time we heard things from out in the world that we listened to but that still didn't mean we believed them" (9).

The first story—opening to the sound of Miss Katie Rainey's voice narrating the events surrounding the conception of King MacLain's twin sons and possibly Miss Katie's own daughter, Virgie Rainey—finds Miss Katie at the height of female vitality, an attraction that draws King to her. The wise woman serves as the generative force, joining the memories of the principal characters, cultivating the plenitude of the lush Mississippi setting and shaping the events of Morgana daily life into myth.[4] Welty allows her seer more power than Cather, for example, gives to Ántonia; Miss Katie creates imaginatively as well as instinctively. Her voice spins a world, showing woman as source of imagination and history; as she tells us confidently in "Shower of Gold," "Me, I have a little girl to sew for" (11). In her power, her homeland shimmers with the gold that surrounds King.

Twice watcher maidens warn the reader against approaching these stories with logical, linear patterns of thought. Nina Carmichael of "Moon Lake" realizes that learning comes from the emotions not the intellect, and Cassie Morrison of "June Recital" sees Miss Eckhart's art as "more than the ear could bear to hear or the eye to see, even in her" (59). Miss Katie's woman's language spins out the world and meaning itself. Miss Katie sits on her throne by the road, where she offers her produce and her tales with equal generosity to both neighbors and passing strangers. The first story comes to the reader as a gossipy, familiar personal conversation, an oral history, arising from the face-to-face small-scale bounded community. The individual perspectives in the later stories are limited, none having the omniscience of Miss Katie to weave her stories. In tone, too, the stories move from the comic springtime tone of "Shower of Gold" to the somber autumnal tone of "The Wanderers." Welty celebrates the seer's golden world through the contrast of the first narrative—joyous, creative, and maternal—with the succeeding voice of "The Whole World Knows," a tale of adultery, suicide, and broken communication. The progression of the story cycle shows Katie's world of abundance shrinking to the introspection of King's son. Kreyling considers Ran's story to take place in a new Morgana ruled by money and technology, a Morgana that has lost the golden glow in the lives of inhabitants like Ran who live "neglected lives" (*Achievement*, 100–101). In a land giving off the scent of sour pears, the prayer to the father and the cry to the brother receive no answer. Ran lives in the town, captive to public opinion, married to the faithless Jinny Love, who, within the cycle, illustrates the conventional acquisitive femininity of the town girl.

The last story, "The Wanderers," details Miss Katie's death and funeral. The narrating female voice is stilled as "The Wanderers" portrays the destruction of the woman's garden by the assaults of the outside world's machines and tools. The weakening and death of Miss Katie, and the exile of her daughter symbolize the fallen Morgana. At the story's beginning, she looks anxiously for her daughter Virgie, whose random, sexual adventures have occasioned the gossip that torments Miss Katie in her old age. Her family now consists only of Virgie herself; she has founded no lineage in the fallen Morgana. A slight stroke—like that of Perseus, like that of the metronome—weakened Miss Katie, and she no longer sits on her throne. As she dies, she bids her female Eden farewell, preparing to sell off her garden in the emerging commercial Morgana, her foot, like Granny Vaughn's in *Losing Battles* marking the seconds, the rhythms of life: "Dying, Miss Katie went rapidly over the list in it, her list. As though her impatient foot would stamp at each item, she counted it, corrected it, and yet she was about to forget the seasons, and the places things grew" (235). Dying, Miss Katie catalogs the creations of a life's labor and care, both natural art through the list of flowers and domestic art through the quilts and crocheted tablecloth she names. Welty suggests, as she includes each by name, a passing world full of beloved natural and crafted objects, which will now be sold off—Virgie's legacy, a whole world for sale. At the last, she, like Granny Weatherall, confuses herself with her daughter with one last sexual vaunt; she knows that her barren daughter will be exiled from her garden: "Mistake. Never Virgie at all. It was me, the bride—with more than they guessed. Why, Virgie, go away, it was me" (236).

As Miss Katie celebrates and relinquishes the work of her hands, Welty shows the passing of the mother's garden, destroyed by the deadly harvesters who now come to Morgan's Woods. The distanced narrative voice notes that the road still runs from Morgana to Vicksburg and Jackson, but now the "wrong people" drive by swiftly in "heavily loaded" trucks, carrying the weapons that will destroy Katie's natural world, the saws and axes that ready the trees for the mill. The third person narrative points to the change: "They were not eaters of muscadines, and did not stop to pass words on the season and what grew, and the vines had dried" (242). Welty creates a pastoral landscape menaced by technology; "the machine in the garden" in Leo Marx's words, is, in fact, the woman's garden. As with her predecessors, Welty shows the female-centered domestic world opposed to an invasive large-scale national social order.

As with Cather's Nebraska, Porter's Texas and Mexico, Naylor's Willow Springs, Jewett's New England, and Glasgow's Virginia, the women of Mississippi serve as stable center of the home place, creating the civilizing home despite the wandering male, bearing and raising the children, and keeping the peoples' history. And these stories, like Cather's *My Ántonia,* show the threat to communal action and customary activities of the neighborhood from a rationalized, impersonal technological society.

Welty offers a contrasting female character to Miss Katie's sensuous, fleshly generosity. Miss Eckhart, the German piano teacher, of "June Recital," presents another role for the woman: the artist-teacher. A lonely foreigner in provincial Morgana, Miss Eckhart lives in a rented apartment with her tyrannical mother. Her relationship to her mother shows the separation of the two roles in this cycle. Miss Eckhart combines the artist with the teacher, a figure who allows the author to place her art within an ongoing woman's community. All four works in this discussion have central characters who teach or who have taught: Robbie Reid of *Delta Wedding,* Miss Eckhart in *The Golden Apples,* Miss Julia Mortimer and Gloria Short in *Losing Battles,* and Becky Thurston McKelva and Adele Courtland of *The Optimist's Daughter.* The older women-teachers share several positive characteristics: dedication, self-sufficiency, generosity, and a passion to share their knowledge with the next generation, especially the daughters. In the teachers' lives, the demands of romance and male-centered marriage are antithetical to their commitment to the next generation, therefore none combine teaching with marriage. Miss Katie's home place and Miss Eckhart's art here are seen as opposite commitments but nonetheless inextricably tied; as Miss Katie achieves creativity through her coming-of-age, Miss Eckhart too has been touched, and the music comes like the "red blood" of sexual initiation and birth. These contrasting but ultimately cooperating commitments are both essential to the continuation of the magical Morgana civilization; after Miss Eckhart's exile and after Virgie takes up piano playing at the Bijou, Morgana has no life, as Marilyn Arnold notes, and Miss Katie dies.

Only in the last novel, *The Optimist's Daughter,* will Welty find the assurance of the full home place and place its influence in the artist-daughter's life. Until then, the artist and the mother are separated, unable to join. Like Mademoiselle Reisz of *The Awakening* or Thea Kronborg of *The Song of the Lark,* Miss Eckhart retains her dedication to art as her primary attachment, her solace in exile. Like such figures as Porter's Aunt Eliza and Cather's Thea and Alexandra, she expands her temporal body as she transcends the limitations of the individual.

As a teacher of music, Miss Eckhart tries to bring Virgie Rainey's abundant energy into the community of art, to make her, like Cather's Kronborg, one of the eternal daughters of music. That Miss Eckhart hopes to bring her "daughter" Virgie into a union as creative, as momentous, as that of marriage is indicated by the ritual nature of the June recital; a "ceremony" we are explicitly told. From Welty's description of the preparations for the ritual which will portray Virgie's initiation—she is thirteen—it is apparent that the recital is a sort of wedding. The girls attend her in their rainbow of newly stitched dresses; the women appear in their Sunday dresses to offer the community's support, the house is heavy with flowers, and gold chairs await the guests. After Virgie plays, she undergoes a change, which parallels the sexual initiation and Miss Eckhart's own artistic creativity, "the red of the sash was all over the front of her waist, she was wet and stained as if she had been stabbed in the heart, and a delirious and enviable sweat ran down from her forehead and cheeks" (74). Fearing that she has lost her daughter, Miss Katie says, "Oh, but I wish Virgie had a sister!" (74). Miss Eckhart functions here as the traditional mother of the bride, welcoming guests, dispensing refreshments, and accepting congratulations at the reception after the recital.

In "June Recital" music becomes the language of connection, a force as momentous as birth and death, and a force beyond the limits of time and place. As Cassie views Miss Eckhart, she senses, "If the sonata had an origin in a place on earth, it was the place where Virgie, even, had never been and was not likely ever to go" (56). Music, then, defeats time and the vicissitudes of the individual life in much the same way that maternity does. Throughout the cycle, music functions as a more elemental, more "natural" communication than language in the modern environment, a theme most notably apparent in "Music from Spain." But other examples abound. For example, by accepting the dedication to music, Miss Eckhart, unlike the other musicians in the book, loses her own personal life and the possibility of biological maternity. In contrast, the "glimmering" Mrs. Morrison, trapped in a prosaic marriage and spending her days at Rook parties, tells Cassie that she could have sung. Like Glasgow's Eva Birdsong, Catherine

Morrison has sacrificed her voice to her marriage, a romantic sacrifice that ultimately leads to her suicide. Easter of Moon Lake, King's daughter, plans to be a singer, and Cassie Morrison sings her own theme, "By the Light of the Silvery Moon," as Virgie plays hers, "*Für Elise.*" Music assumes a greater importance in *The Golden Apples* than in Welty's other extended narratives, representing immediate connection, incapable of misunderstanding and freed from paternal legalisms.

Soon after Virgie's "grace," she refuses the commitment promised by the recital, instead playing the piano at the movies. She now belongs on the insubstantial screen with the Gish and Talmadge sisters, a "shadow of her former self." Having refused to be controlled by Miss Eckhart's metronome, the representative of mechanical time, Virgie now sits "nightly at the foot of the screen ready for all that happened at the Bijou, and keeping pace with it" (59). Her art for sale, she produces tunes in time to the screen's flickering. Like Virgie's sexuality, music shrinks to "fun" in modern Morgana.

In *One Writer's Beginnings,* Welty identifies with Miss Eckhart but claims Virgie at her most intense as the embodiment of her fictional subject. Like Cather's Marie Tovesky and Porter's Aunt Amy, beautiful young women who fill their life with passionate romance, Virgie lives intensely in her present emotions. Her free expression of female emotion and sexuality cannot build a community or perform a concert; she represents the active fleeing element of life, the "glimmering girl" who inspires art. She is nature, art's object, passing by. Yet this elemental force needs the woman's garden of community or the framing of art. The appearance of the lost girl incident in *Delta Wedding* first announced this motif; Virgie's youthful sexual adventures develop it, and Rachel Sojourner's life and death in *Losing Battles* brings the theme to its fullest expression.

If Virgie represents the active female principle, life passing, always in motion, Cassie Morrison depicts the organizing, reflective watcher— moon to Virgie's sun. Her pale coloring contrasts with Virgie's glittering sexuality. Because myth in Welty is allusive not allegorical, Cassie also shows aspects of the gods' messenger Iris with each color of the rainbow on her petticoat when "the gathering past" and the "pellucid" poetry overtakes her, as King overtakes Mattie and, we suspect, Miss Katie (McHaney, 604). She takes control of the female narrative voice from Miss Katie whose "Shower of Gold" directly precedes "June Recital," as creativity passes from the mother-woman to the artist-daughter. Through evidences of her conformity, Cassie might be considered an example of the repressive nature of the solidly conventional middle-class of Morgana, yet Kreyling is surely closer to Welty's intent when he concludes that, despite her own negative maternal heritage, Cassie, like many another positive female character, claims those steadfast virtues submerged in the social competition, patience, reverence, and loyalty. She appears as the guardian of the female memories (*Achievement*, 86). Cassie is, after all, the messenger whose memories connect the art of "The Song of Wandering Aengus" with the glowing life that Virgie represents. Cassie, the quiet watcher, shares several key experiences with the author; Welty, for example, felt the impact of literature through Yeats's poem and also emphasizes her own "sheltered life" (*One Writer's Beginning*, 81, 104). Unlike Jinny Love, Cassie has no desire to coerce Virgie into accepting her conventional life. Like her "sister" Virgie, she refuses marriage and commemorates the mother.

Several symbolic motifs used in *The Golden Apples* unite it with Welty's other novels and connect her work with the other women in this discussion. Again these motifs indicate the connection of the home place with the natural world. With all its plenteous wonder, Miss Katie's garden offers the primary example of the central floral imagery of *The Golden Apples*. But Cassie's commemoration of her dead mother by a garden also indicates female solicitude as does Virgie's presentation of the fragrant magnolia to Miss Eckhart each day and the girl's crowning her with a garland of flowers. Virgie's floral tribute finds its reflection in the country woman's offering of a night-blooming cereus to Virgie as she sets out, in each case the giving of the blooming plant is silent homage to creativity from one woman to another. Because the old woman's offering for her piano playing at the Bijou reminds Virgie of the triviality of her service, she rejects it, whereas the teacher accepted the floral tributes, however ironically given, as a gift from her daughter of music.

As in *Delta Wedding*, the theme of flight and bird imagery is central. The hummingbird is explicitly a symbol of Virgie, so much so that the last story was originally entitled "The Hummingbirds." At Miss Katie's passing, the hummingbird comes to remind Virgie of the persistence of life even in the house of death. Cassie meditates on Virgie's relationship to life through the imagery, which yields insights to her own place in the scheme of things. Watching the hummingbird, which represents Virgie, the flash of emotion passing, Cassie vows that she will not trap the "tangible and intangible" fairy bird. Instead, she, like the artist, will hold him in memory, everlasting: "Let him be suspended there for a moment each year for a hundred years—incredibly thirsty, greedy for every drop in every four o'clock trumpet in the yard, as though he had them numbered—then dart" (67). Cassie's refusal to trap the bird—as Audubon's fatal love demands in "A Still Moment" and as the young hunter intends in Jewett's "A White Heron"—makes her the figure of the recording female daughter-artist. It is enough for Cassie to acknowledge the bird's vitality; she need not possess it. As "The Wanderers" closes, Cassie says to Virgie, "A life of your own, away—I'm so glad for people like you and Loch" (272).

Finally, after youth and passion have passed and after the possibility of conception has diminished, the middle-aged Virgie takes stock of a life that has rejected both the commitment to maternity and to the dedication to artistry or education. She feels trapped in her own time. In a scene reminiscent of Thea's epiphany in Panther Canyon, she floats and bathes in the Big Black River. As she swims, she reconciles life and death, seeing herself immersed in time through the loss of her mother. When emotion and continuity have left the physical world, Virgie looks inward. The black seer Minerva, a figure of wisdom, steals away Virgie's material legacy from her mother; she teaches "Venus" to look to memory in the fallen world from which the mother's hand has been withdrawn. As the rain falls, Virgie sits with Minerva, resolving the duality of experience, becoming for a moment both Perseus and Medusa, both feeling and guiding the stroke of time.

Welty's autobiographical account focuses its attention on maternal home and family; *The Golden Apples* centers on the female-ordered home as well. "Shower of Gold" finds the old female-headed families and their spoken histories intact; "The Wanderers," shows them aged, scattered, dead or dying. Yet as Virgie takes leave, she salutes the graves of all the old families, last rites, as she undertakes her exile. Past forty, childless, motherless, without home or art, Virgie sets out on the American quest. As she rises up to take the long road of the homeless American wanderer, Miss Katie's care, Minerva's wisdom, Miss Eckhart's lessons, and Cassie's benediction accompany her.

Welty's penultimate novel, *Losing Battles* (1970), resounds with women's voices. Readers are surrounded by a thriving oral female community with no doubt that the guiding creative imagination is female. Margaret Jones Bolsterli observes that the women of both the clan and the teaching profession form the rock-solid strength that sustains the community (153). She elaborates the specifics of the particularly female nature of the authorial vision, citing Welty's attention to the details of food preparation and sewing and asks rhetorically if a male writer could understand that domestic concerns are "serious" (154–55). (The woman's garden could be added as well to the analysis.) In *Losing Battles* women's arts and voices are stage center for the human drama, and Welty the author and director of the assembled cast. Welty's writing displays the marks of the woman's traditional community: the colloquial female histories, the celebrations of the wise woman and maternal source, the richness of the female garden, and continuity of the generations. These characteristics are in ascendance in this novel with one exception: the mother's gardens are blighted by the forces outside. Welty chose the poorest section of Depression Mississippi as the setting, reducing the community to its essence, "to show them when they had really no props to their lives, had only themselves" (Bunting, *Conversations*, 50).

Two female rituals stand at the center of the novel, Granny Vaughn's ninetieth birthday reunion and Miss Julia Mortimer's funeral. The paired rites introduce the major actors of this drama. Commentators such as Sara McAlpin, Jane L. Hinton, Elizabeth M. Kerr, and Joseph Childers have written on the central place family holds in *Losing Battles*, and Kreyling and Sheila Stroup have noted the battle between the forces of myth represented by Granny Vaughn and those of history represented by Miss Julia. Welty herself explicitly denies that *Losing Battles* represents a "battle for identity" because the individual is both submerged and victorious, "because you can't really conceive of the whole unless you *are* an identity. Unless you are very real in yourself, you don't know what it means to support others or to join with them or to help them" (Bunting, *Conversations*, 48–49). Welty suggests that those who are subject to the modern social order tend to define the self as made of imposed identities and purchased life-styles.

Like many another matriarch, Aunt Shannon of *Delta Wedding* for one, Granny has rejoined the female generations by raising her grandchildren to adulthood after her daughter's death. Her life is celebrated

by the voices of her huge family—an indication of the persistence of
the mother's community; she herself lives in several times simultaneously, her dead in her mind along with the living family. For example,
she confuses the wanderer hero of the family, Jack Renfro, with her
young grandson, Sam Dale, killed in the First World War—repeatedly
the males in Welty's novels are killed by the wars fought "outside,"
blinded or imprisoned by its legalistic language. A sybilline figure,
Granny, like Miss Katie, is rich in quilts, the stitching together of many
women's life stories. For her, experience retains the layered sense of
time and the presence of the living family's stories, rather than the
linear narrative left by Miss Julia. Noting this difference, Kreyling
marks the family's ability to reshape current events to archetypal patterns to defeat the passing of time and thus shape the future by the
ongoing present, concluding that "these are the weapons the mythical
consciousness uses against the historical in *Losing Battles* ("The Foes,"
644). Granny, for example, seeks to restore the female lineage in the
present time, to bring the orphan Gloria Short and her daughter Lady
May into the Vaughn clan by naming Gloria the child of the dead son
Sam Dale and the "lost girl," the beautifully named, fox-haired Rachel
Sojourner. Because of her daughter's loss, Granny feels she has no
lineage, no just commemoration, even though the reunion includes
grandchildren, thirty-seven or thirty-eight great-grandchildren, and
many others. As the narrative develops, the reader discovers that the
old woman wants to go "home" to the time of her abundant strength
when she picked up her daughter's family and began all over again.
The end of the birthday brings the old woman to the realization that
all her grandsons leave her, as the males take off on their wanderings
and their wars. The end of the day finds Granny screaming at her
departing family, "Parcel of thieves! They'd take your last row of pins.
They'd steal your life if they knew how. . . . Thieves, murderers, come
back," she begged. "Don't leave me!" (342–43). Granny has lost her
battle, having moved aside for the new generations, but in another
sense, she survives. Despite age and infirmity, Granny still moves to
the rhythms of life. After she sings all the verses of an oracular song,
Granny is lifted up by her family to a table and begins her dance of
continuing life and time passing: "She danced in their faces" (297).
Aging Demeter still dances, but now the land has "gone back" on her
family, renewal comes instead from the serene female narrator's art.

Instead of the lost Fisher King, Welty, and Porter as well, shows modern barrenness to have at its base the woman's search for the daughters, for human continuity.

Granny's opposite, Miss Julia Mortimer, also serves as caretaker of the generations, teaching the reluctant children carpentry, knitting, horticulture, and swimming along with writing and arithmetic. She expresses her female creativity in influencing the children and thus the community, through her chastity, her controlled sexuality; Hardy calls hers a "priestly vocation" ("Marrying Down," 106). One of the characters in *Losing Battles* observes, correctly, of Miss Julia's life, "But would *she* have been as satisfied, with only a husband to fuss over instead of a whole nation of ignorant, squirming schoolchildren?" (327). She shares much of the sense of mission found in earlier individualistic heroines of independent achievement such as Dorinda Oakley, Nan Prince, or Alexandra Bergson. She looks to the future of Mississippi and to the nation; Miss Julia accepts a much more abstract faith, emptied of immediate emotion.

Kreyling contrasts Miss Julia Mortimer's historical beliefs with Granny's mythic consciousness, observing that, unlike the cyclical patterns of Granny's home, the historical mind of Miss Julia's schoolroom tries to assert her "dream" of order ("Foes," 646). The schoolteacher owns the linear rationality of Welty's male "optimists." As passionate as Miss Eckhart in her dedication to a universal community, Miss Julia pledges herself to the future just as surely as Granny Vaughn. Indeed, Miss Julia's largesse spreads to the whole state; she keeps and milks cows, tends the woman's garden, and sends peach cuttings throughout Mississippi as she seeks with the help of her chosen "daughter" Gloria Short "to give some of her abundance away" (234). Unlike Granny, Miss Julia's community extends beyond blood and place, thus she leavens the individualistic competition with nurture. There are, however, comic aspects to her portrayal. Kreyling cites as an example of Miss Julia's "isolate determinism" her decision to continue classes in the midst of a hurricane ("Foes," 539), and Seymour Gross points out that Miss Julia believes "every mystery can be solved" like other of Welty's optimists (201). If Granny is ignorant of scientific and intellectual knowledge, Miss Julia is at least equally ignorant of emotional and natural realities. Granny's birthday celebration and Miss Julia's funeral—her last name forecasts her fate—represent Banner's biggest celebrations, calling their wandering descendants back to the female center.

Like her antagonist, for two types of women are here in battle for the female soul of Gloria Short, Miss Julia loses her battle. Left alone with no family to protect her, she is at the mercy of a bullying caretaker, one of her former students. Miss Julia's last testament is fittingly a written document using legal terminology and read by Judge Moody, who Kreyling characterizes as "a man of the written word and justice rather than oral communication (hearsay) and family ties" ("Foes," 646). As he reads it, Miss Julia appears before the group, transcending the writing as the family sees her face in living reality. Her written testament is as expressive of her personality as Granny's dance is of hers: "Now that the effort it took has been put a stop to, and I can survey the years, I can see it all needs doing over, starting from the beginning" (287–88). With Miss Julia's epiphany, we experience the exaltation of the artist's memory very much like Porter's in "The Grave." Like Granny, Katie Rainey, and Ellen Fairchild, Miss Julia accepts the circularity of woman's experience, and she acknowledges the "something" that dawns out of the communal experience. Despite the family's scorn, Miss Julia leaves behind her own communal legacy. With this discovery, Welty comes to the same place as Porter at the end of the Miranda cycle; she grows back to her own beginnings.

The third female character in *Losing Battles*, Gloria Short, sets out on a path shared with earlier protagonists facing a barren social landscape. Because the orphaned Gloria has no received family background, she finds herself open to adoption by the two female models, Miss Julia and Granny. Miss Julia seeks to "pass the torch" to the girl she educated and loved; she takes Gloria in to her own home and sends her to the teachers' college. When Gloria announces she will marry Jack, Miss Julia tries to dissuade her by logical argument. The family too names her as one their own. After the ominous watermelon baptism by the female Beechams, Gloria is considered a member of the family—an identification she refuses. As one of the women, Aunt Beck, later observes to Gloria, "You don't have to answer to the outside any longer." Because her parentage is unknown, Granny insists that Gloria was born of a romance between a "lost girl," Rachel Sojourner, and the dead grandson hero of the family, Sam Dale. In a statement very like that of Robbie Reid in *Delta Wedding*, Gloria tells her husband, "I'm here to be nobody but myself, Mrs. Gloria Renfro, and have to do nothing with the old dead past. And don't ever try to change me" (347). Like her fictional male counterparts, she retreats to form her own alternate world, safely away from the "old dead past." As with the other authors here, the determination to separate permanently from the female community is depicted as futile or dangerous. Welty, like her colleagues, doubts that the Edenic domestic haven can exist apart from the mother's home: "[Gloria's] the most naive soul there" (Bunting, *Conversations*, 49). Like earlier women writers, Welty considers marriage without attachment to female kin to be as foolish a notion as planting a cut flower. Despite her desire to be a self-made individual, Gloria has absorbed the lessons of both Granny and Miss Julia. As she grows wiser through the stroke of time, Gloria will integrate the two models in her own life. The theme of the story is, after all, "the unreliability of the individual perspective," as Fleischauer observes (78).

With *The Optimist's Daughter*, Welty moves like Porter toward the drama of individual consciousness, as she expands female memory through connection to the home place as creative source. As Minerva wisely stole away Virgie's material legacy from Miss Katie, so here Laurel can at last leave behind the breadboard given in homage to her mother Becky from Laurel's dead husband Phil; she needs no "raft," no object for she has cast off into living memory. Both wanderers carry home with them, memory a shelter in exile, a hope for new connections and new creativity.

Shaped from a short story published in *The New Yorker* in 1969, her next, and to this time, last novel, *The Optimist's Daughter* (1970), contains Welty's most complete fictional statement on the relationship of female protagonist to family and traditional role.[5] Welty has acknowledged how close the events of her mother's life touch on those of Becky McKelva and how heartfelt is the study of the relationship of the artist-daughter to the female generations, and *One Writer's Beginnings* indicates how close the tie between fiction and biographical fact.

Wanda Fay Chisom McKelva formerly of Madrid, Texas, and Becky Thurston McKelva, the second and first wives respectively of Judge Clinton McKelva, are brought into direct comparison through the observations and recollections of Becky's daughter, Laurel McKelva Hand, now widowed and working as a fabric designer in Chicago.

Judge McKelva has in his last years unaccountably married the vulgar outsider Fay. Set in the mid-1960s, the action of the novel starts with the judge's illness and death in New Orleans during Carnival, continues through his funeral in Mount Salus, Mississippi, and ends with his daughter's repudiation of his "optimism" or false progressive vision, represented by his telescope and his mantel clock. After an eye operation, he loses the will to live and dies as Wanda tries to rouse him because of her boredom at her hospital vigil during Mardi Gras.

Through the course of the narrative Laurel learns that she is her mother's daughter as well, a mother who had no optimism at all because of her connection with life and death. As in previous narratives of the female artist's development by Cather, Jewett, and Porter, Welty's protagonist, a textile designer, cannot reach her full creativity until she discovers its relationship to her female heritage. As previous critical usage has noted, this novel moves inward from Welty's more pictorial earlier works, but nonetheless we remain in the mother's, and the grandmother's, garden throughout much of *The Optimist's Daughter*, and once more the voices we hear are almost exclusively female—not only those of Fay and Laurel—but also those of Laurel's former bridesmaids and Becky's garden club. The only living males who appear are the distant Dr. Courtland, the dying Judge McKelva, and the woozy Major Bullock, all defined by their public roles. Laurel—the floral name is surely no accident—returns to take away her cuttings of memory; her viewpoint in the first sections is that of a commenting witness as befits her sensitive, but emotionally distanced, viewpoint. Still trapped in the false vision of filial piety, unable to forgive her parents their humanity, Laurel is cut off from the creative power of her mother's legacy, the wisdom of the natural and domestic world.

To reach her potential as an artist, Laurel must undertake a quest back through time to painful truth. Her guide, Miss Adele Courtland, is the gentle spinster teacher and next-door neighbor who continually explains others' motives to the early conventional Laurel. She connects human experience to the natural world as did the other teacher Becky before her. In this novel, to be mother is to be teacher and to be teacher is to be mother as Welty examines what can be carried out of the house of childhood and memory to the cold Northern city. Commentary has suggested that Adele may well be another semiautobiographical figure such as Miss Eckhart, and Welty herself has already identified some of the autobiographical components in Laurel's experience. Miss Adele shares many characteristics with Louisa Goddard of Glasgow's *They Stooped to Folly.* Here the mature author guides her younger self much as the authorial voice of Miranda commented on her childhood. The artist thus becomes mother to the tale.

The last two parts of the novel depict Laurel assessing her place in the mother's community and the distant city. Like Virgie and other female protagonists, Laurel will find her own way in a world cleared of emotional landmarks; her parents and husband have left her behind in a world to which Fay holds future title. But we must also understand that Laurel at first seeks the control and order her father's public life represents, as the title emphasizes. She overcomes her intellectual detachment from the horror and messiness of human relationships, to become like her female family less "optimistic."

The extended scene in Becky's garden prepares us for Laurel's understanding of her artistic birth. As Laurel tends her mother's iris, four elderly ladies, the survivors of Becky's garden club, sit at their ease among nature and discuss Laurel's situation with the frankness allowed by long and loving acquaintance. Birds and flowers mark this as the vacated but still blessed home of the mother: "Cardinals, flying down from low branches of the dogwood tree, were feeding here and there at the ladies' crossed feet. At the top of the tree, a mockingbird stood silent over them like a sentinel" (125–26). Elizabeth Evans notes that Laurel sits silent at the "still center" of the novel as "[t]he trappings of the world are shut out" (115). As their voices go on, Laurel removes the weeds from the garden. With each one, she hears the mother's voice bringing order to existence, as she herself must learn to seek the blossom and reject the weeds of resentment and distance. All gathered celebrate Becky's climber, a root that is "a hundred years" or older, But in spring, the root "strong as an apple tree," her maternal legacy, sometimes bloomed most.

This legacy arose from the grandmother's West Virginia mountain home which, like Porter's grandmother's home, is found on no map. When the child Laurel recoils from the scene of the birds feeding from each other's crops, the old woman explains, "They're just hungry like we are" (166). Later as she discovers the years of yellowed letters from her grandmother hidden away in the old nursery-sewing room, she finds one that tells Becky that she would like to send Laurel a pigeon, that it would eat out of her hand "if she'd let it."

To understand the grandmother's and the teacher's wisdom garnered from nature, Laurel will journey back to the room of her physical and artistic beginnings, finding in that innermost room the mingled love and hate, use and affection, the hard truth about marriage that her optimist father could not accept when he, like the social order, turned to Fay's easy attraction. And she will reclaim the home place. Both grandmother and teacher instruct Laurel in the lessons of the female garden to save her from following Fay.

Her antagonist Fay bears more than a passing resemblance to those women of the modern consumer society such as the Peacock sisters of *The Ponder Heart*. Kreyling notes that such characters are diminutive, kittenlike, with a propensity to decorate with pastels (as if softening out unpleasant physical fact). He adds that both the Peacocks and Fay "stock a house, already furnished with the personal objects of a more domestic woman, with the chrome and electric marvels of a mechanical age. And both share a kind of agelessness, an appearance of lasting youth that somehow signifies the extent of their spiritual growth" (*Achievement*, 112). As we have seen with earlier happiness hunters, this modern sisterhood thrives on display, novelty, and "romance," although not necessarily sexuality. They have no understanding of custom, and place no value on received personal relationships. Fay finds no use for either because, as she says, echoing Gloria Short, "The past isn't a thing to me. I belong to the future, didn't you know that?" (207). In an interview with John Griffin Jones, Welty discusses the connection of people such as Bonnie Dee and Wanda Fay—the observations apply as well to the young Gloria and the Memphis Robbie Reid, who have both left behind their teachers' pasts. To a observation by the interviewer that Wanda's and Bonnie Dee Peacock's greatest "affliction" is that they have no communal memory, Welty replied, "They don't understand their own experience. And they would have to understand it in order to have it in their memory. Their memory hasn't received it because it hasn't meant anything" (*Conversations*, 335–36).

The impoverished modern child-woman has no social history, no pattern for womanly achievement, instead she serves as a "consumer" of both goods and lives. A woman of modern mass society, Fay gains her ideas of elegance from the newspapers and the movies; newness and notice offer her the most profound experiences, the old and the discreet seeming "boring" and "stuffy." She shows, for example, an initial antipathy to the funeral ritual until she perceives its opportunity for a "scene" in which she is the central actor. Fay discovers appropriately attractive mourning garb in black satin, and she considers hysterics, kisses, and embraces of the judge's body at the public funeral to be suitable manifestations of grief. All her efforts are directed toward her public appearances; she has no private life. In the same spirit, she denies that her family is living until the awful Chisoms appear at the McKelva door with a pickup truck bearing the modern motto, "Do Unto Others Before They Do Unto You" (109). Fay claims ownership of the judge's house immediately, implying that the old friends and Laura will in some way cheat her of her material due. Instead of the old-fashioned camellia the judge placed on Becky's grave, his own in the "new" section will no doubt be adorned with "indestructible plastic Christmas poinsettias." Her behavior, however, comes from her family past; Evans has contrasted the Chisoms' manifestations of human greed and naked hunger, symbolized by Bubba's hands wrapped around his ham sandwich, with the Mount Salus mourners' sense of decorum and ritual (32). The Chisoms' unmediated human need classes them with the Grandmother's pigeons; humanity arises from the *care* which Becky brought through her discretion and domestic arts. In her belief that all civilization comes from the carefully preserved domestic arts, Welty connects with the earlier authors.

Laurel offers little doubt as to her opinion of Fay, yet the gentle voice of the old teacher Miss Adele Courtland defends the second wife, saying that Fay is only following *her* maternal example and honoring the judge according to her social experience. The modern social order offers her few examples of communal care, not even the most elementary one of the family. Fay can only examine events from the single perspective of their effect on promoting her public notice. And beneath the crudity of the Chisoms and their daughter Fay is the naked human hunger that Laurel herself cannot face. After his betrayal through his detachment from Becky's dying—a detachment which Laurel as his daughter and a professional shares—the failing "sight" of Judge McKelva propels him to address that hunger for life by his unfortunate marriage to the birdlike Fay. The marriage of the Judge and Fay, therefore, in the terms of the narrative, represents the yielding of the old moribund paternalistic Southern culture to modern competitive genderless individuality. Unlike the women friends, Becky and Adele, the judge finds no way to acknowledge that hunger and contain it within an ongoing community. At the beginning of the narrative his daughter finds herself in the same circumstance; she must learn to give the past its due, and to move forward in the present.

In her desire to save her mother's life from Fay's casual curiosity, Laurel searches through the Judge's public papers, looking for his letters from his wife, but she finds he has destroyed them: "But there was nothing of her mother here for Fay to find" (145). After the funeral guests leave her alone in the McKelva house, Laurel faces her mother and her memory. Laurel at first wants revenge on Fay, thus "following" her through a blindness similar to her father's. Driven inward by a chimney swift trapped in the house, a representative of Laurel's confinement in her childlike relationship to her parents and her unrealistic memories of Phil, Laurel retreats further into the private space of the house, back to her mother's room. There Laurel discovers a door to memory; Becky has saved all her letters from the judge. Those letters bring Becky back to her daughter and free Laurel to claim her female past and bring it into her art.

As discreet as Fay is blatant, Becky practices all of the domestic arts, making clothes, growing roses, and baking bread. But she also hates, and she also feeds, like the pigeons, like the roses, greedily and deeply, from the life around her. At the end, Becky, blinded, screams "Lucifer! Liar!" to her husband because he cannot accord her dying its majesty, and because of her anger at death itself. Like Granny Vaughn and Granny Weatherall, Becky wants more of life, and she understands that the male myth seeks to trick her into an easy, false death. These scenes of naked need have caused Laurel to turn her eyes, to lose the mother who sat a generation before with her own mother and her own child high in the mountains. The grandmother's place, an ideal "up home," taught both with flowers and music and nourished them with bread.

Like Cassie Morrison of *The Golden Apples*, Laurel plays with all the colors of the rainbow in her profession of textile designer. In the nursery, which significantly served later as a sewing room, Laurel finds the connection between maternal heritage and daughter's art by recounting the creation of the "most beautiful blouse" Becky ever sewed.

The fabric was spun and dyed with pokeberries gathered by Laurel's grandmother and designed and sewn by Becky. The final product was the result of grandmother's garden, mother's domestic talents, and daughter's imaginative art, a microcosm of the female creative process of the writers here discussed. The child Laurel's artistic activities emerge from these beginnings, her plenitude of creation reflect the female creative lineage seen in Miss Katie, Ellen, Granny Weatherall, Miss Sophia Jane, and Granny Vaughn:

> When her mother—or, at her rare, appointed times, the sewing woman—
> sat her in her chair pedalling and whirring. Laurel sat on the floor [of
> the sewing room] and put together the falling scraps of cloth into stars,
> flowers, birds, people, or whatever she liked to call them, lining them
> up, spacing them out, making them into patterns, families, on the sweet-
> smelling matting, with the shine of firelight, or the summer light, mov-
> ing over mother and child and what they both were making. (159)

Welty has given no more accurate description of the female authorial task; she plays upon her own chosen repeated symbolic motifs of flowers and birds as well as her own fictional concerns of the female family and friends. Taking the scraps falling from the mother's own sewing, the daughter creates a small world as she lines her creations up, spaces them out, and forms them into artistic patterns. And she portrays the gift of imagination as issuing directly from the example and presence of Becky; her art comes from the falling scraps of the mother's domesticity, just as Welty ties her own written art to Chestina's stories. The choice of a textile designer once again displays the female imagination of the narrative voice by using the metaphor of weaving to deal fictionally with the creation of her own art.

Through the immediacy of this emotional, feminine reunion, Laurel, like Miranda at the end of "Pale Horse, Pale Rider," finds herself existing in a state of being between the material world and the emotional reality. Laurel calls her dead husband to her. In the vision, Phil holds his mouth open, like Becky, like the pigeons, wanting more life. Through her understanding of Becky, Laurel can face his hunger and turn to her own life, discovering and channeling the hunger that drives her own art, now moving outward from the female creative source. After these visitations, Laurel sleeps and dreams of her lost husband, as she, unlike her father, faces Phil's anger and her own and gains back her lost and fitting mate. The reconciliation with her mother allows her to move into public life. Laurel now realizes that she can leave the house because artistic memory keeps both physical and spiritual experience vital, replicating the cycles of life. In her last novel to this date, Welty recapitulates the journey to the origins of female creativity.

The Optimist's Daughter is yet another woman's book where literary art and authorial experience intersect. The parallels between the lives of Becky Thurston McKelva and Chestina Andrews Welty are many and obvious: the desperate raft trip to Baltimore, the granddaughter's visit to West Virginia, the mother's adoring brothers, her harrowing last illness and blindness, and the nature of the mother's grave concern for her husband and daughter. Issuing from a mountain "up home," the grandmother's and the mother's legacies inform Laurel's art. Once the protagonist understands this connection, she can leave the mother's garden to create her own world. This is a story the writers most often tell as they look back over their artistic careers; it represents their ultimate wisdom. In all the earlier writers, as well as Welty, the writers find their resolution of gender and creativity with the understanding of the home place. Welty writes at the end of her autobiography that memory joins all of experience and all the beloved, living and dead, and she obliquely defends the home place from her own life: "As you have seen, I am a writer who came of a sheltered life. A sheltered life can be a daring life as well. For all serious daring starts from within" (104).

[Miranda] finds herself in a vast space of glowing light.

Daughter. The word comes to cradle what has gone past weariness. She can't really hear it because she's got no ears, or call out because she's got no mouth. There's only the sense of being. Daughter.

—Gloria Naylor
Mama Day

7.

Lead On with Light

GLORIA NAYLOR

THE OUTLINES of the wise woman's loving community in American remains an attractive one for the woman writer, although increasingly problematic, given the atomized and regimented social order. As before, this fictional ideal allows the woman writer in America simultaneously to create a model for her own creativity and to point the way to more cooperative, egalitarian community. The evolving body of work of Gloria Naylor suggests that the patterns of plot, characterization, and attitudes toward language persist to the present. Naylor's personal history differs from the other women authors in this discussion in several important respects: she grew up as the child of poor black parents in New York City.[1] The several strands of her cultural background unite to give her writing an emphasis unique among this group, although the underlying imaginative paradigm shares many of the same outlines.[2] Naylor, for example, never accepts the ideal of the heroic individual as a model for her female protagonists. Instead, her first novel, *The Women of Brewster Place* (1980), portrays a woman's community gathered around the maternal figure of Mattie Michael, a community brought together from an urban world of broken neighborhoods and disrupted families. The society Naylor depicts is an infernal mix of uncaring bureaucracies and male violence, a society whose fragmentation is indicated by the work's structure, "a novel in seven stories."

In a famous passage in *The Souls of Black Folk*, W. E. B. Du Bois writes of the conflict of African-American identity: "One ever feels his twoness—an American, a Negro; two souls, two thoughts, two unreconciled strivings" (215). Despite obvious and crucial differences in their respective histories, women in America, like African-Americans, have felt a split in their consciousness between the perceptions of themselves that the dominant cultural discourse attempts to impose and those generated by the testimony of their own experience. Commentators as early as abolitionist Frederick Douglass and Du Bois himself have understood the connection in the situations of the two marginalized groups in the larger society. Decades ago, sociologist Gunnar Myrdahl in his classic *An American Dilemma* detailed the similarity in the stereotypical portrayals of both groups, noting that women and African-Americans both were distinguished from the assumed cultural norm of the white adult male by their appearance, making their isolation from central decision-making groups easily achieved. He points out that they are often characterized negatively in very similar terms, which justify their social subordination (Vol. II, 1078). More recently, commentators such as Audre Lorde and Elizabeth Fox-Genovese have noted the difficulties of reconciling the identity of individual promoted by the dominant discourse and the identity of race or gender.

With the African-American woman author, however, the problem multiplies. Lorde, a black lesbian poet and cultural critic, writes of the difficulties particular to the feminism of women of color. As Lorde pungently proclaims, "Black feminism is not white feminism in blackface" (*Sister Outsider*, 60). The woman of color, whether African-American, Latina, Native-American, or Asian-American, finds it necessary to sort out authentic portions of her self-image and reject the false images projected by sexism and racism, for, as Lorde insists about her ethnic group, black America has no need to repeat the mistakes of white America.

Henry Louis Gates writes that the problem of twoness posed by

DuBois extends to literature. Black writers learn to write by reading, and the texts that serve as models are those of the Western canonical tradition, therefore works of African-American literature share more resemblances than differences with other Western texts. Naylor herself speaks directly to the problem of literary "influence," which she found a particularly complicated one as a black female child. If women must overcome patriarchal influence to discover an authentic voice, the black woman must overcome patriarchal influence and racial oppression, both of which insist that her contribution conform to the existing models of Western male literary achievement. As Naylor grew up, her literary education offered her no examples of writing black men, let alone black women writers: "I read Emerson, I read Poe, I read Hawthorne, Fitzgerald, Faulkner, Hemingway. My God! Wonderful writers, wonderful writers! And never having read anything that reflected me" (*American Audio Prose Interview*). Like the white women authors in this discussion, Naylor found herself turning to models from classic European and American sources gained in her early literary education and revisioning them into patterns that reflected her ethnic and gender identities. Naylor identifies, for example, the landscape of Dante's *Inferno* as the model for her modern suburban hell in her "apocalyptic" second book *Linden Hills* (1985) and various aspects of Shakespeare's *King Lear* and *Romeo and Juliet* as important influences on her latest book *Mama Day* (1989). As Cather uses classical and biblical sources, as Welty, Glasgow, and Jewett use classical references, and as Porter uses Roman Catholic, Mexican, and biblical references, so Naylor reaches to her earlier education in the traditional canon.

Only much later did Naylor realize the diversity and richness of the African-American experience in literature and discover the work of women who, like herself, shared the two marginalized identities of female and black. As Calvin Hernton notes, black women writers must cross a sexual mountain, for "the world of black literature in the United States has been a world of black men's literature" (195). Naylor remarks that in the year of her birth, 1950, Gwendolyn Brooks received the Pulitzer Prize, but she never heard of Brooks in school. Not until she was twenty-seven years old did she discover that there were black women literary artists. Toni Morrison's *The Bluest Eye* (1969) was a "watershed" book for the young author, making her aware of a tradition of black writing women (*American Audio Prose Interview*).

Elaine Showalter notes that literary subcultures go through three stages, imitation of the models of the dominant discourse, protest against the morality and standards of those usages, and finally self-discovery, the reclamation of an authentic voice of the community. In the last stage, the existence of an artistically skilled, *and widely read,* body of work gives rise to the beginning of a true, independent literary tradition (*A Literature of Their Own,* 13). Showalter's model serves to illuminate Naylor's career. Her first books show the righteous anger seen in Showalter's protest stage (designated "Feminist" in women's writing) as the author protests both the impersonal indifference of the bureaucratic society to black women's suffering and the harsh models of competitive male achievement, which offer woman as the ultimate trophy and the available conquest; in her latest book she turns instead to the final stage of art (the *female* mode) as *Mama Day* speaks with the voice of the black woman and her community. Black texts, Gates insists, have a crucial difference in their use of the vernacular; the language that Gates presents has significant connections with the oral, pictorial local language of the home place (*Signifying Monkey,* xxii–xxiii). Through use of the vernacular voice, Naylor achieves the third stage of Showalter's evolution.

The women in the first novel, *The Women of Brewster Place,* are meant, as Naylor asserts, to represent "a tiny microcosm of the black female experience" (*American Audio Prose Interview*). No matter how diverse the women in age, talents, and experience, the wall seals them in behind barriers of racism and sexism, defines the limits of their aspirations, and shields the rest of the city from their influence. Losers all in the social competition, the black women of Brewster Place succeed first in creating a community and finally in tearing down with their bare hands the isolating wall.

Moreover, in *Brewster Place,* Naylor portrays the hate and fear that such men as Eugene hold toward Mattie's influence on "his woman" Ciel, as the author depicts exclusive male possession of the wife as the reward granted to each man, if he chooses to grasp it, in the competitive individualistic culture. And through the brutal gang rape of Lorraine, Naylor connects violence against women directly to the cultural ideal that privileges male aggression, acquisitiveness, and dominance. The fact that Lorraine has chosen to live with her female lover Tee, rather than a man, offers a justification for her rape to the gang; she has committed the ultimate sin in refusing to keep to her "place" as a woman in a masculine-dominated social setting. That the attack represents a homophobic attack is certainly correct, but it also represents an attack on any women who does not accede to subordinate status in a relationship with a man, who claims primary attachment to a woman, whether that be lover, sister, mother, or friend. Like Jewett's Mrs. Tolland, the refusal of Lorraine and Tee to conform has excited the curiosity and enmity of the conventional women around her, especially the gossiping churchwoman Sophie, who spies on Lorraine and her lover. Barbara Smith has noted the ambivalence at the heart of this story; Lorraine suffers the most violent fate, and the pair are both shown in an exclusively heterosexual context—although Tee often mentions a homosexual social club. Even as she identifies the homophobia motivating the attack, Smith neglects the overreaching sexism that underlies that hate—the Big Man's demand for dominance, which the young men emulate in the dead-end alley.[3]

As Smith notes, Mattie and her lifelong friend Etta are moved by the presence of Tee and Lorraine to examine their own attitudes toward love between women. When Mattie, the elder wise woman, muses that she has loved some women more deeply than any man and that some women have loved and labored for her more earnestly, Etta demurs, insisting that her experience is "different" from that of "the two." But Mattie insists, "Maybe it's not so different. . . . Maybe that's why some women get so riled up about it, 'cause they know deep down it's not so different after all" (141). But both Etta and Mattie, feeling the intensity of their own relationship, retreat, refusing to examine the mingled love, attraction, and responsibility they feel toward each other. As Eve Sedgwick has suggested, in contemporary society close relationships between women are only socially acknowledged after primary allegiance to the male is first sworn; otherwise the relationship is classified as "deviant" and therefore to be shunned. Nonetheless, like Louisa Goddard and Victoria Littlepage of Glasgow's *They Stooped to Folly*, Mattie and Etta share the deepest relationship of their respective lives, yet paternalistic social practice offers no publicly validated form for the celebration of that friendship and love. Love between women having either emotional or sexual intensity, or both, is ignored and reviled, finally attacked as illegitimate. This is the point of Naylor's narrative, and indeed Lorraine is not shunned by Kiswana, the political activist. Even Etta, who rejects Mattie's discussion of their love, understands that Sophie's attempt to eject Lorraine from a neighborhood meeting attacks female rebellion of all types. (As in Jewett and Cather, the churchwoman acts as the local militia for male leadership, enforcing conformity.)

Naylor connects the street violence on Brewster Place with the violence she perceives at the center of the American ruling bureaucracies. The young men leading urban gangs find no wide fields or deep forest to conquer, no boardroom to dominate as validation of their "success" as men in the social competition; instead they, like such female creations as Wharton's "mannequin" Lily Bart, see themselves as figures of fashion, having their existence primarily through life-style. Naylor shows that violence against Lorraine affirms the leader C.C. as a model of triumphant masculine initiative: "She had stepped into the thin strip of earth that they had claimed as their own. Bound by the last building on Brewster and a brick wall [the true end of the American social order in contrast to the fabled endless nature], they reigned in that unlit alley like dwarfed warrior-kings" (169–70). Naylor connects the dominance of the CEO with the display of force by C.C. and his followers. In Naylor's view, the neighborhood "dwarfed warrior-king," the socially subordinated male "cheated" of his perceived masculine birthright, asserts his dominance over woman in imitation of the Big Men, who now have expanded technological phalli for scattering "iron seed" into the womb of the supine earth. Naylor offers a suggestion for the cause of urban male violence. Denied the individual notice celebrated in cultural myths perpetuated by daily news and sportscasts, celebrity biographies, and television and movie narratives, without a "stateroom, armored tank, and executioner's chamber" of their own, the disenfranchised male still can find a way to assert his individual dominance within the social dead end of Brewster Place.

In contrast to these men, Naylor creates the fatherly figure of Ben, the gentle janitor who befriends Lorraine and who dies because of the violence against her. In contrast to C.C. and the other male figures who emulate the values of the dominant men, Ben refuses to return the cruelty the white world has visited upon him. In the South from which he fled, Ben has been cheated by the landowner, who promises Ben more land if he will ignore his daughter's sexual abuse by the white man. His wife Elvira accuses him of unmanliness because he will not accede to Mr. Clyde's demands, and ultimately his daughter is lost to the world of Memphis, sending back the money Elvira craves. Ben becomes an alcoholic, a figure of no great influence even on Brewster Place, yet in his compassion he illustrates—as do other masculine "failures" such as Asa Timberlake of *Beyond Defeat*, Mr. Elliott of *Two Lives*, William of *The Country of the Pointed Firs*, and Ray Kennedy of *The Song of the Lark* among others—that men as well as women can shelter and care. Unfortunately, these men spend much of their time shedding the cultural messages of hypermasculinity. But Ben is the one Brewster Place inhabitant who says to Lorraine, "I got nothing, but you welcome to all of that. Now how many folks is that generous?" (149). Together, they form a father-daughter relationship until violence tears them apart.

Mattie herself was started on her long road to Brewster Place by an unmarried pregnancy and a beating by her heartbroken father. She and her son Basil are sheltered by Miss Eva, who takes her in as a daughter. Miss Eva anticipates in her generosity and wisdom the woman Mattie herself becomes in the present time of the story. Despite her age, Miss Eva remains the lusty, humorous woman of her youth. She tells Mattie that she's had five husbands and "outlived 'em all," and her old house still glows with the laughter of her absent son's girl child, the aroma of a pot roast, and the gleam of brightly polished surfaces. She becomes the mother that Mattie, Basil, and her own granddaughter all need so desperately as she bonds together a family from the damaged urban setting. Like Grandmother Fincastle, Nannie and Sophia Jane, Mother Blackett and Almira Todd, Ántonia, and other wise women, Miss Eva holds the warmth of life after the beauty and passion of youth have passed. As Mattie realizes, Miss Eva replaces the mother she lost when she left her home. Thirty years later, as Mattie prepares to take Miss Eva's place, she remembers the lessons the old woman taught her, and she too in her turn takes over the task of sheltering the lost and the weak. Mattie, however, has no home or family of her own now; it must all be redone by will and emotion. Late at night and alone, her prayers are addressed to "the wisdom of a yellow, blue-eyed spirit who had foreseen this day and had tried to warn her" (42).

Cast aside by a succession of men, Mattie's girlhood friend, Etta Mae Johnson, places her last hope for a "respectable" life on enticing Reverend Moreland T. Woods into marriage. A rebel like Amy Rhea, Virgie Rainey, and Clara Vavrika, Etta Mae was "a black woman who was not only unwilling to play by the rules, but whose spirit challenged the very right of the rules to exist" (59). Etta is driven out of the small town from which they both come, moving from man to man as she seeks always to better herself economically and socially. She breaks the rules by accepting them with a vengeance; she seeks the big stake by identification with a powerful man. Like her male counterparts, Etta wants to rise in the social scale, and she will do it by treating the opposite sex as a commodity. For a woman, however, the game runs out, and age comes. Abandoned by Reverend Woods after their sexual encounter, Etta realizes that she is trapped in Brewster Place, that as with Mattie, Tee, and Lorraine, she has no place more to go. As she walks into Mattie's house, she hears Mattie's records, and she realizes someone has waited up for her. Once again, the wise woman gathers in the lost sister, offering love and comfort after the wars of romance and passion. As the three wise women shelter Nelly Deane, as Grandmother Fincastle aids Ada, as Almira Todd comforts Mrs. Tolland, Mattie brings Etta Mae home, into the small woman's space allowed in the modern American city. Unlike the earlier rebels who disappear from the community's history, Etta Mae's life will be difficult, but it will not be solitary because she and Mattie will together keep Brewster Place alive, fighting the conventionality within the community and the indifference and bigotry without.

Like Jewett, Welty, Cather, Porter, Gilman, and Glasgow, Naylor shows a persistent suspicion of the male-led church, although not the faith itself, as an instrument of control for women by the social leadership. In *Brewster Place*, as in Jewett's "The Foreigner," the female churchwoman enforces the morality of the male leadership against Lorraine. And both *Brewster Place* and *Linden Hills* have scorching portraits of male clergy who cynically violate the tenets of their religions through self-indulgence. The "spawning" of the impersonal, legalistic rules of remote complex organizations and the lethal seed of the "dwarfed warrior-kings" contrast with the birth of children and dreams engendered by the women's community. Discord comes from the bureaucratic outside, either directly or through those who accept its judgment of value. Romance, as before, brings the women into unwed maternity, disappointment, or bitter marriage.

Like the domestic novelists so long before her, who created reconstituted female networks, Naylor portrays women of spirit and determination remaking their community and re-forming their families. And in the passion for justice of Kiswana Browne, formerly of Linden Hills, Naylor indicates that Brewster Place will not fall. When she visits, Kiswana's mother is offended by her daughter's repudiation of her suburban Linden Hills existence, and by her daughter's characterization of her own past, but in an emotional exchange, the mother concludes that she raised her children so that no one would ever slight them, and "that's not being white or red or black—that's being a mother" (86). Suddenly, Kiswana has an epiphany similar to that of Vickie Templeton at the end of "Old Mrs. Harris": she "suddenly realized that her mother had trod through the same universe she herself was traveling. . . . She stared at the woman she had been and was to become" (87). (In the taped interview Naylor says that she could not entirely condemn Mrs. Browne, so she put her in the outer ring of Linden Hills.) In *The Women of Brewster Place*, Naylor places a strong emphasis on shared identification between women, while depicting the oppression of the urban bureaucracies. In Brewster Place, threatened by mandates, legalisms, and distant judgmental bureaucracies, the living community embraces black women and men of all ages and circumstances except those tied to the morality of *Linden Hills*. The woman's community, but not the home place, lives despite the urban bureaucracies: "*It watched its last generation of children torn away from it by court orders and eviction notices, and it had become too tired and sick to help them. . . . But the colored daughters of Brewster, spread over the canvas of time, still wake with their dreams misted on the edge of a yawn*" (192, emphasis Naylor's).

Naylor's second book, *Linden Hills*, pictures the author's inferno of success, the competitive and isolated lives of the black "winners" of the competitive consumer culture. When asked if Tupelo Drive, the inner circle of her Hell, reflected her southern childhood, Naylor answered that its name represented instead the two pillars found at the entrance of the lower Hell in the City of Dis. Linden Hills represents a male-controlled American dystopia in contrast to the ideal female pastoral of Mama Day's Willow Springs. As with Dante's *Inferno*, the guides to the infernal landscape are a pagan poet, Willie, the unbeliever from the outside, and a young poet seeking salvation from his sinful heritage, Lester. Like Dante, Lester cannot renounce Linden Hills until he has viewed the center of its evil.

Naylor has identified a loss of communal memory and "a geographical center" as a crucial factor in negative self-images of black people (*American Audio Prose*). The author considers that individual identity arises out of a group unity based on a shared oral tradition of family and neighborhood history, out of distinctive local foods, colloquial speech, and codes of behavior. Naylor identifies the loss of the oral tradition, the mother tongue, the family interaction, as dissolving the "communal ties, familial ties, spiritual ties," the connections that shape an enduring sense of individual identity. She recalls that her own family, despite their poverty, gave her a sense of self which came out of their struggles and experiences in the South.

Whereas Naylor identifies the women of Brewster Place as having "very strong communal ties," the black citizens of Linden Hills seek to leave their pasts and their communal identities behind. As they rise in material success and social esteem—both central markers of success in the social competition—they descend ever further down toward the deepest Hell of Luther Nedeed's undertaking parlor. In Naylor's words, these bonds of identity "all melted away the farther they come down" (*Linden Hills*, 16). If Mama Day can be said to preside over a harmonious female pastoral, Luther Nedeed rules over a competitive consumerist Hell.

The first Luther Nedeed, he who reportedly sold his wife and children into slavery to get a stake, soon discovered that the future was "white," that the white male leadership would determine the definitions of "success." He decided that success, defined as an acknowledgment of black individual achievement in the market economy, would be the overriding cultural value. A deformed, froglike creature, Luther constantly renews himself through the single son named for himself who is born of a nameless mother. He indicates the nature of marriage at the center, for the son is shaped and schooled by him, and the succession of wives are always and only known as Mrs. Nedeed.

Naylor paints the perfect male material achiever through the limning of Luther Nedeed. With deft satiric touches, Naylor portrays the deity of Linden Hills and, by implication, the modern social leaders, the Big Men, writing that within the social competition it becomes clear that the great power is simply the "*will* to possess. It had chained the earth to the names of a few and it would chain the cosmos as well" (17). The white leaders find no need to destroy the leaders of Linden Hills because they understand that they both serve "the same god" (17).

On the outer rings are such people as Winston and David, lovers torn apart by Winston's marriage, which will "prove" his heterosexuality and thus advance his career; Catherine Ward calls them Naylor's Paolo and Francesca. As a result of his betrayal of David, his bride, and himself, Winston is promised a deed to the deepest rings of Linden Hills. In contrast to Winston's failure of love, Naylor offers us the abiding love between Willie Mason and Lester Tilson, the two comrades who will walk together out of the hell of Naylor's Linden Hills. Like Mattie and Etta in *Brewster Place*, Willie and Lester have the most intense and sensitive relationship in the narrative. They bring to each other their dreams and their fears; together they seek a definition of manhood that will defeat the sterility and calculation of the personal relationships they see on Tupelo Drive. Willie is the oral poet, the living voice of the black community, whereas Lester writes his poems in reflection of his Linden Hills education. Lester's family lives on the outer rings, the space allotted the uncommitted, those who are neither good nor evil.

The Tilsons have had a sure guide in the person of old Grandmother Tilson, who had warned them that the price of living in Luther's infernal suburb will be their souls. The original Luther first tried to buy her land and lease it back to her, but the old wise woman drove him off. As Ward writes, "She warned her children and neighbors that they were in danger of losing the 'mirror' in their souls, of forgetting what they 'really want and believe'" (74). The Tilson women show the gradual disintegration of the family from the courageous old grandmother to the status-seeking granddaughter. This is the limbo that Lester lacks the will to flee at the narrative's beginning.

The loving relationship of Lester and Willie contrasts as well with that of Maxwell Smyth and Xavier Donnell, the young men on the way up in the corporate structure and on their way down in Linden Hills. In contrast to the young poets' discussions on morality and poetry, the young executives' relationship with each other hinges on such matters as how long each waits to respond to the ring of a doorbell. Maxwell, who is Xavier's "mentor," warns his colleague to avoid marrying black women because they either refuse to assume a subordinate role,

or—even worse—they "let themselves go," refusing to be the mannequin they both demand as a complement to the success. In Maxwell's
own life, he does not allow himself to have sexual relations often because of the loss of isolation and the potential loss of control. In fact,
he has disciplined his body so completely that it resembles the perfectly
working machine; as he walks in the cold December air, he "seemed
to have made the very elements disappear, while it was no more than
the psychological sleight-of-hand that he used to make his blackness
disappear" (102). The man who joins the top of the bureaucratic structure becomes the perfection of Weber's rationalized manager, and as
Ward points out, ironically enough, this mechanical man becomes a
type of the Dantean glutton, his appetite, however, is not for food or
drink, but rather for the endless power of the white male leadership.

As the aspirant to this life, Xavier justifies his choice to Lester who
tells him that their ideal of progress is spelled "W-H-I-T-E" and that
he and Maxwell are merely tokens who allow the system to continue
without essential alteration. Xavier responds that a photographic
spread in the "men's" magazine *Penthouse* proves him wrong. It features a nude dark woman with a short "Afro" haircut, who is shod with
leopard-skin boots and little else. She is pulling on a chain. At the end
of the eight-page feature she is shown having reeled in the chain as
she stands with her foot on a white hunter. Maxwell says triumphantly
that today it's *Penthouse*, but tomorrow the American world. But Lester
and Willie realize that the spread implies that black people live in a
jungle, that the living woman has been changed into "breathless body"
(115), and later Willie remembers that his shame comes from the model's resemblance to his own sister. Where Maxwell sees cultural acceptance in the spread of commodification of black women in the mass
media, the young men understand that now both black and white
women have a chance to be "sold out." Both Willie and Lester feel
their connections to their racial identity and to their female family,
despite Lester's rejection of his mother's upwardly striving in the outer
rings of Linden Hills.

In the lower rings, Laurel Johnson Dumont dies crumpled in the
bottom of her empty winter swimming pool, crushed after taking her
arching swan dive into death, her last flight. Lester and Willie find her
body by following her grandmother's plaintive call to the child who has
been unable to hear her for so many years. As with many previous

female characters in this discussion, Laurel has no available parents, her mother dead, her father in love with a selfish young woman. Her grandmother takes her into her small home for wonderful summers. There she discovered her two loves, music and swimming. As with such women writers as Welty, Cather, Chopin, Carson McCullers, and Porter, music and dance, here synchronized swimming, becomes for the protagonist the undiscovered voice: "It was difficult to tell whether her body was making the music or the music her body" (223). Laurel finds the creativity, the harmony missing in her life away from her grandmother's house. In her grandmother's home she reaches the fullest expression of her own personality.

As Laurel moves away, attends university, and attains success, she accumulates the markers of her progress: Phi Beta Kappa key, featured articles in the *New York Times* business pages, a wealthy marriage to a scion of the Linden Hills Dumonts. Laurel slowly realizes how many times she has had no time for her grandmother. Upon her return to Roberta Johnson's home, however, she thinks of it as "little more than a shack" compared to her Linden Hills house, and the grandmother's place smells like old age (230). Laurel discovers that the woman's space in the competitive social order is small indeed. When her grandmother asks her why she has returned, Laurel responds that when people are in trouble, "[D]on't they go home?" (231). But Roberta Johnson reminds her that the small house is not her home, and Naylor continues, "So Laurel went home. And home was Linden Hills. If she had any doubt, she could look at her driver's license, or call up the post office just to be sure" (231). Home is now defined by bureaucratic designations, not by personal relationships. Her grandmother's world and her life seems dingy and shrunken compared to the jewels, automobiles, and elegant clothes of Tupelo Drive. In many respects, Laurel Dumont's story has parallels with that of Wharton's Lily Bart. Like Lily, Laurel feels a tie to the small personal space allowed to women within the social structures, but nonetheless finds herself inevitably shaped by the consumer culture. Women here, as there, function as ornaments to their husbands, with the addition of the wives' own success now validating and expanding their husband's own power. Like Lily Bart, Laurel, the prize, is rootless, "the number of places she couldn't claim, dizzying" (233). Despite her accomplishments in the reigning social bureaucracies, Laurel, like Lily Bart so many years before, is finally an object of display.

Bit by bit Laurel tries to get back to her family and her history, but given Naylor's firm contention that the individual identity is shaped by and inseparable from the communal ties, she finds there is no foundation on which to rebuild. She gives up, in their turn, her profession, her social circle, her husband, her possessions. She stays on alone in her husband's empty house. Now she frantically shuts out the world with music, choosing Mahler above all, appreciating music as knowledge, as discrimination, as *expertise*, in contrast to the bodily joy of her youth at her mother's house, within nature. On a final visit to save her child, Roberta makes explicit the woman author's attitude toward language and music when she remarks that Billie Holliday and Bessie Smith communicate emotional truths inexpressible by "plain talk." When the lost modern daughter notes that Holliday and Smith were alcoholics and drug addicts and thus poor examples for her own controlled life, the grandmother asserts connections between generations of black women:

> "No, you ain't never had to worry, like a lot of us did, about Jim Crow or finding your next meal, but if that's all you hear in them songs, then you don't know as much about music as you think you do. What they *say* is one thing, but you supposed to hear is, 'I can.'" Roberta came and stood over her. "'I can,' Laurel, that's what you supposed to hear. It ain't a music that speaks to your head like some of this stuff you been playing, or to your body like the rock music of these kids. But it speaks to a place they ain't got no name for yet, where you supposed to be at home." (236)

Roberta explicitly asserts the passing of experience from one generation of women to another. From the example of female creativity, at no matter how much cost, the daughters learn to live and to create. In her life at the center, Laurel learns to shun their black female messages coming directly through music; instead she listens to the music of European males.

Laurel has lost touch with her heritage as a black woman. In her success, Laurel believes, like other autonomous female protagonists, that she is different, insulated from the failures of the other women in her community. Instead of the Linden Hills demand for excision of her maternal past, the records of Smith and Holliday sing of that past, illuminating the strength of the black women who sing despite the best efforts of the white, male-controlled social bureaucracies to ignore or to trivialize their experience. Those voices, if she would listen, would sing her home to Roberta, connecting her with those before who have joyed in the face of defeat, who have refused to retreat.

Laurel makes a last attempt, begging Roberta to tell her the old stories, to spin out the black female past, and to give her back her own childhood. She has internalized the morality of the massed, materialistic social order around her. The weight of her loss and depth of her entrapment only adds to her depression, as she listens to the stories she realizes that she has "nothing inside her to connect up to them" (239). Finally, like Lily Bart, Laurel's rootlessness overcomes her, she realizes that she has no way back, no solid earth to sustain her growth. When Luther comes to evict her from her house because her husband is gone and she has none of "his" children, she realizes that she has never really had an independent existence separate from that of her husband in Linden Hills. Like so many other dependent women, this modern woman finds herself with no identity that expresses her self and her female history. Her argument with Luther was only a reflex, but now Laurel realizes the meaning of time in hell through Luther's words: "She had never lived in a house in which she had never lived" (246). Unlike Lily Bart and Edna Pontellier, Laurel cannot even dream her way back to the home place in death. In her last moment she can only dream of a cessation of pain. Her last hope is a flight to oblivion, "Once she got down, she'd be free" (248).

The deepest rings of Nedeed's inferno are composed of those who have completely renounced that communal memory, Laurel Dumont, Professor Daniel Braithwaite, and finally Luther Nedeed. As Naylor notes, those on the upper reaches lose their family ties, next they lose the social, personal ties, next the spiritual, religious ties, and finally all traces of their ethnic heritage as they strip away all traces of the received communal identities to enter the social competition. The old history professor Dr. Braithwaite occupies the ring well within sight of Luther's undertaking parlor, because he has converted the living memory of the black people into the rational associational language for his own self-advancement: "He's this dried-up voyeur—that's the worst kind of academic you can have, someone who goes through life, sapping and sapping and storing knowledge" (*American Audio Prose Interview*). Unlike the living stories of Mama Day, Dr. Braithwaite disconnects memory from emotion, embalming it into the dry, associational language, trapping it in impenetrable jargon that excludes those who are "outside." As Willie, our poet guide to the underworld, tells us, universities have fences to "get you used to the idea that what they have in there is different, special. Something to be separated from the rest of the world" (45). Willie sees that he must never be a hired pen like the historian. Dr. Braithwaite's language, like the barrier around the university, serves as a fence against the anger of the unheard, the blacks and the women of Linden Hills. If memory of the community is the key to an enduring self for members of marginalized groups as these women writers suggest, then the Braithwaites who rewrite those memories into palatable tales of deserved failure, enduring weakness, and lost rebellions deserve opprobrium. Or even worse, those memories disappear into convoluted language, reified into a social problem within a complicated methodology. For these academics give over, in Mary Douglas's words, the "lineages and ancestral shrines" to the control of the dominant discourse safely sanitized of all emotion. They justify the group's losses, stressing how they could have been avoided, planting their roots in helplessness, showing how "progress" can be measured.

The metaphor for Braithwaite's memory are his dead willow trees. Because they blocked his view of Nedeed and his house, because the living memories of blacks and women separated him from success, Braithwaite had them killed. Now he can imagine they will bloom for half a year, during winter, just as he can believe his histories reflect lives. He has killed his living knowledge of the community so that he could more easily keep the deadly Nedeed in sight. He need no longer suffer guilt. Through the dried, blasted nature of Dr. Braithwaite's grounds, Naylor protests the jargon-filled academic language, which pretends detached intellectualism and erases the pain of experience. Braithwaite's preserved, embalmed trees resemble the perfumed, cosmetic-covered corpses that are Nedeed's true female loves—the ultimate compliant mannequins. The two deadly creations of the two successful men prepare us to enter the vital female pastoral of *Mama Day*.

At the time of the action of *Linden Hills*, the latest Luther has imprisoned his wife and son, who he suspects of "belonging" to another man, in his cellar, an abandoned embalming parlor without food and with only limited water offered in small amounts for "good behavior." After the boy's death by starvation and dehydration, his distracted mother takes a journey back through the trunks holding the abandoned diaries, clothes, and photographs, the only records of the earlier anonymous wives. The first Mrs. Nedeed bemoans her enslavement by her husband as more absolute than that of slavery itself, a later wife begins to cook enormous amounts of food, finally seeking to poison her husband, and a third progressively disappears from photographs of herself with her family. Only in her own extremity does the last Mrs. Nedeed discover their names, finding the female connections that allow her to destroy Luther and his kingdom.

Here, as in the domestic and introspective novels by women, female voices reach out to each other over time and distance, their respective miseries in marriage exposed. Luwana Packerville's diaries turning to madness, Evelyn Creton's domestic labor turning to poison, Priscilla McQuire's photographs turning to blankness, and finally Willa Prescott, through their words and images, turning to the avenging angel who destroys Luther's kingdom in a fiery conclusion on Christmas Eve. Starting in 1837, Luwana Packerville's entries hidden in her Bible begin Willa's journey back. Luwana's writing creates a fictional sister "Luwana" in her loneliness because "together we can weather those tiny tempests that blow through a woman's world" (122). She was first a slave bought by Luther; her son is freed by her husband but not she. Naylor reveals through this circumstance her perception of the truth of upper-class marriage. Slowly, Luwana realizes that she has exchanged one slavery for another, "From his birth, he has been his father's son in flesh and now in spirit. But I tremble daily, for I fear it is even more than that. . . . Believe me, I am not losing my mind but it is not just that he is Luther's son, he *is* Luther" (123). "Luwana" answers that there is nothing in her sister's marriage that "is not repeated in countless other homes around you" (123). Through the buried tales of the successive Mrs. Nedeeds, Naylor builds up a critique of marriage at the social center. Like Chopin, Wharton, Gilman, Cather, and Glasgow, Naylor shows marriage within the material competition placing the wife on a shelf as one of many possessions who display the husband's achievement. As Willa—the present Mrs. Nedeed—regains her strength, she remembers her own shopping trips to New York as she struggled to make "it" change. Naylor parodies the slogans that alienate the woman from her own body through the profitable manipulation of fantasy, "steal a little thunder from a rose," "paradise regained," "say it without a word," and "believe in magic" (149). For all the ministrations of the potions, "it" never changes as she becomes increasingly peripheral in Luther's self-expansion.

At the end, Willa changes from the "she" of the early passages, claiming her own identity. She refuses to be Mrs. Nedeed as she recovers the names and stories of her predecessors and sisters, claiming their strength and histories, finding her way out of his jail of imposed definition. Margaret Homans discusses Willa's emergence from the "cave" as a re-vision of male myth, turning it into a birth tale. Willa finds in their shared domestic tragedies the "mirror," a cooking pot, which will allow her to see herself clearly. Then Naylor brings her character to her own birth through her lost female community; as she sleeps, she dreams herself past the human limitations of material reality. The author rewrites a creation myth, whose destructive power recalls the Great Mother in her negative aspect; through this figure she prepares us for the creative power of Sapphira Wade and Miranda Day: "She breathed in to touch the very elements that at the beginning of time sparked to produce the miracle some called divine creation and others the force of life" (288). She passes beyond the "ovaries, wombs, and glands" to reach the cosmic creativity that will destroy Luther's hell: "Out, toward the edge of the universe with its infinite possibility to make space for the volume of her breath" (288). Naylor tells us that it is a "birth" out of the thunder that Sapphira and Miranda can summon, and she awakes Willa Prescott Nedeed.

That Luther Nedeed anticipates the healing of Mama Miranda Day is suggested by the contrasts between them. He is an undertaker, she is a midwife. He dominates the residents of suburban Linden Hills, she nurtures the neighbors of communal Willow Springs. He values material success, she honors communal ties. He refuses the black spiritual, historical, and cultural past, she keeps its traditions and memories. The final conflagration that destroys Luther, his mad wife, and dead son, an unholy family whose death on Christmas Eve clears the way in Naylor's fiction for the serenity and wisdom of Mama Day's ideal island community. This sequence of books brings to mind Glasgow's last two books, *In This Our Life* and *Beyond Defeat*, in which the venality and impersonality of William Fitzroy's Queenborough yields to the generosity and acceptance of Kate Oliver's pastoral Hunter's Fare. In both, the hellish, unholy family of the male leader is changed into the chosen, blessed community of the female figure of warm autumn.

As with preceding women authors, Naylor turns to the home place in *Mama Day* (1988). In Mama Day's Willow Springs, Naylor summons a separate, democratic community wrested from a white slavemaster and landowner by the first mother and wise woman, Sapphira Wade.[4] Through sisters Miranda, again an unmarried "seer," and Abigail, the mother of three daughters, Peace, Hope, and Grace and granddaughter Cocoa, Naylor shows the harmony between the single artist-woman and the mother-woman. As Gilman did so long ago, Naylor insists that biological maternity does not define or enclose participation in motherhood. When Cocoa is threatened by death, Miranda tells George that no mother could feel more pain or pride in "Baby Girl" as she grew. Because the sisters complement each other's femininity, the sisters combine without rancor or jealousy to bring to life and happiness their child, Ophelia-Cocoa-Baby Girl—the daughter's multiple names a litany of love. Cocoa reflects that together they were the perfect mother. In the separate island community, Willow Springs, Miranda works through nature, midwife and death dealer, daughter of the Mother Goddess as she redefines the received categories of gender conventions and rejoins the human community.

Mama Day opens with a narrative celebration of the female seer Miranda, and her foremother, the founder of Willow Springs, Sapphira Wade. A voice tells the reader of the island women's world, found on no map, lying just off the coast of South Carolina and Georgia and then the narrating voice—defined as neither male nor female—in the preface enjoins us to hear the maternal language of Mama Day and Sapphira Wade. Naylor seeks to bring the reader immediately and intuitively into Willow Springs as she insists on direct personal communication. Miranda's voice, or more precisely the voice of the community—she is the oracle—merge with the reader's own emotions and memories, a part that the mainland has taught the reader to ignore: "Think about it: ain't nobody really talking to you. We're sitting right here in Willow Springs, and you're God-knows-where. It's August 1999—ain't but a slim change it's the same season where you are. Uh, huh, listen. Really listen this time: the only voice is your own" (10). The community's voice comes close, enters the reader's experience, demanding that he or she, black or white, young or old, reach back, to remember the wise woman. Although the voice clearly arises from the black community, it invites the reader into the homes as the seer's legend is passed, as the community members fix their autos, prepare their dinners. With the insistence on the oral nature of the printed narrative and its direct, immediate, even telepathic transmission, the writing daughter Naylor attempts to transcend the limits of modern language and summon the connecting strength of myth. And in her refusal to classify the opening narrator as belonging to either gender, Naylor insists that the home place welcomes men as well as women. The mystery of religion is once again merged with the acts of the daily life as the domestic acts and manual labor of the working man and woman are elevated to the sacred.

The narrating voice recollects the college-educated Reema's boy, who returns from the mainland to study Willow Springs's customs and language. This figure allows Naylor to juxtapose Mama Day's maternal language with the impersonal associational language represented by the writing of Reema's boy—he is known on Willow Springs by his mother's name—and the language and calculation of the mainland investors who seek to persuade Miranda to sell the island for "development." Reema's boy "rattled on about 'ethnography,' 'unique speech patterns,' 'cultural preservation,' and whatever else he seemed to be getting so much pleasure out of while talking into his little gray machine" (7). When the academic books arrive, the inhabitants discover that Reema's boy writes condescendingly of Willow Springs's legends, calling it "asserting our cultural identity" and "inverting hostile social and political parameters." The narrating consciousness laughs off the corrupt and limited modern language, which separates itself from the morality and emotions of the maternal home and prepares us for Mama Day's own narrative of her salvation of her beloved Cocoa. Tracing the woman's lineage back to the first mother, the narrator looks forward to the next century. The author relinquishes control of the narrative, telling us that the story comes from within, from our own memories, our own voice.

In *The Signifying Monkey*, Henry Louis Gates contrasts the "speakerly text" of Zora Neale Hurston with the ideal of the individual text found in Richard Wright. Gates posits that difference in voice comes from the attitudes of both toward the black culture around them, Wright, in Gates's opinion, believing that the only representative of "the ideal individual black [self]" was the author himself. Further, Gates observes that Wright's humanity is "achieved only at the expense of his fellow blacks" (183). Accordingly, Wright uses the strategies so prominent in the white male canon, the recourse to "realism" or the depiction of social arrangements as they exist and the recreation of the self-made man. Hurston, in contrast, allows the community to speak for itself through the agency of the author herself, creating a "transcendent, ultimately racial self, extending far beyond the merely individual" (183). Gates depicts Hurston and Wright at opposite poles of African-American literature, fellow artists who carried on a critical debate through reviews as well as through the fiction itself.[5] A trained anthropologist and folklorist, Hurston understood the power of the language of the black community from her own intellectual work; in addition, her protagonist Janie Crawford of *Their Eyes Were Watching God* as a woman of color—the member of two marginal groups, understood the consolations offered by her woman friend, and she suspected the romantic attentions of material achievers like Jody Starks, who would view her as a possession. Unlike Wright's acceptance of competitive individualism, Hurston understood the terrible isolation of the single human being and reached toward connection. If, as Calvin Hernton contends, the black literary tradition has until this point been as dominated by male voices as the white canon, this poses even more difficulties for the black woman facing white male structures.

Hurston's language itself reflects the attempt to bring the mother tongue into literature, to bridge the gap between reader and author and fictional community. Indeed, the local language arises from groups who retain some of the communal identity within the bureaucratic society.[6] In line with Gates's theory of transmission of fictional patterns, Naylor acknowledges Hurston's influence when she came to write the crucial storm scene in *Mama Day*. She gained confidence in the ability of the communal voice to carry the narrative through her reading of the flood scene in *Their Eyes Were Watching God*. As Andree McLaughlin writes, African-American women must refuse the Western images and ideas that deny full humanity to those who in their persons or their lives challenge white, male, Christian dominance, and the materialistic pyramid. McLaughlin calls for black women to redefine themselves in their entirety, which includes, as do the other visions here, the men, children, and natural world: "By symbolmaking, ideamaking, and worldmaking, they are creators in a preeminent sense" (176). The critic concludes that these women along with other women of color can defeat that dominant world view by recourse to "the traditional world views and fearlessness of their maligned foremothers" (176). Along with other feminist critics and women artists, McLaughlin identifies these new constructions as leading to "real change in the real world through real means" (176).

Naylor's *Mama Day* moves toward this ideal as the author seizes the voice of the community. The communal voice of Hurston, her courageous defiance of both black male and white definitions, has empowered Naylor, as well as other African-American women authors, to write out of their experience of doubled marginality as woman and black, and like Hurston, Naylor reaches back to the local language, which exists at the margins of the competitive bureaucratic social order. By refusing the authority of the scientifically detached introspective author, Naylor, like the other women here, negates the idea of the self-created genius and instead insists on the vitality of woman's communal voice.

Hidden away from the American mainland, connected only by a fragile bridge, Willow Springs enriches the New York of Cocoa and her husband George. As with Porter's "Pale Horse, Pale Rider," the bridge demarcates the separation of the two worlds, a function served by the mountain in Glasgow's *Vein of Iron*, Gilman's *Herland*, and Welty's *The Optimist's Daughter*, the vast plains in *My Ántonia*, and the ocean in Jewett's *The Country of the Pointed Firs*. In all, the natural world shelters the other place at the same time as the author indicates the imaginary nature of the hidden home as well as its different relationships and beliefs.

As with Van of *Herland*, George serves as the reader's guide to Willow Springs. A city man, George grew up without a mother or father; instead he received the just and impersonal guidance of Mrs. Jackson of the Wallace P. Andrews Shelter for Boys. She teaches her charges the affective rules for survival in the city: "Our rage didn't matter to her, our hurts or disappointments over what life had done to us. None of that was going to matter a damn in the outside world, so we might as well start learning it at Wallace P. Andrews. There were only rules and facts" (24). Mrs. Jackson is the perfect mother of the abandoned children of the bureaucratic society; she offers fairness and promises control as long as her children follow the rules. Although harsh, her punishments for misdeeds are dispassionate; emotional reaction and personal relationships will only hinder her charges in the city outside. George represents the man of the regimented social order; like Mr. Elliott of McIntosh's domestic novel, he must learn the morality of the home place. When he meets the mothers of his bride, George realizes that he has come back to a home he never knew, but at some level mourned. As he crosses the bridge from the mainland, that good man knows that he enters "another world," the other world in which nature enters the breath and blood of each person, spanning the divide between environment and human being. George knows that "it all smelled like forever" (175), and when Abigail blesses him, he realizes that no woman had ever called him her child before. As Cocoa tells him, he has come home.

Naylor suggests that George's lonely life represents the emotional costs to men as well as women of the mother's loss. Although Hazel Carby calls for a return to the urban setting for verisimilitude in the portrayal of the lives of urban blacks, Naylor's career suggests that portrayals of black rural communities, even the ideal home place, represents more than a facile "romantic" vision of the folk, just as in the earlier white women's writing it represents more than simple "nostalgia" (175). As Barbara Smith notes, Alice Walker, Toni Morrison, Margaret Walker, and Zora Neale Hurston incorporate such folk arts as root working, folk medicine, midwifery, and conjure into their narratives to capture the distinctive experience of black history and community. Smith offers this concise observation: "The use of Black women's language and cultural experience in books *by* Black women *about* Black women results in a miraculously rich coelescing of form and content and also takes their writing far beyond the confines of white/male literary structures" (174). Smith concludes that critics would find many connections within bodies of work by African-American women. White women too can find segments of their experience and history in books by black women; there are many roads to and from the home place.

Although Mama Day still believes in the male deity as the first creator, she imagines a powerful female partner. In Miranda's extremity,
when Cocoa is threatened with death, she knows she must summon
the Mother, but she cannot name her. Her name has been lost. To free
her mind, Mama Day sets her house in order, prayer mingling with
and arising out of her domestic rituals. Frantically, she searches
through a catalog of names, "Samantha," "Sarena," "Salinda," "Sa-
vannah," as she moves around her home touching the sacred cooking
vessels, asking her familiar, Cicero the rooster, cleaning away the outward dust of male experience to get back to the creator. She prays to
the "Father and the Son as she'd been taught. But she falls asleep,
murmuring the names of women. And in her dreams she finally meets
Sapphira" (280). Through her prayer, her devotion to the homely tools
of her power, Miranda finally reaches back to the mystic ancestress
who first won the island from the white slaveowner. The goddess
whose name is never "literally said" is the "guiding spirit for that island" (*American Audio Prose*). Arising out of a historical memory, a
racial memory as well as a female memory, Sapphira's name comes
only when Miranda passes through rationality, through male myth,
coming at last through dreams to the first seer. As she sleeps, in
dreams, Sapphira comes, nourishing Miranda, calling her "daughter,"
giving her the female power of working with nature. Naylor makes it
clear that Sapphira Wade, like any deity, cannot be described except
through her identity as a conjure woman of African ancestry. Like the
Virgin Mary in her many manifestations, Sapphira takes on the complexion of the worshipper: "satin black, biscuit cream, red as Georgia
clay: depending on which of us takes a mind to her" (3). Unlike Mary,
the ever-virgin handmaiden, however, the fully sexual Sapphira, like
all the female demigoddesses in this study, is independently creative
and restorative within her own realm: "She turned the moon into salve,
the stars into a swaddling cloth, and healed the wounds of every creature walking on two or down on four" (3).

Now Miranda can command the thunder in the thrilling storm scene
as the mother deity and the seer battle the false arts of obsessive passion. As Naylor has remarked, she originally feared that this central
scene could not encompass the symbolism and power of the storm if it
was written in the community's voice. Depicting the turmoil in the
mother god's community as the daughter passes toward death, the

hurricanes arise from the coast of Africa, Sapphira's birthplace. Naylor intends this hurricane to serve as the central metaphor of the Middle Passage, and she wondered as she contemplated this sophisticated metaphor if the local, communal "world view" could carry it to completion. Then remembering Hurston's flood in *Their Eyes Were Watching God*, she gained the confidence to allow the community to speak for itself.

Like the female elders in Jewett, Porter, Welty, and Glasgow, Sapphira and her female descendant Miranda guard the gates of birth and death, bringing her healing powers of growth to the natural world. Like the male deity, Sapphira has her own day of commemoration, Candle Walk, whose nature implicitly comments on the mainland's commercialized Christmas, a holiday most notably portrayed in Naylor through Luther's fiery demise. The story of Candle Walk's founding comes from a local legend, which says that when God threw down the island from heaven, he brought along some stars. The mighty conjure woman, Sapphira Wade, tells the deity to let them stay, so that she can lead on with light. Thus the ritual of celebration asks each member to carry a candle and a gift as they walk from house to house in a ceremony something like the Mexican *posada*. Instead of exchanging purchased gifts among friends, the members of the community carry a gift, however modest, as long as it is homemade or the product of the earth. These gifts are given to the needy and the lonely as the givers walk about on Candle Walk.

In Willow Springs the women carry the memory, the magic, and the creative power of the ideal community. Together Sapphira, Cocoa, and Mama Day form a sort of woman's trinity with mother, daughter, and spirit. The antagonist of the narrative is Ruby, a woman jealously in love with a younger man, transformed into an evil sorceress; Naylor portrays Ruby's obsession as the source of disorder and evil within the community. The supposed conjure man, Doctor Buzzard, is in fact an ineffectual figure of fun.

Naylor implies that the home place, existing in "no state," enriches the America outside despite its distance and isolation. Cocoa, for example, sees New York not as a city, but as a collection of small towns; her childhood experience of the mothers enables her to humanize the impersonal urban setting. Her experience with Willow Springs accompanies her to the city, but George's childhood leaves him unable to understand the mores of Mama Day's island as his experience with the gambling circle illustrates—he exposes and defeats an ancient male charlatan, robbing the old man of one of his few illusions. When the mainland developers seek to buy the island, promising jobs and prosperity for Willow Springs, Miranda sends them packing from her women's world because "even well-meaning progress and paradise don't go hand in hand" (185). The regimented, impersonal society and its language gain no foothold on Sapphira's island.

At the narrative's climax, Naylor depicts the wise woman struggling to convey her meaning in modern language. When Miranda tells George that he must undertake a quest to save his wife, Cocoa, who is bewitched and dying from Ruby's sexual jealousy, the city man replies that she is talking in metaphors. Through Miranda's anguish, Naylor portrays the modern emptying of effective ritual communication from literature, as she dismisses the elegant, aesthetic concept of metaphor as belonging to the present leisure entertainment of intellectual literature. She concludes that she is speaking of efficacious ritual speech and acts: "The stuff folks dreamed up when they was making a fantasy, while what she was talking about was *real*" (294). Naylor portrays the shared symbolism that holds the bonding power of the community, that ritual language charged with emotion when understood and underlined with belief. The language Miranda summons is literature in its truest sense, possessing force and consequence in the real, natural world; it breaks out of the library's walls; it defies explanation and explication. Naylor evokes the language of the face-to-face woman's community, calling up the immediate emotion, the efficacy of shared ritual. In Mama Day's "paradise," communication and law come from old tales and memories, lived ties between neighbors, and continuity between the female generations; by recourse to both Miranda's creativity through the garden—work with the natural world and through the quilt—art through the spirit, Naylor returns to the metaphors found in many writers from the beginnings of women's introspective fiction in America. The characterization, the ongoing generations of women, their bodies and spirits, and the setting, kitchen and garden, recall previous women's work. In *Mama Day* we envision, along with George, "paradise," but the author locates her haven in a island found on no American map.[7] Through the other-worldly content, magic and metaphor, and the rejoined generations, contemporary women authors like Naylor restore the home place to the American literary landscape.

We pass through death and violence to come back where we started, with Miranda in the future August, waiting the daughter's return, waiting for the millennium's end, easily in the past and memory as she communicates with her dead sister through the rustling of the trees and the unspoken language. Like Cather's hidden Ántonia or Glasgow's isolated Kate Oliver, Miranda is aged, tired with her prodigies of work, but she still lives and still summons in living memory her dead, like Miranda of "Pale Horse, Pale Rider" and Laura of *The Optimist's Daughter*. And she still waits for the daughter's return.

Stepping out into a wintry literary world, the
writing daughters walk for us, looking for the
seer's footsteps, under the skeleton bowers,
among last summer's broken stalks. Led by
flashes of Demeter's robe, gold and purple,
living, warming the dark shadows, they find
their way back. They will renew her garden.
                        —H. F. L.

8.

Conclusion

CROCUSES

WHAT ELEMENTS OF PLOT or characterization account for the endurance of this plot over time and through difference of authorial circumstance? Clearly it arises from an ongoing dialogue between the competitive individualism of the dominance discourse and women's own
experience of relationships. To the present Carol Gilligan's controver-
sial work explains that women continue to hold generally stronger ties
than men to the private sphere of female family and friends and to
a communal, relational language which appears to share significant
characteristics with Bernstein's model of the restricted code. Noting
that men tend to emphasize rules and fairness—possibly because of
their generally greater closeness to the bureaucratic center that spins
out impersonal rules—whereas women tend to stress relationships—
perhaps because of longer social immersion in communal, domestic
roles and the strength of the mother-daughter tie—Gilligan calls for a
correction by both sexes of historic mistranslations of gender language
and meanings: "Yet in the different voice of women lies the truth and

ethic of care, the tie between relationship and responsibility, the origins of aggression in the failure of connection" (173). Although it should be said that men also partake of the committed, personal communities, their greater participation in the public sphere with its impersonal rules and rationalized workplace has inclined them to extend those conditions to ever larger areas of their lives. Gilligan's work has generated both admiration and dissent, yet the work of Douglas and Bernstein forms a cultural explanation for her findings, which refuses a purely biological one. Gilligan's position has been modified recently to reflect more clearly cultural impact on female adolescent development, which is suggestive for the direction taken by the careers of women writers. The failure to see the different reality of women's lives and to hear their different language comes in part from an assumption that there is a single field for cultural heroism, that of the vocational and social competition—in sum, the field of the successful entrepreneur, the star professional, and the top manager, and their literary double, the westering frontiersman. The male quest to move away from family and history is particularly valorized under American liberal individualism, as is suggested by a dozen cultural messages from the picture of the lonely Marlboro Man to the booming sales of the latest celebrity biography to the musings of the current academic superstar. The women authors of this discussion insist that the exclusive focus on the winner of the social competition is not only morally shortsighted, but foolishly inhuman.

The women of whom I write celebrate the local language and mourn the increased devaluation of the emotional ties they shared with other women as they celebrated the marriages and births of the family, and as they mourned the passing of the older generations and celebrated the coming of the new. They seek in their mature fiction to reconstitute the family in an ideal home place far from the urban, industrial, technological American center. They portray lives of larger-than-life female figures of continuity and connection who exemplify attributes the authors believe are crucial to a full human life and a just human society. In the yearning for the woman's community that drives their narratives, and in the fictional dialogue that re-creates women's voices, readers hear the living local language restored and triumphant. Carroll Smith-Rosenberg indicates that women's networks of care survived within the middle class as well as the minority and working-class communities during the years in which most of these writing women grew and wrote ("Love and Ritual," 60–61). Thus their memories held models of female care and connection which, through the idealized home place, enthroned woman in body and spirit at the center of a loving, egalitarian, female community. In a social order in which women have historically received little acknowledgment for their contribution, these writers have preserved the legacy of the female community through the home place, even though the associational language offers few modes of expression for their cultural vision. In writing of women's communities in English and American fiction, Nina Auerbach, for example, remarks on the oblique, clouded nature of women's literary language; I believe that this different language arises out of the shared assumptions of the separate communities. The two languages receive metaphorical representation through the home with its communal language presided over by an aging female seer, an ideal place, which is juxtaposed with institutions governed by impersonal rules directed by a white male: Dr. Hildesheim's hospital in Porter's "Pale Horse, Pale Rider," Wick Cutter's railroad in Cather's *My Ántonia*, Cyrus Treadwell's factory in Glasgow's *Virginia*, William Fitzroy's factory in *In This Our Life*, and Dr. Courtland's hospital in *The Optimist's Daughter*, among others.

The wise woman serves two purposes in the writing of these women; she insists on women's contributions to the creation and continuance of a distinctly American civilization, and she validates the female authors' choices. She empowers the writing woman by reclaiming at least part of the power of the male deity. In books like *The Golden Apples*, *The Optimist's Daughter*, *The Country of the Pointed Firs*, *My Ántonia*, *The Old Order*, *Vein of Iron*, *Herland*, and *Mama Day*, the wise woman creates a world by her labor and, more importantly, by her elemental creativity. That creative legacy passes in *The Optimist's Daughter*, *Herland*, *Vein of Iron*, *Country of the Pointed Firs*, *The Old Order*, and *The Song of the Lark* to her artist-daughters. It is not the playful, youthful Muse, waiting to be wooed and won, that acts as the force behind art, but the serious, mature female ideal. At the same time, her presence in these writers posits the feminine, not the masculine, as the expected, natural creative force. The female goddess shares with the male deity the creative power, insisting that the contributions of woman as well as man are required to shape the ideal American homeland. These writers thus reclaim and justify their own creative task, taking their place in their families' history.

This group of women writers from the domestic novelists to the present share an underlying didactic purpose. As I suggest earlier, the home place envisioned an American community within a pastoral setting in which the claims of individual rights would be balanced with the demands of civic virtue. The self-conscious women writers here indicate in their plot that the home place would refuse the injustice of the paternalistic community as well as the oppression of the material competition of the social structure. Although it promotes women's relationships as its primary good, the seer's home shelters all who seek its protection. Cooperation, decorum, and nurture are the desired qualities, unlike the competition, fashion, and blame of the social order they left behind. It is a consciously imaginary social order, based in the memory of female family and friendships.

The concept of responsibility in the wise woman's domain extends not only to the people within her care but to the natural world as well. Unlike the consumption of resources and space represented by the chain saws, automobiles, and guns—the technological order—and the brutality represented by the untouched wilderness, the home place represents the cooperation of human being with nature, promising abundance to the mutual enrichment of both. The wise woman rejects the machines, chain saws and guns, that destroy the home place and its garden, and the authors portray as suspect those vehicles, automobiles and railroad cars, that carry the children, and thus the American future, away from the home place. They abhor equally the harshness of undomesticated nature. The wise woman is a good housekeeper, preserving the best of the old women's crafts and nurturing the natural landscape. In several of the works the authors explicitly connect the domestic setting with the world just outside.

The flower garden finds a connection with the patchwork quilt as the female home offers the example and the origins of woman's arts. The garden shows that hollyhocks and roses grow harmoniously together, just as wise woman and artist-daughter build different but uniquely beautiful lives side by side. Sewing, and especially quilting, becomes an apt figure for the way these women must reconstitute the female histories in a scattered social order. And they also reclaim male myth, cut it to fit their experience, and reshape it into the finished work. A significant group of these works, Jewett's *The Country of the Pointed Firs*, Welty's *The Golden Apples*, Cather's *O Pioneers!* and *My Ántonia*, Naylor's *The Women of Brewster Place*, as well as Porter's "Miranda" stories, represent in their form, a story cycle united through character and theme, the process of quilt design. Each is shaped of seemingly diverse stories stitched together by the woman author to create a unified work of art, suggesting how the claims of individual rights and social responsibility can be reconciled in the home place. These works of art are often faulted as an artistic failure to sustain the imaginative strength demanded by the creation of a novel; such criticism arises from a failure to discern that their writers are about another artistic task, one which reflects their experience of the scattered bureaucratized society. At the center of the narratives stand the central female figures, Miranda Gay, Mattie Michael, Almira Todd, Miss Katie Rainey, Alexandra Bergson, and Ántonia Shimerda who draw together the seemingly divided stories into an artistic work in a parallel to their labor to unite the community.

Is the home place a vision progressively harder to realize? On this point the authors show little consistency, ambivalence often troubling the individual author on this point. Eudora Welty and Katherine Anne Porter, two of the later writers, suggest that the home place now exists as living source of strength in the memory of the artist-daughter, and Willa Cather in her final years saw social devastation, but Gloria Naylor as recently as 1988 has created the home place in full strength issuing from the communal voice. Ellen Glasgow, Charlotte Perkins Gilman, and Sarah Orne Jewett create timeless communities, which we are encouraged to imagine as ongoing without regard to modern time. Certainly as the associational language of the specialized vocations spin out more and more bodies of esoteric jargon and as the individual is increasingly beholden for the necessities of life to bureaucracies rather than to personal relationships, the home place becomes more difficult to re-create.

Increasingly, as numerous literary critics have noted since the beginning of the twentieth century, the human being is isolated within a discrete block of time without moral benchmarks. Nonetheless, as the fiction of Naylor and other contemporary authors illustrate, this plot still speaks to the American woman author and her reading public. Perhaps, as the work of Nancy Chodorow suggests, so long as the actual physical and emotional ties are particularized, the mother-daughter relationship offers a counter in the flesh to the individualistic social messages. In the most concrete and dramatic possible way, the child learns that body cannot be left behind, replaced like a worn gear, because it offers a crucial part of identity for men as well as women. Moreover, they insist that human beings must live in a social context and that friendship between equals, not the romance of dependency, offers the most enduring rewards. This is true whether the friendship lies between men and women or between women. Once again it needs to be said that, although nostalgia underlies some of these narratives, they also represent an attempt to create not only an ideal of human relationships, but also an emotional reality partaking of communal ritual. Thus they summon in a fragmented world feelings of security, mystery, and decorum.

The women writers in this discussion understand that there are no human beings who make themselves, that death and birth are realities, and life—even space—has its limits. They assert that the individual arises from an interdependent social context and that he or she cannot in fact leave the experience of the past behind to start anew endlessly. Finally they understand that society needs to balance the demands for individual rights with responsibilities to loved ones and the others who shelter the individual and whom she or he shelters in inevitable times of weakness and fear. Moreover, they understand that the American nation was made up of little neighborhoods following in the wake of Daniel Boone's fabled demand for "elbow room," neighborhoods and civilizations formed out of family recipes, wedding quilts, faithful letters from the East, and carefully preserved rootstocks and herbal remedies from dooryard gardens.

Initially the women writers here, particularly the earlier writers, Jewett, Glasgow, and Cather, explicitly seek to join that culturally valorized male tradition of the protagonist's deadly movement "west" and "away," to write in what Showalter calls the "Feminine" phase and only later do they achieve the "Female" phase, "a turning inward freed from some of the dependence of opposition" (*A Literature of Their Own*, 13). The building of this female authorial language in the United States comes from the effects of several historical, cultural circumstances.

Because women in greater numbers remained in communal, domestic relationships longer than men, because they were denied the full definition of independent social actor, and because of the mother-daughter bond, women writers portrayed human interconnection in their fiction to a greater extent than their writing brothers, searching for a language and a narrative that expresses their historic past and their own artistic traditions, some of which grew out of their domestic arts. These writing women seek a language vibrant with emotion, which reflects woman's communal experience and past history as a remedy for the impersonal elaborated public speech that values differentiation and innovation—in a word, separation. Their attempts to evoke such experiences have met with out-of-hand dismissals of "sentiment" or their narratives invite misreadings. Yet the women included here explicitly identify the home place as an alternate human ideal, not as Old Home Week. And it needs to be said that it is at least as "realistic" to many women's experience, even now, as the tales of the adventuring American individual have accurately reflected the realities of most men's lives.

From the domestic writers onward, many American women authors reached toward their memories of the wise woman's domain, purifying them of paternal definitions, and restitching them, creating new woman's designs of complexity and artistry. The introspective artists in this study left us with a record of women's lives, which, although fictional, are nonetheless true in an emotional, imaginative sense. As all these literary workers understood, lives of women forgotten by history had, along with the pain and undeniable oppression, moments of grace, joy, and strength, moments when they felt the loving bonding and heard the voice of the home place. The women authors in this discussion place the local experience of our own female families within a larger American feminine context, joining it to an ongoing literary tradition as they connect physical fact with loving memory. Jewett, Cather, Glasgow, Porter, Welty, and Naylor share a belief in the female pastoral home with its sustaining creativity and personal connections as a model for the loving, just human community and, equally significant, as a model for their own authorial labors. As writing daughters these authors sought to discover their own place within the generations; they recovered the connections between the mother's gardens, the grandmother's quilts, and their own women's art. They found patterns of art that escaped the long shadows of the great adventuring male protagonists of Hemingway, Faulkner, Melville, and Whitman; they rewrote American history to bring women's experience to its center. Through them, we go back to find out what woman's stories and what female examples brought us to our present day. From writers such as Welty and Porter we can learn the informing power of the female self, leading us to examine our own lives. Only with this examination can we tell our own stories, adding a patch to the quilt of the past.

These narratives seek to bring us back to our own lives, to our own female families' experiences, through immersion within their communal language and their specifically feminine vision of creativity. These women, intending to affect the lives of their readers, reject the idea of literature as a leisure entertainment, safely "fictional," thus having no designs of the world, having no ability to effect change. Infusing their writings with remnants of ritual, initiating us into the customs of the home place, they deny that each story is an individualized narrative having no reference to our own lives. The writers bring us as readers into an ongoing lineage of women. They challenge us, as they educate the writing daughters of the respective literary works, to examine our own histories, to restore our collective past as women, to rewrite cultural narratives of female victimization and marginality. In my own life, these writers have encouraged me to think that my own experiences might well connect with some of the readers' own. The following memories is the patch I will add to the American women's quilt. It is mine but, because of these writers' fiction and autobiographies, I know, not mine alone.

When, after ten years as a housewife, I returned to academic life, I held the notion that this experience would, in some undefined way, place the daily, often relentlessly menial, details of my life as a woman and mother in a larger framework. Somehow I hoped to find a way to join together my work "at home" with my new life in library and classroom. Soon enough I found myself reading a range of works on women's lives, among them cliometric books based on official records—all that was left behind of the sorrows and joys of many women. Recording the quantifiable data from working-class or farm women's lost lives—their "obscure destinies," in Willa Cather's wonderful phrase—the details those scholars noted were familiar in their description of dreary physical facts and tasks. And yet . . .

The working-class and farm women I knew in my past as neighbors and family were not victims, despite the hardness of their lives, the commands of their beloved, or endured, husbands, brothers, and fathers, and the incursions of the great world. They were and are strong, vital women with resources and sorrows of their own, and their struggles connect with ours.

This is some of what I remember. When I was a child in the 1940s, my family owned a small family farm in northeastern Illinois, near the village of Plainfield; my maternal grandparents and single aunts and uncles lived a quarter of a mile down the road on a tenant farm owned and somewhat offhandedly managed by a corporation in Chicago headed, we were told, by a philanthropist. My married aunts—my mother's sisters—lived nearby. My grandmother didn't have electricity or central heating in her farmhouse—the ice would be on the wash basins when we awoke—and our house didn't have running water in the early years.

Indeed, as those logically argued texts indicated, our mothers, aunts, and grandmothers worked hard, especially if they were immigrant, minority, working-class, or farm women, asking and receiving little quarter for their "femininity" in their lives' struggles. Serving as a passive satellite in the ornamental "domesticity" of consumption and appearance was an unknown luxury to these women and many others like them. One of the yearly tasks for my female family, for example, was the harvesting and putting up of fruit. On that day, often blazing hot, high Illinois summer, bushels of peaches would be carried into the kitchen, the cook stove, still hot from breakfast, fed more wood, the great pots set to boil, and the mounds of peaches peeled, pitted, and cut so that the family would have food against the long winter. My mother did such tasks with the help of her mother, her sisters, and, in times of special stress such as childbirth, a "hired girl," the daughter of a neighbor. Seasonal work such as canning of fruits and vegetables, the butchering and canning of meat, or the care of hatching chicks was added to the accustomed routine of homemaking.

My mother and grandmother had hands stained dark from paring fruit; they sat wearily, feet up, over coffee before starting supper—both observable, undeniable physical facts—but they also had their sisters and their gardens and their crafts to sustain them. Each Sunday afternoon, the women of the family would sit around my grandmother's dining room table, mending and quilting, exchanging Kiefer pears for

Yellow Transparent apples from a sister's orchard, or trading outgrown children's clothes. The whole time, the talk flew, circling and dipping—talk of the daily woman's business to be sure, but also doings of family and lifelong neighbors. These are small events, unworthy of public note, indeed impossible to record, but nonetheless stitches that joined lives. From that table, through the dislocations and anxieties of the Great Depression and World War II, the five sisters arose and entered the public world, often for the support of their families, men and children. My grandmother remained on the sharecropping farm, bringing them back to that table. The whispers and the touches wove together their past and present, the living and the dead. There was a feeling connection to their lives, an abiding emotional support, which bore those women up in times of trouble. They were always there, one or all, when there was need, no matter the depth or bitterness of a former falling out. I felt ties between women that were stronger than death or distance then, and I feel it now.

The ties between those women gave a continuity and shape to their lives that elevated daily tasks into a history, a history that they have left to me and my daughters. Having understood their strength as living presence, I could borrow it in this new competitive, impersonal setting. Like other women from marginalized groups I could replace pity—horrible, condescending word!—with pride, in examining the experiences of my female family. The stories and labor of my grandmother, mother, sister, aunts, and girl cousins joined with the research and academic writing of the feminist "gang of five" at the University of Michigan: Rosemary Kowalski, Marilyn Ferris Motz, Mary Corbin Sies, Barbara Winkler, and myself. As we discussed our own academic work at Michigan, we talked often of our female families. Like the authors in this discussion, we needed to find our way back, to find the connections with our female families, and to join our experience as women with that of our colleagues. We sought to explore those connections, to enliven our studies with emotional memory. These discussions seemed crucial to the success of our educational labors in the largely male-controlled university world of passive lecture hall, isolated library carrel, and competitive seminar table. Daughters and sisters all, we experienced together the joy of accomplishment, the patterns of women's memories, and the lightened weight of disappointment in an impersonal, competitive public life. Public and private worlds touched, our scholarship enriched by those stories from our shared women's past. From them, I learned that there were still dining-room tables and that the struggles of our female families still inspired their daughters' efforts.

Yes, Welty's Becky Thurston McKelva "up home" in West Virginia, or Cather's Ántonia in her hidden Nebraska farm, or Naylor's Miranda in her island Willow Springs do not reflect the realities of twentieth-century farm or urban women of diverse backgrounds and experiences—or their professional, working class, or poverty-stricken daughters, for that matter—any more than Melville's Ahab or Thoreau's woodsman portray the realities of the nineteenth-century or twentieth-century men. Yet both patterns are instructive, raising core elements of cultural and authorial belief to the larger-than-life size of deities and coloring them through their dreams and fears with the bright emotional hues of imagination. And both influence public and private actions. Through the lives and language of the imaginary, but nonetheless living female protagonists and through their creation of an idealized home place, I found echoes of my grandmother's family, placing those small tasks that most women undertake to shape a life in a larger metaphorical pattern that placed woman and their domestic arts at the center of the national literary tradition. These texts bring us to our histories and to the strengths of those who went before us. They inform and empower the daughters to claim a place in an ongoing lineage of creativity, to tell our stories without changing pronouns. They also inspire us to work with men who suffer under the constraints and impersonal rules of competitive individualism.

For we do not make ourselves "from scratch," identity comes from group experience, and the concept of the "self-made" American individual can be a particularly poisonous one if it teaches us to forget or despise those who give the care we have all needed and will need. To acknowledge this fact and call for its remedy by women who primarily realize this cultural lack is not "essentialism," nor does the statement that women share many life experiences constitute denial of significant difference. The ideal imaginative neighborhood insists that the modern bureaucratic society has yielded few examples and even less resources to support the values that women as a group have traditionally put forward.

Despite our differences in background, our past as women does share some important points of contact, foremost of which is the crucial emotional and physical heritage shared by mother and daughter, our consistent devaluation and, often, exploitation by both old paternalistic communities and new bureaucratic experts, our internalization of those received cultural definitions, and finally and most problematic, given the demands of rationalization, our female body. At last, we find in these women writers the joining of our own experience of our female families. We find that the weariness and the frustrations of our mothers had meaning that joins their life to ours, allowing us to salvage their wisdom and their creativity from portrayals of victimization, to acknowledge and reclaim our own past as their daughters. Although at first we flee their lives, like the writers here, we come to see elements that allow us to formulate stories that empower us as individual women and as members of the woman's community. We are freed from the social competition with its "self-made man" and his satellite mannequin with her pouting, constantly dissatisfied painted face. We learn to survive, yes, but more. The "more" comes from our families and our friends, and it is much more than the sum of its parts.

The record of "the other place" remains as an inspiration to writers and scholars, women and men, who follow. As mature artists these women slip the bonds of the male-controlled stories and cultural models that make them voiceless outsiders. They imagine a model for creativity and justice for all. It waits for our daughters and sons and our sisters and brothers, rewriting the past and turning the next page.

Notes

Chapter 1

1. Many of these writers use autobiographical elements. Writing about the interest among marginalized groups in autobiography, Sandra S. Friedman notes that "individualistic paradigms of the self ignore the role of collective and relational identities in the individuation process of women and minorities" (35). The autobiographical content allows these women to witness against male-controlled narratives.

2. As such commentators as Elizabeth Fox-Genovese and Henry Louis Gates, Jr., and such writers as Gloria Naylor and Katherine Anne Porter contend, women and minority writers partake of a dual cultural heritage—that of their local community and that of the national culture. As Fox-Genovese concludes, "Unless we acknowledge our diversity, we allow the silences of the received tradition to become our own. Unless we sustain some ideal of a common culture, we reduce culture to personal experience and sacrifice the very concept of American" ("Individualism" 29).

3. The official communications of the associational language demand the excision of both gender and personal relationships for participation in the public life; at the same time, the continued presence of male pronouns and communal nouns, the assumptions underlying medical experiments, for example, through usage imply the white male as the most representative, and significant, segment of the population. The demand for the erasure of gender is treated in Carroll Smith-Rosenberg's "The New Woman as Androgyne" and Rosalind Rosenberg's *Beyond Separate Spheres*.

Smith-Rosenberg discusses the attempt of professional women, responding to the demands of rationalization, to claim the outlines of the individual who shed all evidences of received identities. Rosenberg's discussion of the movement "toward a sexless intelligence" recounts a progressive movement from the imposed paternalistic roles of "true womanhood" to the emergence of the New Woman, Rosenberg is forced to detail a sad epilog. Many women social scientists had predicted that, once intellectuals understood the arbitrariness of gender classification, its *irrationality*, separate spheres would disappear. As universities gained acceptance as gatekeepers for admission to the top of the growing professional bureaucracies, however, women academics found themselves increasingly marginalized as "the university established itself as a distinctively male institution" (239). Although early feminists may have erred in an essentialist assumption that women were, by nature, more nurturing and community-minded, Rosenberg concludes, it remains true that women have taken responsibility for preserving those qualities. She concludes, "Only when men are willing to endorse the social vision that has long been the particular concern of women will we be able to move . . . beyond separate spheres" (246).

4. In an ingenious and convincing reading of Gilman's "The Yellow Wallpaper," Walter Benn Michaels argues that the narrator is engaged in creating herself. He continues that the creative impulse in market capitalism is "the desire to make something out of oneself, to make oneself out of oneself" (11). Although I will not discuss Gilman's career as a whole, clearly the movement from the ideas driving "The Yellow Wallpaper" (1892) to those underlying *Herland* (1915) replicate the movement seen in other women in this discussion. In the earlier work the woman struggles to give birth to herself in a nursery, to run like her "free" shadow self in nature and outside the walls of the house—leaving behind the daughter; in the later work the woman's home has expanded to become the alternate world itself, bringing in all the community's daughters.

5. For information on the interdependency of the New England settlement, see Kenneth Lockridge, *A New England Town*, and John Demos, *A Little Commonwealth*.

6. For the change from local benevolence to charitable organization, from family-based tasks to impersonal bureaucracies, see these representative sources: Carl Degler, *Against All Odds*, Barbara Ehrenrich and Deirdre English, *For Her Own Good*, Thomas Haskell, *The Emergence of Professional Social Science*, Dolores Hayden, *The Grand Domestic Revolution*, Carl Kaestle and Maris Vinovskis, "From Apron Strings to ABCs," Glenna Matthews, "*Just a Housewife*," David J. Rothman, *The Discovery of the Asylum*, Mary P. Ryan, *The Cradle of the Middle Class*, and of course the landmark study, Robert Wiebe's *The Search for Order*.

7. For discussions of Demeter in American women's writing, see Josephine Donovan, *After the Fall*, Louise Westling, *Sacred Groves and Ravaged Gardens*, and Jane Demouy, *Katherine Anne Porter's Women*.

8. I am in debt to David Hogeberg for his observation that the words "text" and "textile" come from the same Latin root, *textus*, meaning "woven," making the joining implied in sewing and particularly quilting an apt one for describing the oral genesis and subsequent narrative strategy of these works.

Chapter 2

1. Of course, the romance as a form is very much alive and well on the present-day booklists as Janice Radway has amply demonstrated in *Reading the Romance*. The end of the romance is the successful pairing of the woman with her chosen man. Its focus is *not* the establishment of a home or family—a distinct change from the earlier domestic novelists. The emotional tone of these latter-day popular books are the antithesis of the measured passion seen in the earlier writers.

2. Josephine Donovan in *New England Local Color Literature* posits a split in attitude and emphasis between the writers of the New England "local color" and American domestic novel, which is considerably to the latter's disadvantage. Despite its reference to other novelistic traditions, the plot of the domestic novel inevitably addressed American cultural conditions.

3. These sources offer information on the growth of the publishing industry in nineteenth-century America: Hellmut Lehman-Haupt with Lawrence C. Wroth and Rollo G. Silver, *The Book in America*; Mary Kelley, *Private Woman, Public Stage*; Mary P. Ryan, *The Empire of the Mother*.

Chapter 3

1. The question of influence is a difficult one. Clearly, Cather was influenced both personally and professionally by Sarah Orne Jewett. These authors often read each other's work, along with that of many others, men and women. This reading was necessarily influential if only through the shared gender identity. Nonetheless, I believe that the shared cultural context forms the overriding influence in creating the home place.

2. I have consulted the following biographies and memoirs for information on Cather's life: E. K. Brown, *Willa Cather: A Critical Biography*; Edith Lewis, *Willa Cather Living: A Personal Record*; Sharon O'Brien, *Willa Cather: The Emerging Voice*; Phyllis Robinson, *Willa: The Life of Willa Cather*; Elizabeth Shepley Sergeant, *Willa Cather: A Memoir*; James Woodress, *Willa Cather: Her Life and Art*, and *Willa Cather: A Literary Life*.

3. Reprinted in L. Brent Bohlke, *Willa Cather in Person: Interviews, Speeches, and Letters*, 8–11. Correspondent, F. H., *Philadelphia Record*, 10 August 1913, p. 11.

4. Sharon O'Brien's biography takes a psychological approach to Willa Cather's artistic coming-of-age. The emphasis necessarily leads to a diminution of the larger cultural influence.

5. Susan Rosowski in *The Voyage Perilous* characterizes the three as representative of women who "feed upon others" in Cather's work, hindering woman's entrance into the male public world.

6. Inscription by Willa Cather in Carrie Miner's copy of *O Pioneers!* Quoted by Mildred Bennett in "Introduction" of *Collected Short Fiction*, xiii.

7. Willa Cather, "Restlessness Such as Ours Does Not Make for Beauty," interview with Rose C. Feld in *New York Times Book Review*, 21 December 1924. Reprinted in Bohlke, 71.

8. Willa Cather's interview with Eleanor Hinman, "Willa Cather, Famous Nebraska Novelist," *Lincoln Sunday Star*, 6 November 1921, 42–48. Reprinted in Bohlke, *Willa Cather in Person*, 47.

9. Erich Neumann's chapter in *The Great Mother*, "The Positive Elementary Character," delineates the ancient connection of the pottery vases and vessels with the creative, rather than the destructive, aspect of the mother goddess.

10. Carl G. Jung, *Symbols of Transformation*. See especially Chapters 5, "Symbols of the Mother and Rebirth" and 7, "The Dual Mother."

11. Discussions of Cather's *Lucy Gayheart* (1935) and *Sapphira and the Slave Girl* (1940) have been deleted. *Lucy Gayheart*, as Edith Lewis and others have written, was produced under difficult physical and emotional conditions, and Cather herself tired of her slight romantic heroine; *Sapphira and the Slave Girl* shows a dystopian maternal vision under slavery, which contrasts with the American home place, the New Jerusalem, of her "prairie" novels and the New World maternal home of *Shadows on the Rock*. Even in the last novel, however, we see the evil mother replaced by the worthy daughter, who ultimately restores the woman's community in face of an immoral and mendacious social system.

Chapter 4

1. For Glasgow's reading and intellectual interests at the crucial time of her mother's death in the fall of 1893, see J. R. Raper's extensive discussion of the influence of Charles Darwin and Thomas Huxley on the fledgling author (*Without Shelter*, 50–51).

2. *A Certain Measure* contains the observation, "Every Christmas, after I had passed into my second reader, I had received one of these perennial romances" (11).

3. Like Sharon O'Brien's study of Willa Cather and Sarah W. Sherman's biography of Sarah Orne Jewett, Linda W. Wagner traces Glasgow's long search for a positive feminine sense of self.

4. For a discussion of Glasgow's relationship to the Southern Lady cult, see Anne G. Jones, *Tomorrow Is Another Day*.

5. E. Stanly Godbold reports that Glasgow undertook a new course of psychoanalytic therapy in the summer of 1922 (133).

6. C. Hugh Holman, Allen Becker, and Blair Rouse place Glasgow within the Southern literary tradition. Becker and Rouse consider *Barren Ground* to be the harbinger of modern Southern literature.

7. Despite the self-pity that dominates *The Woman Within*, I consider that

the record left behind in *Vein of Iron* and the two subsequent novels to be more truly representative of Glasgow's state of mind in her last years.

8. For a discussion of the frontier myth, see Richard Slotkin's *Regeneration Through Violence* and for a discussion of its relationship to American history, see Slotkin, *The Fatal Environment.*

Chapter 5

1. Throughout this chapter, the biographical information is taken from Joan Givner's *Katherine Anne Porter: A Life.* The chronology of publication and composition is taken from Jane DeMouy's *Katherine Anne Porter's Women* (Appendix, 207–208).

2. Katherine Anne Porter, Review of *Portrait of Mexico*, Diego Rivera and Bertram Wolfe. Unpublished typescript, Katherine Anne Porter Collection, McKeldin Library.

3. Joan Givner relates Porter's creation of Laura, identifying the experiences of Mary Louise Doherty as the source for the Braggioni sequence and for the circumstances of Eugenio's death. The final dream sequence arose out of the author's own experimental use of marijuana (152–56). For a discussion of Laura as an early portrait of Miranda, see Unrue, *Truth and Vision.*

4. Miranda's position as the witness "in-between" has been treated from the earliest criticism; see Robert Penn Warren, "Irony with a Center." Miranda treated from a feminist perspective may be found in DeMouy, "Face to Face" (145–76), and Hennessy, "Katherine Anne Porter's Model for Heroines."

5. I am grateful to Connie Johnson for this insight.

6. Givner has researched Porter very thoroughly and is frank in her opinion of her subject. Note some of the listings in the index: "garrulousness of," "inconsistent literary opinions of," "maliciousness of," "rigid beliefs of," "short interest span of," and "extravagant spending habits of." The truly appalling betrayal of her friend and colleague Josephine Herbst by Porter is detailed by Elinor Langer in *Josephine Herbst: The Story She Could Never Tell* (1983).

Chapter 6

1. See interviews with Tom Royals and John Little in *Conversations* (252–53) for Welty's fullest discussion of the relationship of personal life to literature, and *One Writer's Beginnings* throughout shows the influence Welty's childhood memories had on plot and characterization.

2. John Edward Hardy in an article on "marrying down" fervently champions Robbie's cause (74–77).

3. Thomas L. McHaney discusses the mythological connection which unites *The Golden Apples* into a unified narrative not unlike the novel in effect ("The Multitudinous Golden Apples").

4. As with her stylistic techniques, Welty's use of proverbs indicates Miss Rainey's position as spinner of the communal language in *The Golden Apples*. See Louise Blackwell.

5. Helen Hurt Tiegreen details the revisions made in *The Optimist's Daughter* through an examination of the autobiography and the recent Franklin Mint introduction to the book. She discovers that the ending of the novel finds Laurel gaining an acceptance of her past missing from the story. Tiegreen concludes that the novel offered the author a resolution as well. I would add that this resolution is the particularly one connected to female artistry seen in Welty's predecessors (626).

Chapter 7

1. I use the term "black" in reference to Naylor's heritage and writing since that is her preference.

2. The books on African-American feminism consulted are Joanne Braxton and Andree Nicola McLaughlin, eds., *Wild Women in the Whirlwind*, Hazel Carby, *Reconstructing Womanhood*, Audre Lorde, *Sister Outsider*, Barbara Smith, "Toward a Black Feminist Criticism" in Elaine Showalter, *The New Feminist Criticism:* 168–85, and Alice Walker, *In Search of Our Mothers' Gardens*.

3. Naylor insists that there is enough agony in Brewster Place to make comparison obscene. Is Lorraine's rape more tragic than Ciel's loss of her child? Is Ciel's loss of her child to be judged worse than Mattie's betrayal by her son?

4. In her recorded interview Naylor promises that her fifth book will center on the narrative of Sapphira Wade.

5. *Mama Day* illustrates the problem of multiple group identities. As Elizabeth Fox-Genovese writes in *Within the Plantation Household*, the African-American woman in the slavery era remained caught between the gender rules of the dominant white Southern community and the gender conventions of the slave community.

6. Marget Sands, a scholar on Native American women's sacred writings, has suggested similarities between the morality of the home place and attitudes toward community in those writings.

7. In my teaching, two works elicit the same love, there is no other word for it, *Mama Day* and Cather's "Neighbor Rosicky." These works seem to send the readers back to their own histories.

Works Consulted

Abbott, John S. C. *The Mother at Home; or, The Principles of Maternal Duty*, 1834. Family in America Series, edited by David J. and Sheila M. Rothman. New York: Arno Press, 1972.

Allen, John Alexander. "The Other Way to Live: Demigods in Eudora Welty's Fiction." In *Eudora Welty: Thirteen Essays*, edited by Peggy Prenshaw, 26–55. Jackson: University Press of Mississippi, 1983.

Allen, Paula Gunn. *The Sacred Hoop: Recovering the Feminine in American Indian Traditions*. Boston: Beacon Press, 1986.

Ammons, Elizabeth. "Going in Circles: The Female Geography of Jewett's *Country of the Pointed Firs*." *Studies in the Literary Imagination* 16 (Fall 1983): 83–92.

———. "Jewett's Witches." In *Critical Essays on Sarah Orne Jewett*, edited by Gwen L. Nagel, 165–84. Critical Essays on American Literature. Boston: G. K. Hall and Co., 1984.

Anderson, Mary Castiglio. "Nature and Will in Ellen Glasgow's *Barren Ground*." *Modern Fiction Studies*. Women Writers of the South Issue. 28 (Autumn 1982): 383–95.

Anderson, Quentin. *The Imperial Self: An Essay in American Literary and Cultural History*. 1971. New York: Vintage/Random House, 1972.

Arnold, Marilyn. "When Gratitude Is No More: Eudora Welty's "June Recital." *South Carolina Review* 13 (Spring 1981): 62–72.

———. *Willa Cather's Short Fiction*. Athens, Ohio: Ohio University Press, 1984.

Auerbach, Nina. *Communities of Women: An Idea in Fiction*. Cambridge, Mass.: Harvard University Press, 1978.

Bailey, Jennifer. "The Dangers of Femininity in Willa Cather's Fiction." *Journal of American Studies* 16 (December 1982): 391–406.

Barnes, Daniel R. and Madeline T. "The Secret Sin of Granny Weatherall." *Renascence* 21 (Spring 1969): 162–65.

Bartkowski, Frances. *Feminist Utopias*. Lincoln: University of Nebraska Press, 1989.

Baym, Nina. *Woman's Fiction: A Guide to Novels by and about Women in America, 1820–1870*. 1978. Ithaca, N. Y.: Cornell University Press, 1980.

Becker, Allen. "Ellen Glasgow and the Southern Literary Tradition." *Modern Fiction Studies* 5 (Winter 1959–60): 295–303.

Bellah, Robert N., Richard Madsen, William M. Sullivan, Ann Swidler, and Steven M. Tipton. *Habits of the Heart: Individualism and Commitment in American Life*. Berkeley: University of California Press, 1985.

Bellamy, Edward. *Looking Backward: 2000–1887*. 1888. New York: Modern Library, 1951.

Benedict, Ruth. *Patterns of Culture*. 1934. Foreword by Margaret Mead. Boston: Houghton Mifflin Company, 1959.

Bennett, Mildred. *The World of Willa Cather*. 1951. Lincoln: University of Nebraska Press, 1961.

Bernstein, Basil. *Class, Codes and Control: Theoretical Studies Towards a Sociology of Language*. London: Routledge & Kegan Paul, 1977.

Blackwell, Louise. "Eudora Welty: Proverbs and Proverbial Phrases in *The Golden Apples*." *Southern Folklore Quarterly* 30 (December 1966): 332–41.

Bolsterli, Margaret Jones. "Woman's Vision: The Worlds of Women in *Delta Wedding, Losing Battles*, and *The Optimist's Daughter*." In *Selected Essays*, edited by Peggy Prenshaw, 149–56. Jackson: University Press of Mississippi, 1979.

Bond, Tonette. "Pastoral Transformations in *Barren Ground*. *Mississippi Quarterly* 32 (Fall 1979): 565–76.

Brown, E. K. *Willa Cather: A Critical Biography*. Completed by Leon Edel. 1953. New York: Avon Books, 1980.

Bryant, J. A., Jr. *Eudora Welty*. University of Minnesota Pamphlets on American Writers, No. 66. Minneapolis: University of Minnesota Press, 1968.

———. "The Recovery of the Confident Narrator: *A Curtain of Green* to *Losing Battles* in Eudora Welty." In *Eudora Welty: Thirteen Essays*, edited by Peggy Prenshaw, 56–70. Jackson: University Press of Mississippi, 1983.

Bukoski, Anthony. "Facts of Domesticity in Eudora Welty's Fiction." *Southern Studies* 24 (Fall 1985): 326–42.

Carby, Hazel V. *Reconstructing Womanhood: The Emergence of the Afro-American Woman Novelist*. New York: Oxford University Press, 1987.

Carson, Richard G. "Nature and the Circles of Initiation in *The Country of the Pointed Firs*," *Colby Literary Quarterly* 21 (1985): 154–60.

Cary, Richard. *Sarah Orne Jewett*. Twayne United States Authors Series, no. 19. New York: Twayne Publishers, Inc., 1962.

Cash, W. J. *The Mind of the South*. New York: Alfred Knopf, 1941.

Cather, Willa. *Collected Short Stories: 1892–1912*. Edited by Virginia Faulkner. Introduction by Mildred Bennett. Lincoln: University of Nebraska Press, 1965.

———. *The Kingdom of Art: Willa Cather's First Principles and Critical Statements: 1893–1896*. Edited by Bernice Slote. Lincoln: University of Nebraska Press, 1966.

———. *A Lost Lady*. 1923. New York: Alfred Knopf, 1951.

———. *Lucy Gayheart*. 1935. New York: Vintage/Random House, n.d.

———. *My Ántonia*. 1918. Boston: Sentry/Houghton Mifflin Co., n.d.

———. *My Mortal Enemy*. 1926. New York: Vintage/Random House, n.d.

———. "The Novel Demeublé." In *Not Under Forty*. New York: Alfred Knopf, 1936.

———. *O Pioneers!* 1913. Boston: Sentry/Houghton Mifflin Co., 1962.

———. *Obscure Destinies*. 1930. New York: Vintage/Random House, 1974.

———. *"The Old Beauty" and Others*. New York: Alfred Knopf, 1948.

———. *Sapphira and the Slave Girl*. New York: Alfred Knopf, 1940.

———. *Shadows on the Rock*. 1931. New York: Vintage/Random House, 1971.

———. *The Song of the Lark*. 1915. Lincoln: Bison/University of Nebraska, 1978.

———. "Training for the Ballet: Making American Dancers." *McClure's Magazine*. October 1913: 85–95.

———. *Willa Cather in Person: Interviews, Speeches, and Letters*. Edited by L. Brent Bohlke. Lincoln: University of Nebraska Press, 1987.

———. *The World and the Parish: Willa Cather's Articles and Reviews, 1893–1902*. Edited by William M. Curtin. 2 vols. Lincoln: University of Nebraska, 1970.

Childers, Joseph W. "Character and Context: The Paradox of the Family Myth in Eudora Welty's *Delta Wedding*." *Essays in Literature*. 14 (Fall 1987): 241–50.

Chodorow, Nancy. *Reproduction of Mothering: Psychoanalysis and Sociology of Gender*. Berkeley: University of California, 1978.

Chopin, Kate. *The Awakening*. In *"The Storm" and Other Stories with The Awakening*. Edited by Per Seyersted. 1899. Old Westbury, N.Y.: The Feminist Press, 1974.

Cott, Nancy F. *The Bonds of Womanhood: Woman's Sphere in New England, 1780–1835.* New Haven: Yale University Press, 1977.

Cummins, Maria Susanna. *The Lamplighter.* 1854. Boston: Houghton Mifflin & Co., 1902.

Degler, Carl. *At Odds: Women and the Family from the Revolution to the Present.* 1980. New York: Oxford University Press, 1981.

Demmins, Julia L., and Daniel Curley. "Golden Apples and Silver Apples." In *Eudora Welty: Thirteen Essays,* edited by Peggy Prenshaw, 130–45. Jackson: University Press of Mississippi, 1983.

Demos, John. *A Little Commonwealth: Family Life in Plymouth Colony.* New York: Oxford University Press, 1970.

DeMouy, Jane Krause. *Katherine Anne Porter's Women: The Eye of Her Fiction.* Austin: University of Texas Press, 1983.

Didion, Joan. *A Book of Common Prayer.* 1977. New York: Pocket Books, 1978.

Donovan, Josephine. *After the Fall: The Demeter-Persephone Myth in Wharton, Cather, and Glasgow.* University Park, Pa.: Pennsylvania State University Press, 1989.

———. *New England Local Color Literature.* New York: Frederik Ungar Publishing Co., 1983.

———. *Sarah Orne Jewett.* Modern Literature Series, edited by Phillip Winsor. New York: Frederik Ungar Publishing Co., 1980.

Douglas, Mary. *Natural Symbols: Explorations in Cosmology.* 1970. New York: Vintage/Random House, 1973.

———. *Purity and Danger: An Analysis of Pollution and Taboo.* 1966. London: Routledge & Kegan Paul, 1978.

DuPlessis, Rachel Blau. *Writing Beyond the Ending: Narrative Strategies of Twentieth-Century Women Writers.* Bloomington, Ind.: Indiana University Press, 1985.

Ehrenreich, Barbara, and Deirdre English. *For Her Own Good: 150 Years of the Experts' Advice to Women.* 1978. New York: Doubleday/Anchor Press, 1979.

Eliot, Thomas Stearns. *Selected Essays: 1917–1932.* New York: Harcourt, Brace & Co., 1932.

Erdrich, Louise. *Tracks.* New York: Henry Holt & Co., 1988.

Erikson, Erik H. *Childhood and Society.* 2d ed. New York: W. W. Norton, Inc., 1963.

Evans, Elizabeth. *Eudora Welty.* Modern Literature Series, edited by Phillip Winsor. New York: Frederik Ungar Publishing Co., 1981.

Fike, Francis. "An Interpretation of *Pointed Firs.*" In *An Appreciation of*

Sarah Orne Jewett, edited by Richard Cary. 1961. Waterville, Me.: Colby College Press, 1973.

Fleischauer, John F. "The Focus of Mystery: Eudora Welty's Prose Style." *Southern Literary Journal* 5 (Spring 1973): 64–79.

Folsom, Marcia McClintock. " 'Tact Is a Kind of Mind-Reading': Empathetic Style in Sarah Orne Jewett's *The Country of the Pointed Firs.*" *Critical Essays on Sarah Orne Jewett*, 76–89. Critical Studies in American Literature, edited by Gwen L. Nagel. Boston: G. K. Hall & Co., 1984.

Fox-Genovese, Elizabeth. "Between Individualism and Fragmentation: American Culture and the New Literary Studies of Race and Gender." *American Quarterly* 42 (March 1990): 7–34.

———. *Feminism Without Illusions: A Critique of Individualism.* Chapel Hill: University of North Carolina Press, 1991.

———. *Within the Plantation Household: Black and White Women in the Old South.* Chapel Hill: University of North Carolina Press, 1988.

Friedman, Susan Stanford. "Women's Autobiographical Selves: Theory and Practice." In *The Private Self; Theory and Practice of Women's Autobiographical Writings*, edited by Shari Benstock, 34–62. Chapel Hill: University of North Carolina Press, 1988.

Fryer, Judith. *Felicitous Spaces: The Imaginative Structures of Edith Wharton and Willa Cather.* Chapel Hill: University of North Carolina Press, 1986.

Fussell, Paul. *The Great War and Modern Memory.* 1975. New York: Oxford University Press, 1977.

Garrison, Dee. "Immoral Fiction in the Late Victorian Library," *American Quarterly* 28 (Spring 1976): 71–89.

Gates, Henry Louis, Jr. *The Signifying Monkey: A Theory of African-American Literary Criticism.* 1988. New York: Oxford University Press, 1989.

Gelfant, Blanche H. "The Forgotten Reaping Hook: Sex in *My Ántonia.*" In *Women Writing in America: Voices in Collage*, 93–116. Hanover, N. H.: University Press of New England.

Gianonne, Richard. *Music in Willa Cather's Fiction.* Lincoln: University of Nebraska Press, 1968.

———. "Willa Cather and the Human Voice." In *Five Essays on Willa Cather: The Merrimack Symposium*, 21–49. North Andover, Mass.: Merrimack College, 1974.

Gilbert, Sandra M., and Susan Gubar. *The Madwoman in the Attic: The*

Woman Writer and the Nineteenth-Century Literary Imagination. New Haven: Yale University Press, 1979.

Gilligan, Carol. *In A Different Voice: Psychological Theory and Women's Development.* Cambridge, Mass.: Harvard University Press, 1982.

Gilman, Charlotte Perkins. *Herland.* 1915. New York: Pantheon Books, 1979.

———. *The Home and Its Work and Influence.* 1903. Urbana: University of Illinois, 1972.

———. *Women and Economics: Relations Between Men and Women as a Factor in Social Evolution.* Boston: Small, Maynard & Co., 1900.

———. "The Yellow Wallpaper." In *The Fictional World of Charlotte Perkins Gilman,* edited by Ann J. Lane. New York: Pantheon Books, 1980.

Givner, Joan. *Katherine Anne Porter: A Life.* New York: Simon & Schuster, 1982.

Glasgow, Ellen Gholson. *Barren Ground* 1925. New York: Hill & Wang, 1957.

———. *The Battle-Ground.* Doubleday, Page, 1902.

———. *Beyond Defeat: An Epilogue to an Era.* Edited by Luther Y. Gore. Charlottesville: University Press of Virginia, 1966.

———. *A Certain Measure: An Interpretation of Prose Fiction.* New York: Harcourt, Brace & Co., 1938.

———. *The Descendant.* New York: Harper & Brothers, 1897.

———. *Ellen Glasgow's Reasonable Doubts: A Collection of her Writings.* Edited by J. R. Raper. Baton Rouge: Louisiana State University Press, 1988.

———. *In This Our Life.* 1941. Franklin Center, Pa.: The Franklin Library, 1976.

———. *Letters.* Edited by Blair Rouse. New York: Harcourt, Brace, 1958.

———. *The Miller of Old Church.* New York: Doubleday, 1911.

———. *Phases of an Inferior Planet.* New York: Harper & Brothers, 1898.

———. *The Romantic Comedians.* Garden City, N.Y.: Doubleday, Page, & Co., 1926.

———. *The Sheltered Life.* Garden City, N.Y.: Doubleday, Doran & Co., 1932.

———. *They Stooped to Folly: A Comedy of Morals.* Garden City, N.Y.: Doubleday, Doran & Co., 1929.

———. *Vein of Iron.* 1935. New York: Harcourt, Brace & Co., n.d.

———. *Virginia.* Garden City: Doubleday, Page, & Co., 1913.

———. *The Voice of the People.* New York: Doubleday, Page, & Co., 1900.

———. *The Woman Within: An Autobiography.* 1954. New York: Hill & Wang, 1980.

Godbold, E. Stanly. *Ellen Glasgow and the Woman Within.* Baton Rouge: Louisiana State University Press, 1972.

Greer, Germaine. *The Female Eunuch.* New York: McGraw-Hill Co., 1971.

Griffin, Dorothy G. "The House as Container: Architecture and Myth in *Delta Wedding.*" In *Welty: A Life in Literature,* edited by Albert J. Devlin, 96–112. Jackson: University Press of Mississippi, 1987.

Hardy, John Edward. "*Delta Wedding* as Region and Symbol," *Sewanee Review* 60 (Summer 1952): 397–417.

———. *Katherine Anne Porter.* Modern Literature Series, edited by Phillip Winsor. New York: Frederick Ungar Publishing Co, 1973.

———. "Marrying Down in Eudora Welty's Novels." In *Eudora Welty: Thirteen Essays,* edited by Peggy Prenshaw, 71–97. Jackson: University Press of Mississippi, 1983.

Haskell, Thomas. *The Emergence of Professional Social Science: The American Social Science Association. The Nineteenth-Century Crisis of Authority.* Urbana: University of Illinois Press, 1977.

Hayden, Dolores. *The Grand Domestic Revolution: A History of Feminist Design for American Homes.* Cambridge, Mass.: Massachusetts Institute of Technology Press, 1981.

Heilman, Robert B. "*Losing Battles* and Winning the War." In *Eudora Welty: Thirteen Essays,* edited by Peggy Prenshaw, 157–92. Jackson: University Press of Mississippi, 1983.

Helmick, Evelyn. "Myth in the Works of Willa Cather," *Mid-Continent American Studies Journal* 9 (Fall 1968): 63–69.

Hendrick, George. *Katherine Anne Porter.* Twayne United States Authors Series, No. 90. New York: Twayne, 1965.

Hennessy, Rosemary. "Katherine Anne Porter's Model for Heroines," *Colorado Quarterly* 25 (Winter 1977): 301–15.

Henretta, James A. "Families and Farms: Mentalité in Pre-Industrial America," *William and Mary Quarterly* 35 (January 1978): 3–32.

Hentz, Caroline Lee. *Ernest Linwood.* Boston: John P. Jewett Co., 1856.

Hernton, Calvin. "The Sexual Mountain and Black Women Writers." In *Wild Women in the Whirlwind: Afra-American Culture and The Contemporary Literary Renaissance,* edited by Joanne Braxton and Andree Nicola McLaughlin, 195–212. New Brunswick, N.J.: Rutgers University Press, 1990.

Higham, John. *From Boundlessness to Consolidation: The Transformation of American Culture, 1844–1860.* Ann Arbor, Mich.: William L. Clements Library, 1969.

Hinton, Jane L. "The Role of Family in *Delta Wedding, Losing Battles,* and

The Optimist's Daughter." In *Selected Essays,* edited by Peggy Prenshaw, 120–131. Jackson: University Press of Mississippi, 1979.

Hirsch, Marianne. *The Mother/Daughter Plot: Narrative, Psychoanalysis, Feminism.* Bloomington, Ind.: Indiana University Press, 1989.

Holman, C. Hugh. "April in Queenborough: Ellen Glasgow's Comedies of Manners," *Sewanee Review.* 82 (April–June 1974): 263–83.

———. *Three Modes of Southern Fiction: Ellen Glasgow, William Faulkner, and Thomas Wolfe.* Mercer University Lamar Memorial Lectures, No. 9. Athens, Ga.: University of Georgia Press, 1966.

Homans, Margaret. *Bearing the Word: Language and Female Experience in Nineteenth-Century Women's Writing.* Chicago: University of Chicago Press, 1986.

———. "The Woman in the Cave: Recent Feminist Fictions and the Classical Underworld." *Contemporary Literature* 29 (Fall 1988): 369–402.

Hurston, Zora Neale. *Their Eyes Were Watching God.* 1937. Urbana: University of Illinois Press, 1978.

Jacobs, Harriet [Linda Brent]. *Incidents in the Life of A Slave Girl.* 1861. New York: Harcourt Brace Jovanovich, 1983.

Jehlen, Myra. *American Incarnation: The Individual, the Nation, and the Continent.* Cambridge, Mass.: Harvard University Press, 1986.

Jewett, Sarah Orne. *A Country Doctor.* 1884. New York: NAL/Penguin Books, 1986.

———. *The Country of the Pointed Firs.* 1896. New York: Avon/Penguin, 1977.

———. *Deephaven.* Boston: J. R. Osgood & Co., 1877.

———. "The Foreigner." *The Uncollected Stories of Sarah Orne Jewett.* Edited by Richard Cary, 307–324. Waterville, Me.: Colby College Press, 1971.

Jones, Anne Goodwyn. *Tomorrow Is Another Day.* Baton Rouge: Louisiana State University Press, 1981.

Jung, Carl G. *The Archetypes and the Collective Unconscious.* Translated by R. F. C. Hull. 2d ed. 1968. Princeton University Press, 1980.

———. *Four Archetypes: Mother, Rebirth, Spirit, Trickster.* Translated by R. F. C. Hull. 1959. Princeton: Princeton University Press, 1973.

———. *Symbols of Transformation.* Translated by R. F. C. Hull. 1956. Princeton: Princeton University Press, 1976.

Jung, C. G., and C. Kerenyi. *Essays on a Science of Mythology: The Myth of the Divine Child and the Mysteries of Eleusis.* Translated by R. F. C. Hull. 1963. Princeton: Princeton University Press, 1969.

Kaestle, Carl, and Maris A. Vinovskis. "From Apron Strings to ABCs: Parents, Children, and Schooling in Nineteenth-Century Massachusetts."

In *Turning Points: Historical and Sociological Essays of the Family,* edited by John Demos and Sarane Spence Boocock, 539–80. A special supplement of *American Journal of Sociology.* American Journal of Sociology. 84(1978), published in book form. Chicago: University of Chicago Press, 1978.

Kaplan, Charles. "True Witness: Katherine Anne Porter," *Colorado Quarterly* 7 (Winter 1959): 319–27.

Kelley, Mary. *Private Woman, Public Stage: Literary Domesticity in Nineteenth-Century America.* 1984. New York: Oxford University, 1985.

Kerber, Linda. *Women of the Republic: Intellect and Ideology in Revolutionary America.* Institute of Early American History and Culture. Chapel Hill: University of North Carolina Press, 1980.

Kerenyi, C. *Eleusis: Archetypal Images of Mother and Daughter.* Translated by Ralph Mannheim. New York: Schocken Books, 1977.

Kerr, Elizabeth M. "The World of Eudora Welty's Women." In *Selected Essays,* edited by Peggy Prenshaw, 132–48. Jackson: The University Press of Mississippi, 1979.

King, John O., III. *The Iron of Melancholy: Structures of Spiritual Conversion in America from the Puritan Conscience to Victorian Neurosis.* Middletown, Conn.: Wesleyan University Press, 1983.

Kolodny, Annette. *The Lay of the Land: Metaphor as Experience and History in American Life and Letters.* Chapel Hill: University of North Carolina Press, 1975.

———. *The Land Before Her: Fantasy and Experience of the American Frontiers: 1630–1860.* Chapel Hill: University of North Carolina Press, 1984.

Kreyling, Michael. *Eudora Welty's Achievement of Order.* Baton Rouge: Louisiana State University Press, 1980.

———. "Myth and History: The Foes of *Losing Battles,*" *Mississippi Quarterly.* Eudora Welty Issue. 26 (Fall 1973), 639–49.

———. "Subject and Object in *One Writer's Beginnings,*" *Mississippi Quarterly.* Eudora Welty Issue. 34 (Fall (1986): 627–38.

Lane, Ann J. *To Herland and Beyond: The Life and Works of Charlotte Perkins Gilman.* New York: Pantheon Books, 1990.

Langer, Elinor. *Josephine Herbst: The Story She Could Never Tell.* Boston: Little, Brown, 1983.

Lears, T. J. Jackson. "From Salvation to Self-Realization: Advertising and the Therapeutic Roots of the Consumer Culture: 1880–1930." In *The Culture of Consumption: Critical Essays in American History: 1880–1980,* edited by Richard Wightman Fox and T. J. Jackson Lears, 3–38. New York: Pantheon Books, 1983.

————. *No Place of Grace: Antimodernism and the Transformation of American Culture: 1880–1920.* New York: Pantheon Books, 1983.

Levy, Helen Fiddyment. "Mothers and Daughters in 'The Bohemian Girl' and *The Song of the Lark.*" In *Willa Cather: Family, Community, and History,* edited by John J. Murphy, 163–68. Provo, Utah: Brigham Young University, 1990.

Lewis, Edith. *Willa Cather Living: A Personal Record.* 1953. New York: Octagon Books, 1976.

Lewis, R. W. B. *The American Adam: Innocence, Tragedy, and Tradition in the Nineteenth Century.* Chicago: University of Chicago Press, 1955.

Liberman, M. M. *Katherine Anne Porter's Fiction.* Detroit: Wayne State University Press, 1971.

Lorde, Audre. *Sister Outsider: Essays and Speeches.* The Crossing Press Feminist Series. Freedom, Calif.: The Crossing Press, 1984.

McAlpin, Sara. "Family in Eudora Welty's Fiction," *Southern Review* 18 (Summer 1982): 480–94.

McDowell, Frederick. "The Prewar Novels." In *Ellen Glasgow: Centennial Essays,* edited by M. Thomas Inge, 86–107. Charlottesville: University Press of Virginia, 1976.

McHaney, Thomas L. "Eudora Welty and the Multitudinous Golden Apples." Eudora Welty Issue. *Mississippi Quarterly* 26 (Fall 1973): 589–624.

McIntosh, Maria J. *Two Lives; or, To Seem and to Be.* New York: D. Appleton & Co., 1846.

McLaughlin, Andree N. "Black Women, Identity, and the Quest for Humanhood and Wholeness: Wild Women in the Whirlwind." In *Wild Women in the Whirlwind: Afra-American Culture and the Contemporary Literary Renaissance,* edited by Joanne Braxton and Andree Nicola McLaughlin, 147–80. New Brunswick, N.J.: Rutgers University Press, 1990.

Madden, David. "The Changed Image in Katherine Anne Porter's 'Flowering Judas,'" *Studies in Short Fiction* 7 (Spring 1970): 277–89.

Marrs, Suzanne. "The Metaphor of Race in Eudora Welty's Fiction," *The Southern Review* 22 (October 1986): 697–726.

Marx, Leo. *The Machine in the Garden: Technology and the Pastoral Ideal in America.* New York: Oxford University Press, 1964.

Matthews, Glenna. *"Just a Housewife": The Rise and Fall of Domesticity in America.* 1987. New York: Oxford University Press, 1989.

Michaels, Walter Benn. *The Gold Standard and the Logic of Naturalism: American Literature at the Turn of the Century.* The New Historicism:

Studies in Cultural Poetics, edited by Stephen Greenblatt, no. 2. Berkeley: University of California Press, 1987.

Moers, Ellen. *Literary Women.* 1976. Garden City, N.Y.: Doubleday, 1977.

Mooney, Harry J., Jr. *The Fiction and Criticism of Katherine Anne Porter.* Pittsburgh: The University of Pittsburgh Press, 1957.

Morrison, Toni. *Beloved.* 1987. New York: Plume/Penguin, 1988.

———. *Sula.* New York: Alfred Knopf, 1973.

Nagel, Gwen L. "'This Prim Corner of Land Where She Was Queen': Sarah Orne Jewett's New England Gardens." Papers from the Jewett Conference at Westbrook College. *Colby Literary Quarterly* 22 (March 1986): 43–63.

Nance, William. *Katherine Anne Porter and the Art of Rejection.* Chapel Hill: University of North Carolina Press, 1963.

Naylor, Gloria. "Interview." Audiotape. *American Audio Prose Library,* AAPL 8082. Columbia, Mo.: American Audio Prose Library, Inc., 1988.

———. *Linden Hills.* 1985. New York: Penguin Books, 1986.

———. *Mama Day.* 1988. New York: Vintage/Random House, 1989.

———. *The Women of Brewster Place: A Novel in Seven Stories.* 1982. New York: Penguin Books, 1983.

Nelson, Robert J. *Willa Cather and France: In Search of the Lost Language.* Urbana: University of Illinois Press, 1988.

O'Brien, Sharon. *Willa Cather: The Emerging Voice.* New York: Oxford University Press, 1987.

Olsen, Tillie. *Silences.* New York: Delacorte Press, 1978.

Orenstein, Gloria Feman. *The Reflowering of the Goddess.* The Athene Series. New York: Pergamon Press, 1990.

Ortner, Sherry. "Is Female to Male as Nature Is to Culture?" In *Women, Culture, and Society,* edited by Michelle Zimbalist Rosaldo and Louise Lamphere, 67–87. Palo Alto, Calif.: Stanford University Press, 1974.

Pannill, Linda. "Willa Cather's Artist-heroine," *Women's Studies* 11 (1984): 223–32.

Porter, Katherine Anne. *The Collected Stories of Katherine Anne Porter.* 1965. New York: Harcourt Brace Jovanovich, 1972.

———. *Katherine Anne Porter: Conversations.* Edited by Joan Givner. Jackson: University Press of Mississippi, 1987.

———. *The Collected Essays and Occasional Writings of Katherine Anne Porter.* New York: Delacorte Press, 1970.

———. *Outline of Mexican Popular Arts and Crafts.* Los Angeles: Young & McCallister, 1922.

———. "The Land That Is Nowhere." Unpublished typescript. Katherine Anne Porter Collection, McKeldin Library, University of Maryland.

————. Review of *Portrait of Mexico* by Diego Rivera and Bertram Wolfe. Unpublished typescript. Katherine Anne Porter Collection, McKeldin Library, University of Maryland.

————. "Xochimilco." *Christian Science Monitor,* May 31, 1921. Attributed to Porter by Thomas Walsh.

Poss, S. H. "Variations on a Theme in Four Stories of Katherine Anne Porter." *Twentieth Century Literature* 4 (April–July 1958): 21–29.

Pratt, Annis. *Archetypal Patterns in Women's Fiction.* Bloomington, Ind.: Indiana University Press, 1991.

Rabuzzi, Kathryn Allen. *Motherself: A Mythic Analysis of Motherhood.* Bloomington, Ind.: Indiana University Press, 1988.

Radway, Janice A. *Reading the Romance: Women, Patriarchy, and Popular Literature.* Chapel Hill: University of North Carolina Press, 1984.

Raper, J. R. *From the Sunken Garden: The Fiction of Ellen Glasgow, 1916–1945.* Baton Rouge: Louisiana State University Press, 1980.

————. *Without Shelter: The Early Career of Ellen Glasgow.* Baton Rouge: Louisiana State University Press, 1971.

Redden, Dorothy. "'Flowering Judas': Two Voices," *Studies in Short Fiction* 7 (Spring 1970): 277–89.

Rich, Adrienne. *Of Woman Born.* 1976. New York: Bantam Books, 1977.

Robinson, Phyllis. *Willa: The Life of Willa Cather.* Garden City, N.Y.: Doubleday & Co., Inc., 1983.

Rohloff, Jean. "'A Quicker Signal': Women and Language in Sarah Orne Jewett's *The Country of the Pointed Firs,*" *South Atlantic Review* 55 (May 1990): 33–46.

Romines, Ann. "After the Christmas Tree: Willa Cather and the Domestic Ritual," *American Literature* 60 (March 1988): 61–82.

————. "Domestic Troubles," *Colby Literary Quarterly* 24 (March 1988): 50–60.

Rooke, Constance, and Bruce Wallis. "Myth and Epiphany in Porter's 'The Grave,'" *Studies in Short Fiction* 15 (Summer 1978): 269–75.

Rosenberg, Rosalind. *Beyond Separate Spheres: Intellectual Roots of Modern Feminism.* New Haven: Yale University Press, 1982.

Rosowski, Susan. *The Voyage Perilous: Willa Cather's Romanticism.* Lincoln: University of Nebraska Press, 1986.

————. "Willa Cather's Magnificat: Matriarchal Christianity in *Shadows on the Rock.*" *Literature and Belief.* Willa Cather Issue. 8 (1988): 66–75.

————. "Writing Against Silences: Female Adolescent Development in the Novels of Willa Cather." *Studies in the Novel* (forthcoming).

Rothman, David J. *Discovery of the Asylum: Social Order and Disorder in the New Republic.* Boston: Little, Brown & Co., 1971.

Rouse, Blair. *Ellen Glasgow.* Twayne United States Authors Series, no number. New York: Twayne Publishers, 1962.

Ruddick, Sara. *Maternal Thinking: Toward a Politics of Peace.* 1989. New York: Ballantine Books, 1990.

Ryan, Mary P. *Cradle of the Middle Class: The Family in Oneida County, New York: 1790–1865.* Cambridge: Cambridge University Press, 1981.

———. *The Empire of the Mother: American Writing about Domesticity.* Women and History Series, No. 213. New York: Haworth Press, 1982.

Scura, Dorothy McInnis. "The Southern Lady in the Early Novels of Ellen Glasgow," *Mississippi Quarterly* 31 (Winter 1977–78): 17–31.

Sedgwick, Eve Kosofsky. *Epistemology of the Closet.* Berkeley, Calif.: University of California Press, 1990.

Sergeant, Elizabeth Shepley. *Willa Cather: A Memoir.* 1953. Lincoln: Bison/University of Nebraska Press, 1963.

Sherman, Sarah W. *Sarah Orne Jewett: An American Persephone.* Middletown, Conn.: The New England University Press, 1989.

Showalter, Elaine. *A Literature of Their Own: British Women Novelists from Bronte to Lessing.* Princeton: Princeton University Press, 1977.

Simpson, Lewis P. *The Dispossessed Garden: Pastoral and History in Southern Literature.* Mercer University Lamar Memorial Lectures, No. 16. Athens: University of Georgia Press, 1975.

Slote, Bernice, and Virginia Faulkner, eds. *The Art of Willa Cather.* Papers and comments delivered at "The Art of Willa Cather: An International Seminar," Lincoln, Nebraska, October 25–28, 1973. Lincoln: Bison/University of Nebraska Press, 1974.

Slotkin, Richard. *The Fatal Environment: The Myth of the Frontier in the Age of Industrialization, 1800–1890.* 1985. Middletown, Conn.: Wesleyan University Press, 1986.

———. "Myth and The Production of History." In *Ideology and Classic American Literature,* edited by Sacvan Bercovitch and Myra Jehlen, 70–90. Cambridge Studies in American Literature and Culture. 1986. Cambridge: Cambridge University Press, 1987.

———. *Regeneration Through Violence: The Mythology of the American Frontier: 1600–1860.* Middletown, Conn.: Wesleyan University Press, 1973.

Smith, Barbara. "Toward a Black Feminist Criticism." In *The New Feminist Criticism: Essays on Women, Literature and Theory,* edited by Elaine Showalter, 168–85. New York: Pantheon Books, 1985.

———. "The Truth That Never Hurts: Black Lesbians in Fiction in the 1980s." In *Wild Women in the Whirlwind: Afra-American Culture and the Contemporary Literary Renaissance,* edited by Joanne Braxton and

Andree Nicola McLaughlin, 213–45. New Brunswick, N.J.: Rutgers University Press, 1990.

Smith, Henry Nash. "The Scribbling Women and the Cosmic Success Story," *Critical Inquiry* 1 (September 1974): 47–70.

———. *Virgin Land: The American West as Symbol and Myth.* 1950. Cambridge, Mass.: Harvard University Press, 1970.

Smith, Michael L. "Selling the Moon: The U.S. Manned Space Program and the Triumph of Commodity Scientism." In *The Culture of Consumption: Essays in American History: 1880–1980,* edited by Richard Wightman Fox and T. J. Jackson Lears, 177–209. New York: Pantheon Books, 1983.

Smith-Rosenberg, Carroll, "The Cross and the Pedestal: Women, Anti-Ritualism, and the Emergence of the American Bourgeoisie." In *Disorderly Conduct: Visions of Gender in Victorian America,* 129–64. 1985. New York: Oxford University Press, 1986.

———. "The Female World of Love and Ritual: Relations Between Women in Nineteenth-Century America." In *Disorderly Conduct: Visions of Gender in Victorian America,* 53–76. New York: Oxford University Press, 1986.

———. "The New Woman as Androgyne: Social Disorder and Gender Crisis, 1870–1936." In *Disorderly Conduct: Visions of Gender in Victorian America,* 245–96. New York: Oxford University Press, 1986.

Sprengnether, Madelon. "*Delta Wedding* and the Kore Complex," *The Southern Quarterly* 25 (Winter 1987): 120–130.

"The State of the Art," a forum on the state of black feminism with Nellie McKay, Patricia Hill Collins, Mae Henderson, and June Jordan. *Women's Review of Books,* 8 (February 1991): 23–26.

Steele, Oliver, "Ellen Glasgow's *Virginia:* Preliminary Notes," *Studies in Bibliography* 27 (1974): 265–89.

Stouck, David. *Willa Cather's Imagination.* Lincoln: University of Nebraska Press, 1975.

Stowe, Harriet Beecher. *Pink and White Tyranny: A Society Novel.* 1871. Introduction by Judith Martin. Plume American Women Writers, Series editor, Michelle Slung. New York: New America Library, 1988.

Stroup, Sheila. "We're All Part of It Together. Eudora Welty's Hopeful Vision in *Losing Battles,*" *Southern Literary Journal* 15 (Spring 1983): 42–58.

Tebbel, John. *A History of Book Publishing in the United States.* Vol. 1, *The Creation of an Industry: 1630–1865.* New York: R. R. Bowker, 1972.

Tiegreen, Helen Hurt. "Mother, Daughters, and One Writer's Revisions," *Mississippi Quarterly.* Eudora Welty Issue. 34 (Fall 1986): 605–26.

Toennies, Ferdinand. *Community and Association.* Translated by Charles P. Loomis. London: Routledge & Kegan Paul, 1955.

Tompkins, Jane. *Sensational Designs: The Cultural Work of American Fiction: 1790–1860.* 1985. New York: Oxford University Press, 1986.

Tutwiler, Carrington C., Jr. *A Catalogue of the Library of Ellen Glasgow.* Charlottesville: Bibliographical Society of the University of Virginia, 1969.

Unrue, Darlene. *Truth and Vision in Katherine Anne Porter's Fiction.* Athens: University of Georgia Press, 1985.

Veblen, Thorstein. *Theory of the Leisure Class.* 1899. New York: Kelley Press, 1975.

Voelker, Paul D. "*The Country of the Pointed Firs:* A Novel by Sarah Orne Jewett." In *Appreciation of Sarah Orne Jewett,* edited by Richard Cary, 238–48. Waterville, Me.: Colby College Press, 1972.

Waggoner, Hyatt H. "The Unity of *The Country of the Pointed Firs.*" In *Appreciation of Sarah Orne Jewett,* edited by Richard Cary, 162–69. Waterville, Me.: Colby College Press, 1972.

Wagner, Linda W. *Ellen Glasgow: Beyond Convention.* Austin: University of Texas Press, 1982.

Walker, Alice. *The Color Purple.* New York: Harcourt Brace Jovanovich, 1982.

———. "Everyday Use." In *The American Tradition in Literature,* edited by George Perkins, et al., vol. 2, 2004–10. 7th ed. New York: McGraw-Hill, 1990.

———. *In Search of Our Mothers' Gardens: Womanist Prose.* New York: Harcourt Brace Jovanovich, 1983.

———. *The Temple of My Familiar.* New York: Harcourt Brace Jovanovich, 1989.

Walsh, Thomas F. "Xochitl: Katherine Anne Porter's Changing Goddess," *American Literature* 52 (1980–81): 183–93.

Ward, Catherine C. "Gloria Naylor's *Linden Hills:* A Modern Inferno," *Contemporary Literature* 28 (Spring 1987): 67–81.

Warner, Susan [Elizabeth Wetherall]. *The Wide, Wide World.* 1852. Philadelphia: J. B. Lippincott & Co., 1892.

Warren, Robert Penn. "Irony With a Center," In *Katherine Anne Porter: A Critical Symposium,* edited by Lodwick Hartley and George Core, 51–66. Athens: University of Georgia Press, 1969.

———. "Love and Separateness in Eudora Welty." In *Selected Essays,* 156–69. New York: Random House, 1958.

Watkins, Floyd C. "The Journey to Baltimore in *The Optimist's Daughter,*" *Mississippi Quarterly* 38 (Fall 1985): 435–41.

Weber, Max. *Economy and Society: An Outline of Interpretative Sociology.* 3 vols. Translated by Ephraim Fischoff, *et al.* Edited by Guenther Roth and Claus Wittich. New York: Bedminster Press, 1968.

———. *The Protestant Ethic and the Spirit of Capitalism.* 1904. Translated by Talcott Parsons. New York: Charles Scribner's Sons, 1958.

Welter, Barbara. "The Cult of True Womanhood, 1820–1860." In *Dimity Convictions: The American Woman in the Nineteenth Century,* 21–41. Columbus: University of Ohio Press, 1976.

Welty, Eudora. *Conversations with Eudora Welty.* Edited by Peggy Prenshaw. Jackson: University Press of Mississippi, 1984.

———. *Delta Wedding.* 1946. San Diego: Harvest/Harcourt Brace Jovanovich, n.d.

———. *The Eye of the Story: Selected Essays and Reviews.* New York: Vintage/Random House, 1979.

———. *The Golden Apples.* 1949. New York: Harcourt, Brace & World, Inc., n.d.

———. "Introduction." *The Optimist's Daughter.* Franklin Center, Pa.: The Franklin Library, 1980.

———. *Losing Battles.* 1970. Greenwich, Conn.: Fawcett Publications, Inc., 1971.

———. *One Writer's Beginnings.* The William E. Massey, Sr. Lectures in the History of American Civilization, 1983. Cambridge, Mass.: Harvard University Press, 1984.

———. *The Optimist's Daughter.* 1972. New York: Vintage Books, 1978.

———. *The Robber Bridegroom.* 1942. New York: Harcourt Brace Jovanovich, 1970.

———. *"The Wide Net" and Other Stories.* 1941. New York: Harcourt Brace Jovanovich, 1971.

Westling, Louise. "Demeter and Kore, Southern Style," *Pacific Coast Philogy* 14 (November 1984): 101–107.

———. *Sacred Groves and Ravaged Gardens: The Fiction of Eudora Welty, Carson McCullers, and Flannery O'Connor.* Athens: University of Georgia Press, 1985.

Wharton, Edith Newbold Jones. *Age of Innocence.* 1920. New York: Charles Scribner's Sons, 1968.

———. *The Buccaneers.* New York: D. Appleton-Century Co., Inc.: 1938.

———. *The Fruit of the Tree.* New York: Charles Scribner's Sons, 1907.

———. *The Gods Arrive.* 1932. New York: Charles Scribner's Sons, 1969.

———. *The House of Mirth.* 1905. Modern Standard Authors Series. New York: Charles Scribner's Sons, 1951.

———. *Summer: A Novel.* New York: D. Appleton & Co., 1917.

Wiebe, Robert H. *The Search for Order, 1877–1920.* New York: Hill & Wang, 1967.

Williams, Raymond. *The Country and the City.* New York: Oxford University Press, 1973.

Winkler, Barbara Scott. *Victorian Daughters: The Lives and Feminism of Charlotte Perkins Gilman and Olive Schreiner.* American Culture Program, Occasional Papers in Women Studies, No. 13. Ann Arbor: University of Michigan Press, 1980.

Woodress, James. *Willa Cather: Her Life and Art.* Lincoln: University of Nebraska Press, 1970.

———. *Willa Cather: A Literary Life.* 1987. Lincoln: Bison/University of Nebraska Press, 1989.

Wroth, Lawrence C., and Rollo G. Silver, *The Book in America: A History of the Making and Selling of Books in the United States.* 2d ed. New York: R. R. Bowker Co., 1972.

Yaeger, Patricia S. "'Because a Fire Was in My Head': Eudora Welty and the Dialogic Imagination." *PMLA*, 1984. *Mississippi Quarterly.* Eudora Welty Issue. 39 (Fall 1986): 561–86.

Index